Tr You tes

Steven J. Fleck, PhD
Physical Conditioning Program
United States Olympic Committee

Human Kinetics Publishers

Library of Congress Cataloging-in-Publication Data

Kraemer, William J., 1953-
    Strength training for young athletes / William J. Kraemer, Steven
J. Fleck.
        p.   cm.
    Includes index.
    ISBN 0-87322-396-9
    1. Exercise for children.   2. Isometric exercise.   I. Fleck,
Steven J., 1951- . II. Title.
    GV443.K687   1993
    613.7'042--dc20   92-22624
                                                                          CIP

ISBN: 0-87322-396-9

Acquisitions Editor: Brian Holding; **Developmental Editor:** Holly Gilly; **Managing Editor:** Marni Basic; **Assistant Editors:** Laura Bofinger, Julie Swadener, and John Wentworth; **Copyeditor:** Julia Anderson; **Proofreader:** Tom Rice; **Production Director:** Ernie Noa; **Typesetter:** Julie Overholt; **Text Design:** Keith Blomberg; **Text Layout:** Tara Welsch and Kimberlie Henris; **Cover Photo:** Wil Zehr; **Cover Designer:** Jack Davis; **Printer:** United Graphics

Human Kinetics books are available at special discounts for bulk purchase. Special editions or book excerpts can also be created to specification. For details, contact the Special Sales Manager at Human Kinetics.

Printed in the United States of America   10   9   8   7

Human Kinetics
Web site: http://www.humankinetics.com/

United States: Human Kinetics, P.O. Box 5076, Champaign, IL 61825-5076
1-800-747-4457
e-mail: humank@hkusa.com

Canada: Human Kinetics, Box 24040, Windsor, ON N8Y 4Y9
1-800-465-7301 (in Canada only)
e-mail: humank@hkcanada.com

Europe: Human Kinetics, P.O. Box IW14, Leeds LS16 6TR, United Kingdom
(44) 1132 781708
e-mail: humank@hkeurope.com

Australia: Human Kinetics, 57A Price Avenue, Lower Mitcham, South Australia 5062
(08) 277 1555
e-mail: humank@hkaustralia.com

New Zealand: Human Kinetics, P.O. Box 105-231, Auckland 1
(09) 523 3462
e-mail: humank@hknewz.com

Contents

About the Authors

William J. Kraemer, PhD, has more than 20 years' experience with both the practical and scientific aspects of resistance training. He is the director of research for the Center for Sports Medicine at The Pennsylvania State University, where he is an associate professor of applied physiology. He has also coached football and wrestling and taught health and physical education at the junior high through university levels.

Dr. Kraemer received his PhD in physiology and biochemistry from the University of Wyoming. He is a past president of the National Strength and Conditioning Association (NSCA) and has received that organization's presidential and executive director awards for outstanding contributions to the field of strength and conditioning. He received the NSCA's Outstanding Sport Scientist Award in 1992.

Dr. Kraemer is an American College of Sports Medicine fellow and in 1992 was elected to the Board of Trustees for Basic and Applied Science. He is also a member of the American Alliance for Health, Physical Education, Recreation and Dance (AAHPERD). He serves as editor-in-chief for the *Journal of Strength and Conditioning Research* (formerly the *Journal of Applied Sport*

Science Research) and is a member of the editorial board for *Medicine and Science in Sports and Exercise*. He is also a reviewer for the *National Strength and Conditioning Association Journal*, the *International Journal of Sports Medicine*, and many other publications.

Steven J. Fleck, PhD, heads the Physical Conditioning Program for the United States Olympic Committee's training center in Colorado Springs, Colorado. His work designing resistance programs for national and international caliber athletes makes him an expert in the field of strength and conditioning. He earned his PhD in exercise physiology from The Ohio State University.

Dr. Fleck is a member of NSCA's research committee, the Certified Strength Conditioning Specialist board, and a past vice president for basic and applied research. He has also served as associate editor of the *National Strength and Conditioning Association Journal*. In both 1988 and 1990 he received NSCA's President's Award for Outstanding Service, and in 1991 he was recognized as their Sports Scientist of the Year.

Dr. Fleck is an American College of Sports Medicine fellow and the associate editor for the *Journal of Strength and Conditioning Research*.

Preface

The average person hears and reads a lot regarding the right way to train and the best program to use. The volume of information about strength training, which can also be called resistance training or weight training, can be very confusing at times. This text will attempt to clarify various concepts and show that often *right* and *wrong* are easy to pinpoint but *why* is sometimes more difficult to answer.

With the increased use of resistance exercise programs over the last 15 years, athletes and fitness enthusiasts alike have started to focus on sport- or need-specific programs. No longer should you pull out an old power-lifting routine for someone who is interested in starting a strength training program; if that person is not a power lifter, his or her needs and goals will not match the program's goals. Program design has become sophisticated and scientific, so that the goals, needs, and abilities of the individual are assessed prior to development of a strength training program. Because scientific studies can only serve as guidelines, a program's appropriateness depends upon the judgment of the program developer. As a program developer, you must incorporate factual information, common sense, and the exercise prescription process in the program design. Remember, this is an individualized process.

Chapter 1 uses research findings to explain why strength training is appropriate for children. Chapter 2 explains some of the important physiological concepts involved in children's growth and development as they apply to developing strength training programs. Chapter 3 describes the concerns you should address when developing a child's strength training program. Chapter 4 explains the specific components of program design, and chapter 5 teaches you how to teach resistance exercises to children.

More than 100 resistance exercises are explained and illustrated in chapter 6. The exercise descriptions, grouped according to the body part that is strengthened, include starting position, movement, spotting and safety, and muscles strengthened. Chapter 7 incorporates the exercises into basic training programs for 16 different sports and activities.

There is a glossary at the end of the book that clearly defines the more technical strength training terms. Words listed in the glossary are italicized the first time they appear in the text.

Many parents, teachers, physicians, and coaches are faced with the need to become involved with strength training for children. The most common question they ask is, ''Where can I find some information or someone to talk to who knows how to put a program together?'' It's difficult to try to address children's needs without knowledge of child development and understanding of strength training for children. We hope that this text will provide some insight into the program design process for children and will act as a resource for your questions.

Acknowledgments

This book was initiated to fill the need for a practical resistance training guide for young athletes. The demands and rigors of this project were greater than we anticipated, but with the help and support of many different people, some of whom didn't even know they provided encouragement, we persisted and have created a book that can serve as a practical guide for young people.

Many colleagues and friends have supported our efforts in the development of this book. We would like to thank Rainer Martens for his support and belief in our work with resistance exercise. To the staff at Human Kinetics who make it all happen, we appreciate your patience, support, and enthusiasm in bringing this book to completion. We would particularly like to thank Holly Gilly, our developmental editor, and Brian Holding and Marni Basic.

A special thank you goes to Mike Nitka and the students at Muskego High School in Muskego, Wisconsin, for their help with our exercise pictorials. To the graduate students at Penn State, thank you for your continued help and support during the process of this work. Thanks to Andrew Fry for his efforts with some of the graphic art.

To the many of our professional colleagues who have helped each of us in our careers, we sincerely appreciate your friendship and support through the years. Special thanks to Gary Dudley, Mike Stone, Jay T. Kearney, Howard Knuttgen, Carl Maresh, and Tom Baechle for their helpful comments during the writing of this book.

Chapter 1

Strength Training for Children: The Controversy Resolved

Position stands by the National Strength and Conditioning Association, the American Orthopedic Society for Sports Medicine, and the American Academy of Pediatrics suggest that children can benefit from participation in a properly prescribed and supervised *resistance training** program. The major benefits are

- increased muscular *strength,*
- increased local muscular *endurance* (i.e., the ability of a muscle to perform multiple repetitions against a given *resistance*),
- prevention of injury during sports and recreational activities, and
- improved performance capacity in sports and recreational activities.

*Words in the glossary are italicized the first time they appear in the text.

Although scientific and medical authorities have supported children's participation in resistance exercise programs, they have cautioned parents, teachers, and coaches about the need for proper program design, competent supervision, and correct teaching of exercise techniques, areas that are paramount for safe and effective programs. Many of the controversies concerning children's participation in resistance training programs that have arisen over the past 10 years have been related to these concerns. As scientific and medical authorities gain greater understanding about resistance training for children, unrealistic fears are starting to diminish.

Strength Building in Childhood

Part of the early controversy was whether children can really improve their muscular strength. The first studies performed were unable to demonstrate strength gains in children who completed a resistance training program (Vrijens, 1978). The lack of strength changes demonstrated in various studies over the years may have been due to poorly designed resistance training programs or poor experimental designs. Building upon previous scientific studies, more recent investigations show that muscular strength improvements are indeed possible in children, including prepubescents (Blimkie, 1989; Ramsay et al., 1990; Sale, 1989; Sewall & Micheli, 1986; Weltman, et al., 1986).

A more complicated question, which is of great scientific interest, is related to the cause of strength improvements in children. To date, the scientific evidence points to the important role the nervous system plays in producing strength gains in children (Ramsay et al., 1990); children gain strength by improving the functional ability of the nervous system rather than by dramatically increasing the size of the muscle. This at least appears to be the case for resistance training programs lasting 6 months or less; what happens over longer periods of time remains unknown. Therefore, *hypertrophy*, or an increase in muscle size, is more difficult for children to achieve over short training periods than for adults. This is especially true of prepubescent children.

Because large increases in muscle mass beyond normal growth are not possible in younger children, it is important that they do not participate in resistance training based only on the hope of getting big muscles. This can especially be a problem for younger males who see older boys (16 or 17 years old) with defined larger muscles. Don't allow a young boy to believe that lifting weights will, within a few months, give him the muscle size and look of the older boys he sees. As children grow older and go through puberty, especially males, they are able to increase muscle size which can then become a goal of training.

Although increases in muscle size beyond normal growth do not typically occur in younger children, a child's muscles can still benefit from resistance training, because resistance exercise improves and enhances muscular function, thus improving performance and physical fitness.

Misconceptions About Strength Training for Children

Much of the controversy that has surrounded resistance training for children has been due to

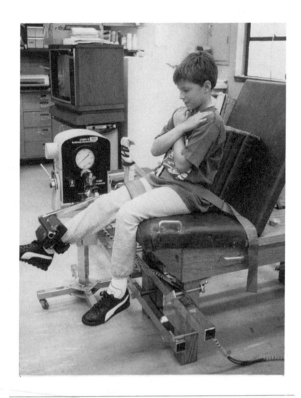

Children's strength levels make dramatic increases due to their growth during the maturation process, even without exercise training.

many misconceptions about resistance training. Television and popular magazines promote striking images of competitive lifters straining to lift as much weight as they can or of bodybuilders posing in a competition with their large muscles bulging. These are examples not of resistance training but rather of specific sports that utilize resistance training, yet many people believe that competitive *weight lifting* and *bodybuilding* are what resistance training is all about. You can see why professionals and parents may have developed tentative if not cautious attitudes concerning children and resistance training. However, the goal of resistance training does not have to be to lift as much weight as possible one time or to develop large muscles. Other goals of resistance training for children or for anyone can be to improve muscular fitness, prevent sport injury, and enhance sport performance. Children need guidelines and some special considerations, but they can safely and effectively perform resistance training.

In the past, weight training was thought to be unsafe for children, but now many scientific and medical professionals think this was an overreaction; furthermore, it was not consistent with the needs of children and did not reflect the actual risks involved in resistance training. Young athletes were being injured in youth sport activities, and it was obvious that their bodies were not able to meet the physical demands of the sports they were playing (Micheli, 1986). Resistance exercise provides a potent tool to help reduce the severity of athletic injury and possibly prevent injury.

Many professionals are concerned when children lift maximal or near-maximal weights. This concern about how much weight is lifted by a child for a particular exercise is reflected in the various professional position stands. Although *maximal strength testing* (lifting as much as possible for one repetition) for clinical evaluation or research under the supervision of trained professionals has not resulted in injury, chronic maximal strength training (lifting only 1-3 *repetition maximum* [RM] resistances) over a training period may be different. Therefore position stands recommend that prepubescent children lift weights that can be lifted at least six *repetitions* or more. At what age a child can start to use weights heavier than can be lifted for at least six repetitions largely depends upon the child's individual maturation and training experience.

Power lifting, Olympic weight lifting, and bodybuilding are competitive sports. The goals of these sports are related to adult training capabilities and adult values. In addition, the goals of bodybuilding are related to the development of muscle size and definition. Medical and scientific professionals have typically discouraged the involvement of children in such adult competitions because the heavy training loads required for success are not thought appropriate for children. Competition in the sport of power lifting comprises three lifts: the bench press, the squat, and the dead lift. The winner of the competition is the person who can lift the most weight for 1 repetition in each of these lifts. In the sport of weightlifting (also known as Olympic lifting), the competition surrounds maximal strength performance in two lifts called the snatch lift and the clean and jerk. Again the goal is to lift the most weight for one repetition in each lift. Although training for such competitions, where the point is to lift as much weight as possible, is inappropriate for children, the lifts used in these sports, when performed with the proper supervision, correct exercise technique, and appropriate resistance, are suitable for children. Remember, prepubescent children should not lift maximal or near-maximal weights.

Lifting maximal or near-maximal resistances (weights that can be lifted less than six repetitions), especially during a child's developmental years, might expose a child to possible injuries related to the long bones and the back. This perceived risk is even greater when children are unsupervised, because they may not understand and use proper lifting techniques, safety spotting, and appropriate program design.

The sport of bodybuilding consists of a competition in which judges score an individual on a variety of physical attributes including muscular size, symmetrical muscular development, muscle definition, and the ability to perform various muscular poses. Because children typically do not make large gains in muscle size, bodybuilding can represent somewhat unrealistic, if not physiologically unattainable, competitive goals for the prepubescent child. Conversely, the principles used in bodybuilding, which emphasize the importance of exercising all of the various muscle groups, symmetrical development of the upper and lower body musculature, and a disciplined diet and lifestyle, are positive aspects of the sport that should be part of any good training program. Thus it is important that you identify the specific aspects of any training program or training goal that may or may not be appropriate for a child. In addition, remember that exercise programs need to demonstrate an overall balance in total fitness, including not

Be sure children can tolerate the resistance training program they are participating in. Proper progression, program monitoring, and supervision are essential to meet the changing needs of children and prevent any inappropriate exercise stress.

just strength but flexibility and cardiovascular development.

Historically, people involved in weightlifting, power lifting, or bodybuilding have been consulted to help develop programs in resistance training. Such lifters or ex-lifters have been the source of empirical and anecdotal information for years. Thus many resistance training programs have reflected a strong influence from the competitive lifting sports. Even today, most of the experts have backgrounds in various forms of competitive lifting or are former athletes who engaged in serious resistance training to enhance their athletic performances. Personal lifting experiences and sound scientific principles can positively influence the development of a resistance training program.

Children's Introduction to Strength Training

Children are introduced to resistance training in many ways. One of the most common is receiving a set of weights for a present; another is receiving a membership to a YMCA or health club. A number of factors should be considered by coaches, parents, or instructors before a young person becomes involved in a resistance training program:

- Is the child psychologically and physically ready to participate in a resistance training program?
- What resistance training program should the child follow?
- Do the child and the supervisor understand proper lifting techniques for each exercise in the program?
- Do the child and the supervisor understand the safety spotting techniques for each lift in the program?
- Does the child understand safety considerations for each piece of equipment used in the program?
- Does the resistance training equipment fit the child properly?
- Does the child have a balanced physical exercise training program (i.e., does the child participate in cardiovascular activities and other sports in addition to resistance training)?

Basic Strength Training Guidelines for Children

The possible dangers involved in resistance training are related to inappropriate exercise demands placed on the child. Although there are general guidelines for resistance training, you must consider the special needs of each individual. In essence this means you must design a program for each child's needs that employs proper exercise techniques and safety considerations.

Resistance training is a training method in which external resistances are lifted to enhance the muscle's functional abilities. All resistance training programs are not alike, nor are their goals, because goals are related to the individual's needs. Proper program design along with knowledgeable supervision makes resistance training safe, rewarding, and fun. Improved physical function will in turn enhance physical fitness, health, injury prevention, and sport performance. Perhaps an even more important outcome is the child's development of an active lifestyle. Proper exercise behaviors can contribute to better health and well-being over a lifetime.

With the increasing participation of children in a wide variety of youth sports from football and gymnastics to soccer and track, there is a significant need for better physical preparation to prevent sport-related injuries. Resistance training has the most potential of any physical activity to address this need. Concerns about injury from a properly supervised and prescribed resistance training program should be minimal, considering the great potential for improving the child's ability to tolerate sport stresses, improve performance, and avoid athletic injury.

When you introduce resistance training to a child, keep in mind his or her physical and emotional maturity. As with any sport or exercise program, a child should have a thorough exam by a physician. A child must then be mentally and emotionally ready to undergo the stress of exercise training. There is no standard age at which a child can start a resistance training program. Typically, if the child can participate in other sport programs, he or she is ready for some type of resistance training program (see Table 1.1). The child must be able to follow directions and perform exercises safely and with proper form. Children with various physical and mental disabilities can also participate in resistance training with appropriate teaching and necessary equipment adaptations. For any child, the program should provide proper instruction and gradual progression in exercise stress (meaning the resistance and the rest allowed; see chapter 4). Remember, the child will need about 2 to 4 weeks to get used to the stresses of resistance training (for example, slightly sore

Table 1.1

Basic Guidelines for Resistance Exercise Progression in Children

Age (years)	Considerations
7 or younger	Introduce child to basic exercises with little or no weight; develop the concept of a training session; teach exercise techniques; progress from body weight calisthenics, partner exercises, and lightly resisted exercises; keep volume low.
8-10	Gradually increase the number of exercises; practice exercise technique in all lifts; start gradual progressive loading of exercises; keep exercises simple; gradually increase training volume; carefully monitor toleration to the exercise stress.
11-13	Teach all basic exercise techniques; continue progressive loading of each exercise; emphasize exercise techniques; introduce more advanced exercises with little or no resistance.
14-15	Progress to more advanced youth programs in resistance exercise; add sport-specific components; emphasize exercise techniques; increase volume.
16 or older	Move child to entry-level adult programs after all background knowledge has been mastered and a basic level of training experience has been gained.

Note. If a child of any age begins a program with no previous experience, start the child at previous levels and move him or her to more advanced levels as exercise toleration, skill, amount of training time, and understanding permit.

muscles and the discipline involved in adherence to a routine).

Don't let the child try to do too much too soon; allow him or her time to adapt to the stress of resistance training. Furthermore, don't be surprised if some children have problems sticking to the program or really don't enjoy it. Interest, growth, maturity, and understanding all contribute to the child's view of exercise training. It is important that the child, in addition to the coaches and parents, understand why he or she is involved in a resistance training program. This requires basic education regarding sensible

goals, needs, and expected outcomes, such as those listed here:

- Improved muscular strength and power
- Little or no change in muscle size in young children
- Improved local muscular endurance
- Positive influence on body composition
- Improved strength balance around joints
- Improved total body strength
- Prevention of injuries in sports
- Positive influence on sport performance

Don't impose a program designed for adults on a child. Such a program is too advanced for the child's physical abilities and needs. In addition, don't overlook the importance of communication. Children and adults often have preconceived (and erroneous) ideas about proper resistance training principles. Various misconceptions (e.g., it only takes a little training to become big and strong, or a strong person is invincible) come from television, movies, magazines, and other people. In addition, a child can pick up wrong signals in an adult environment, especially in the weight room.

Summing Up and Looking Ahead

Training with weights can be fun, safe, and appropriate for a child. Resistance training should be part of a total fitness program that will change as the child's goals and needs change throughout life. Stress the need for adherence to and consistency in training, which require discipline and hard work but allow the child to achieve positive gains through resistance training. At the same time, do not impose adult definitions of hard work on a child. Since each child grows, matures, and thus adapts to resistance training at an individual rate, limit comparisons to other children and allow the child to gain satisfaction in his or her own progress. Programs must be very progressive in nature yet must not overshoot the child's physical or emotional abilities to tolerate and recover from the exercise stress.

In the next chapter we will examine some of the basic concepts involved with the growth and development of children. This will help shape our expectations of a resistance exercise program for children.

Additional Readings

American Academy of Pediatrics. (1990, September). Strength training, weight and power lifting, and bodybuilding by children and adolescents. *AAP News*, p. 11.

Bar-Or, O. (1989). Trainability of the prepubescent child. *The Physician and Sportsmedicine,* **17**(5), 65-82.

Blimkie, C.J.R. (1989). Age- and sex-associated variation in strength during childhood: Anthropometric, morphologic, neurologic, biomechanical, endocrinologic, genetic and physical activity correlates. In C. Gisolfi & D. Lamb (Eds.), *Perspectives in exercise science and sports medicine: Vol. 2. Youth exercise and sport* (pp. 99-163). Indianapolis, IN: Benchmark Press.

Cahill, B. (Ed.) (1988). *Proceedings of the conference on strength training and the prepubescent.* Chicago: American Orthopaedic Society for Sports Medicine.

Clark, D.H., Vaccaro, P., & Andersen, N.M. (1984). Physiological alterations in 7-9-year-old boys following a season of competitive wrestling. *Research Quarterly,* **55**(4), 318-322.

Docherty, D., Wenger, H.A., & Collis, M.L. (1987). The effects of resistance training on aerobic and anaerobic power of young boys. *Medicine and Science in Sports and Exercise,* **19**, 389-392.

Duda, M. (1986). Prepubescent strength training gains support. *The Physician and Sportsmedicine,* **14**(2), 157-161.

Ekblom, B. (1969). Effect of physical training in adolescent boys. *Journal of Applied Physiology,* **27**, 350-355.

Ford, H.T., & Puckett, J.R. (1983). Competitive effects of prescribed weight-training and basketball programs on basketball skill test scores of ninth grade boys. *Perceptual Motor Skills,* **56**, 23-26.

Hejna, W.F., Rosenberg, A., Buturusis, D.J., & Krieger, A. (1982). The prevention of sports injuries in high school students through strength training. *National Strength Conditioning Association Journal,* **4**(1), 28-31.

Hetherington, M.R. (1976). Effect of isometric training on the elbow flexion force torque of grade five boys. *Research Quarterly,* **47**(1), 41-47.

Kraemer, W.J., Fry, A.C., Frykman, P.N., Conroy, B., & Hoffman, J. (1989). Resistance training and youth. *Pediatric Exercise Science,* **1**, 336-350.

McGovern, N.B. (1984). Effects of circuit training on physical fitness of prepubescent children. *Dissertation Abstracts International,* **45**, 452A.

Micheli, L.J. (1986). Pediatric and adolescent sports injury: Recent trends. *Exercise and Sport Science Review,* **14**, 359-374.

National Strength and Conditioning Association. (1985). Position statement on prepubescent strength training. *National Strength Conditioning Association Journal,* **7**, 27-31.

Nielsen, B., Nielsen, K., Behrendt-Hansen, M., & Asmussen, E. (1989). Training of ''functional muscular strength'' in girls 7-19 years old. In K. Berg & B.O. Eriksson (Eds.), *Children and exercise IX* (pp. 69-78). Baltimore: University Park Press.

Pfeiffer, R., & Francis, R.S. (1986). Effects of strength training on muscle development in prepubescent, pubescent, and post pubescent males. *The Physician and Sportsmedicine,* **14**(9), 134-143.

Rains, C.B., Weltman, A., Cahill, B.R., Janney, C.A., Tippett, S.R., & Katch, F.I. (1987). Strength training for prepubescent males: Is it safe? *American Journal of Sports Medicine,* **15**(5), 483-489.

Ramsay, J.A., Blimkie, C.J.R., Smith, K., Garner, S., MacDougall, J.D., & Sale, D.G. (1990). Strength training effects in prepubescent boys. *Medicine and Science in Sports and Exercise,* **22**, 605-614.

Sailors, M., & Berg, K. (1987). Comparison of responses to weight training in pubescent boys and men. *Journal of Sports Medicine Physical Fitness,* **27**, 30-37.

Sale, D.G. (1989). Strength training in children. In C.V. Gisolfi & D.R. Lamb (Eds.), *Perspectives in exercise science and sports medicine* (pp. 165-216). Carmel, IN: Benchmark Press.

Sewall, L., & Micheli, L.J. (1986). Strength training for children. *Journal of Pediatric Orthopedics,* **6**, 143-146.

Shephard, R.J. (1982). *Physical activity and growth* (p. 174). Chicago: Year Book Medical.

Siegel, J. (1988). Fitness in prepubescent children: Implications for exercise training. *National Strength Conditioning Association Journal,* **10**(3), 43-48.

Stanitski, C.L. (1989). Common injuries in preadolescent and adolescent athletes: Recommendations for prevention. *Sports Medicine,* **7**, 32-41.

Vrijens, J. (1978). Muscle strength development in the pre- and post-pubescent age. *Medicine and Sport* (Basel), **11**, 152-158.

Weltman, A. (1989). Weight training in prepubertal children. Physiologic benefits and potential damage. In O. Bar-Or (Ed.),

Advances in pediatric sport sciences (Vol. 3, pp. 101-130). Champaign, IL: Human Kinetics.

Weltman, A., Janney, C., Rians, C.B., Strand, K., Berg, B., Tippett, S., Wise, J., Cahill, B.R., & Katch, F.I. (1986). The effects of hydraulic-resistance strength training in prepubertal males. *Medicine and Science in Sports and Exercise*, **18**, 629-638.

Weltman, A., Janney, C., Rians, C.B., Strand, K., & Katch, F.I. (1987). The effects of hydraulic-resistance strength training on serum lipid levels in prepubertal boys. *American Journal of Diseases of Children*, **141**(7), 777-780.

Chapter 2

Growth and Development

You only have to watch a Little League baseball game to see the dramatic physical and emotional differences among children. Some children are bigger than others; some are faster. One child may become very upset about a missed catch, and another may not really be concerned. The physical differences are due to different genetic potentials and growth rates. It is important for adults to realize that children are not just "little adults." Understanding some of the basic principles of growth and development will allow you to develop realistic expectations of children and will also help you develop goals and exercise progressions. The exercise program must match the child's physical and emotional ability to tolerate the stresses of the training program.

Growth and development of a child involve many factors, not simply a single factor such as height. Also, the child's genetic potential for a given trait (e.g., height) cannot be altered. Still, environmental factors such as nutrition and disease can influence development. Thus a healthy lifestyle involving proper exercise and good nutrition can influence optimal growth and maximize a child's genetic potential.

Maturation has been defined as the progress toward adulthood. A physician considers several areas when examining the maturation of the child:

- Physical size
- Bone maturity
- Reproductive maturity
- Emotional maturity

Each of these areas can be clinically evaluated. The family physician commonly assesses the development of a child based on these areas. Each individual has a chronological age and a physiological age; physiological age is the most important and determines the functional capabilities and performance for that person.

Other factors, such as exercise tolerance, differences between males and females, and adult responsibility, must also be considered when trying to understand children's development.

Physical Size

Physical stature is an obvious sign of growth. Typically, we use measures such as height and weight to assess physical growth from birth to adulthood. It is obvious that all children do not grow at the same rate. Figure 2.1 shows the height growth-rate curves of two males identical in age. This example shows significant size differences at certain ages that are ultimately reduced when the subjects reach adulthood. In Figure 2.2, the pattern of height growth rate is very similar, yet the ultimate stature achieved is quite different. You can observe examples of such responses every day. A boy may be smaller than another boy at ages 11, 12, and 13, but due to similar genetic potentials their height difference in high school may be minimal. Conversely, one child may be the tallest child in the class and may maintain that relationship to his or her classmates into adulthood. The key is the genetic potential for a particular physical trait.

There are many different aspects of physical growth. One child may be taller but another may weigh more and have better muscular development. Each physical trait is dictated by its own genetic pattern for development. Although certain physical traits appear to favor specific sports (e.g., height in basketball), no one physical vari-

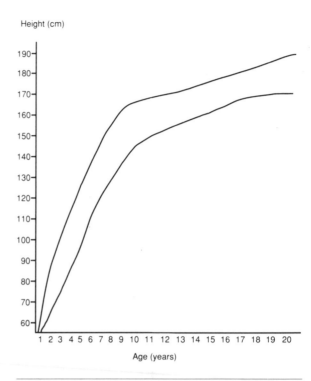

Figure 2.2 Growth curves of two males that remain quite different from birth to adulthood.

able guarantees athletic success. Many times children are pushed into one sport based on a single physical attribute. A tall child may find athletic success in sports such as swimming, rowing, or track and field. This one trait may not truly represent the child's complete physical and mental aptitudes.

You can approximate the child's growth rate by determining at a given age the percent of adult height the child has obtained. Such predictive values have some accuracy but can be influenced by the environment, nutrition, and activity profile. Such predictive charts are only valuable during certain ages. From 3 to 8 years for girls and from 3 to 10 years for boys, the prediction is rather high. When children are older, predictions are accurate only for boys and girls who reach their peak growth rates at approximately 12 and 14 years, respectively. Table 2.1 shows such a chart.

Bone Maturity

Many professionals have feared bone injury in a child who lifts weights, but such fears are outweighed by the physical benefits of resistance training. Bone maturity involves the progression

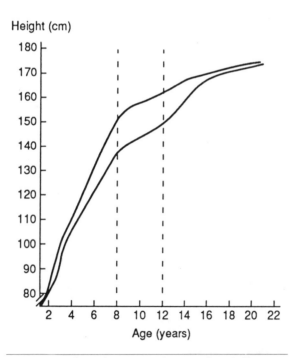

Figure 2.1 Growth curves of two males. Differences during certain years are reduced in adulthood.

Table 2.1

Percentage of Mature Height

Age (years)	Boys	Girls
1	42	45
2	50	53
3	54	57
4	58	62
5	62	66
6	65	70
7	69	74
8	72	78
9	75	81
10	78	84
11	81	88
12	84	93
13	87	97
14	92	98
15	96	99
16	98	100
17	99	100
18	100	100

Note. Modified from Bayley N. 1954. Modern problems in pediatrics: The accurate prediction of growth and adult height, 234-255.

Participation in resistance exercise can help girls avoid osteoporosis later in life.

toward a fully ossified skeleton, that is, solid bone structure. This includes the sealing of growth plates, which determine long bone growth in a child. Bone *mineralization*, which is the deposition of minerals in the bone, determines bone density; this process varies among children. Such changes are evaluated clinically by bone scans. Children who do not have normal bone densities are more prone to skeletal injury. This is particularly true in athletics, because some sports demand toleration of high forces (e.g., football and gymnastics). Bone health is of great importance, especially for girls; *osteoporosis* has been called a "pediatric disease," and young girls should participate in resistance exercise and other physical activities to improve the rate of bone deposition (Loucks, 1988).

Scientific studies indicate that resistance training can influence bone growth in both males and females. Research has shown that young weight lifters have greater bone densities than individuals who do not lift (Conroy et al., in review; Virvidakis et al., 1990). The fear that resistance exercise is detrimental to bone growth appears inappropriate. In fact, resistance exercise can be the most potent exercise stimulus for bone

growth and development. Most bone injuries caused by resistance exercise have been associated with lifting of maximal weights with the use of improper lifting techniques. Thus, proper exercise techniques and training programs can greatly reduce the possibility of any injury. The benefits of resistance training for bone health are greater than the risks.

Reproductive Maturity

Maturity also includes development of a child's reproductive capacity, which dramatically affects growth and development. Changes in hormonal secretions are responsible for many of the significant changes in both boys and girls during pubescence. In males, for example, the increased secretion of the male sex hormone testosterone is related to increases in body weight, muscle size, and strength. As a boy grows older, he will become bigger and stronger without any training at all, due to the influence of hormonal changes alone. Figure 2.3 shows a theoretical relationship between testosterone increase and strength in males. In females, other hormones (e.g., estrogen, growth hormone) may play similar roles. Male testosterone levels, which are 10 to 20 times greater than levels in females, cause the dramatic differences in muscle size and strength between the genders.

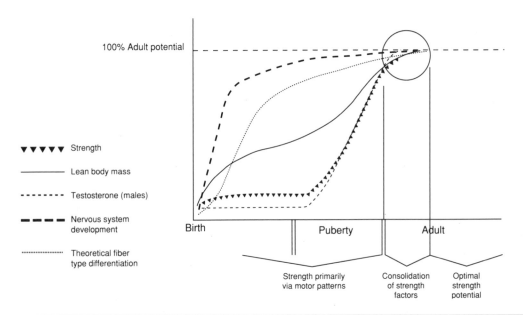

100% Adult potential

▼ ▼ ▼ ▼ ▼   Strength

———————   Lean body mass

- - - - - - -   Testosterone (males)

━ ━ ━ ━   Nervous system
development

·············   Theoretical fiber
type differentiation

Birth

Puberty

Adult

Strength primarily
via motor patterns

Consolidation
of strength
factors

Optimal
strength
potential

Figure 2.3 Theoretical model of strength development factors in males. (Adapted with permission: Kraemer, W.J., Fry, A.C., Frykman, P.N.M., Conroy, B., and Hoffman, J. Resistance training and youth. Pediatric Exercise Science 1:336-350, 1989.)

In young girls, *menarche* is a significant biological marker of increasing reproductive maturity. The onset of the first menstrual flow is the culmination of many hormonal changes that take place in the growing female. In American girls, menarche is observed at about 12.0 to 13.0 years of age. Over the past 10 years, physicians and scientists have questioned the extent to which intense physical activity affects the age of menarche. To date, studies have been unable to draw definitive medical and scientific conclusions. Researchers have observed that certain female athletes and athletes who start to train as prepubescents exhibit later menarche than is normal. Yearly physicals and medical follow-ups are prudent when menarche is delayed because it can impact other growth functions such as bone health. Active young athletes need to have medical examinations that are specific to their needs and that involve the counsel and perspective of a physician trained in sport medicine. Still, research has not definitively demonstrated harmful effects from delayed menarche or sport *amenorrhea*, the temporary absence of menstruation.

Emotional Maturity

Psychological growth is very important, because it interacts with a variety of factors involved with the exercise training process. The child who is in training needs to have the proper interest, attention span, and attitude. As a child grows, he or she exhibits differences in behavior such as group interaction, self-esteem, and mood states. In fact, some children who are 7 and 8 years old may be easier to teach and motivate than those who are 12 and 13 years old. The psychological development of a child will influence the type of activities that he or she can perform safely and effectively and will dictate how much immediate supervision will be needed for various lifts and training methods. The type of program that you can implement will depend upon the child's interest, dedication, attitude, and motivation. Proper teaching progressions, supervision of progress, and positive motivation of a child are important aspects of an exercise training program. Each of these components interacts with the child's psychological mind set.

Almost every child can gain something from participation in a properly designed, prescribed, and monitored resistance exercise program. The child's attitude, interest, and determination to improve are the basic elements of successful participation. Carefully examine your approach to training, your teaching progressions, and the methods you use to monitor the child's exercise toleration. Implement the program with common sense and the best interests of the child in mind. The key is to not do too much too soon.

Exercise Toleration

The importance of the child's ability to tolerate exercise stress cannot be overemphasized. In order for the concepts of individualized exercise prescription, proper supervision, and program monitoring to work, you must communicate with the child; encourage discussion, provide feedback, and listen to the child's concerns and fears. Reflect such interactions in the program development. Use common sense and provide exercise variations, active recovery periods, and rest from training. Do not operate on the belief that more is better.

Start the child with a program that he or she can easily tolerate, and increase difficulty as the child becomes older. Maturation may bring dramatic changes in the child's ability to tolerate resistance training, but don't overestimate the child's ability to tolerate an exercise or sport program. It is better to start out at a conservative level than to overshoot the child's exercise toleration and reduce his or her enjoyment. By using the principles of resistance training, you can design a program that reflects the developmental nature of the child yet does not compromise his or her enthusiasm or physical and mental toleration. By using the proper guidelines for program development, you can implement a resistance exercise program at each stage of the child's development. Remember that the child should not be forced to participate. It is up to you to provide a positive environment that promotes the child's success.

Male and Female Differences

Differences between males and females are obvious in the way they grow. In general, girls mature much sooner than boys. The growth spurt in girls may start as early as age 10 and peak at ages 12 to 13 with the onset of menstruation to soon follow. Conversely, a boy's primary growth spurt occurs between the ages of 12 and 15. Production of testosterone appears to mediate many of the changes that occur in the physical development of muscle and bone of young boys during puberty. Generally boys go through a later growth spurt than girls, catch up to the girls, and eventually surpass them because of a longer growth spurt duration and higher growth rate. This can be seen in Figure 2.4.

An 11-year-old girl can be significantly taller and stronger than an 11-year-old boy, and you

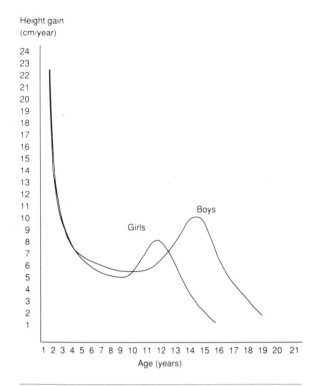

Figure 2.4 Comparison of growth curves for height in boys and girls.

must teach children that such differences are normal. Focus resistance training on the individual's growth, development, and accomplishments, and discourage children from comparing themselves to others. Although this is easy to say, children will want to make such comparisons. It is up to you to explain why individual progress is much more important and then reward it! The greatest thing an adult can do for a child is to express joy and appreciation for the child's own improvement and accomplishment. Promote the idea that the child only competes against him- or herself, and alter the program for each child's specific goals. Focusing on the individual child's progress is the most important factor in long-term adherence to an active lifestyle.

Responsibilities of Adults

Parents are often concerned about the growth of the child for purposes of sport and athletic competition, and they usually desire to see a child grow larger in order to allow for superior sport performance. Thus, many parents become quite obsessed with trying to predict future height and weight of a child. Although it is important that a physician monitor growth rates to make sure that no underlying pathology exists, parents should not try to improve on genetics; a child's genetic basis cannot be altered. Parents should also remember that success in athletics involves more than just a child's size; each sport has particular requirements for success at every level.

Adults should not select a child's activities based only on future professional success. A child can enjoy playing basketball despite the fact that he or she may never be an NBA player. It's up to adults to link sport participation to factors such as fun and fitness rather than to professional or financial success. Resistance training should not be looked at as a tool for sport performance only. It is important that we remember the ''fun'' associated with sport participation and attempt to provide adequate preparation for safe sport participation.

Adults are also responsible for optimizing the child's sport experience. Resistance training along with proper coaching can prepare the child for the demands of sport, whether it is recreational or competitive. So many times we want our children to be successful but do not provide them with the proper tools through appropriate teaching or training methods. Adults must allow children to have fun, to grow, and, to develop, and must provide them with the tools to reach their own potential.

Summing Up and Looking Ahead

Growth and development are multidimensional; prediction of athletic success based on one variable at one point in time is difficult at best and typically does not represent the best interests of the child. Participation in different sports promotes proper physical training, sparks a child's interests, and provides the child with a realistic view of sport. It is up to parents, teachers, and coaches to promote the fun associated with a game and not view it as a future profession. In a time when sports burnout in children is common, the correct attitude concerning the role of sports in a child's life will help make sports participation a positive experience. Furthermore, in a time when youth fitness is at an all-time low, promotion of better physical exercise training can enhance the child's quality of life and help him or her develop habits that will influence health and well-being over a lifetime.

The following poem is about a little boy but can also apply to young girls.

Just a Little Boy

He stands at the plate with heart pounding fast.
The bases are loaded; the die has been cast.
Mom and dad cannot help him, he stands all alone.
A hit at this moment would send the team home.
The ball meets the plate; he swings and he misses.
There is a groan from the crowd, with some boos and some hisses.
A thoughtless voice cries, ''Strike out the bum.''
Tears fill his eyes; the game's no longer fun.
So open your heart and give him a break.
For it's moments like this, a man you can make.
Keep this in mind when you hear someone forget.
He's just a little boy and not a man yet.

—Author unknown

In the next chapter we will examine various administrative and program development concerns.

Additional Readings

Conroy, B.P., Kraemer, W.J., Maresh, C.M., & Dalsky, G.P. (1992). Adaptive responses of bone to physical activity. *Journal of Medicine, Exercise, Nutrition and Health,* **1**(2) 64-74.

Conroy, B.P., Kraemer, W.J., Maresh, C.M., Dalsky, G.P., Fleck, S.J., Stone, M.H., Fry, A.C., & Miller, P. Bone mineral density in elite junior Olympic weightlifters. *Medicine Science in Sports and Exercise,* in review.

Flore, C.E., Cottini, E., Fargetta, C., Giuseppe, D.S., Foti, R., & Raspagliesi, M. (1991). The effects of muscle-building exercise on forearm bone mineral content and osteoblast activity in drug-free and anabolic steroid self-administering young men. *Bone and Mineral,* **13**, 77-83.

Frost, H.M. (1990). Skeletal structural adaptations to mechanical usage. (SATMU): 1. Redefining Wolff's Law: The bone modeling problem. *Anatomical Record,* **226**, 403-413.

Goodship, A.E., Lanyon, L.E., & MacFie, J.H. (1979). Functional adaptation of bone to increased stress. *Journal of Bone Joint Surgery,* **61-A**(4), 539-546.

Kraemer, W.J., Fry, A.C., Frykman, P.N., Conroy, B., & Hoffman, J. (1989). Resistance training and youth. *Pediatric Exercise Science,* **1**, 336-350.

Loucks, A.B. (1988). Osteoporosis prevention begins in childhood. In E.W. Brown & C.F. Bravta (Eds.), Competitive sports for children and youth: An overview of research and issues (pp. 213-223). Champaign, IL: Human Kinetics.

Malina, R.M. (1989). C.H. McCloy research lecture: Children in the exercise sciences. *Research Quarterly for Exercise and Sport,* **60**(4), 305-317.

Micheli, L.J. (1989). The exercising child: Injuries. *Pediatric Exercise Science,* **1**, 329-335.

Plowman, S.A. (1989). Maturation and exercise training in children. *Pediatric Exercise Science,* **1**, 303-312.

Pocock, N.A., Eisman, J., Gwinn, T., Sambrook, P., Freund, J., & Yeates, M. (1989). Muscle strength, physical fitness, and weight but not age predict femoral neck bone mass. *Journal of Bone and Mineral Research,* **4**(3), 441-448.

Roche, A.F., & Malina, R.M. (1983). *Manual of physical status and performance in childhood* (Vol. 1B, physical status). New York: Plenum Press.

Rowland, T.W. (1989). Oxygen uptake and endurance fitness in children: A developmental perspective. *Pediatric Exercise Science,* **1**, 313-328.

Vaughn, J. (1981). *The physiology of bone.* New York: Oxford Press.

Virvidakis, K., Georgiu, E., Korkotsidis, A., Ntalles, K., & Proukakis, C. (1990). Bone mineral content of junior competitive weightlifters. *International Journal of Sports Medicine,* **11**, 244-246.

Chapter 3

Developing and Administering a Strength Training Program for Children

Developing and administering a resistance training program is a very rewarding experience. This chapter discusses factors you must consider if the program is to be successful.

Motivation and Program Philosophy

Every program, whether conducted at home, at school, in a private health club, or in a public recreation facility, must provide an environment conducive to training for children. This requires the development and implementation of a program philosophy that includes motivational considerations and realistic program expectations for children, which should be based on a sound understanding of children's psychological and physiological needs and capabilities.

Providing the Right Motivation

Motivation is a very individual phenomenon that should always be viewed from a child's perspective: what motivates one child may not motivate another. The first step is to get the child genuinely interested in physical fitness. Children who are forced to participate in fitness programs will usually not enjoy the activities and may resent participating. Children who are inappropriately motivated in fitness programs may later turn away from physical activity. Inappropriate motivation is typified by the classic example of a coach assigning exercise as a punishment for unwanted behaviors such as missing a catch or a free throw.

Appropriate motivation hinges on appropriate exercise demands. Don't overshoot the child's physical capabilities or make the experience physically painful. For example, asking a child to perform too many sets during the first training sessions of a program can result in severe muscle soreness. Use proper progression to gradually prepare each child both physically and mentally for sports participation. Each day thousands of young athletes are exposed to sport activities for which they are not prepared physically and mentally. This lack of preparation corresponds to low fitness levels of our youth. Thus, it is important that we positively promote fitness activities in order to promote better health habits and safer participation in sports.

Children need a considerable amount of education concerning what fitness, training, and sports are all about before they start a full program of exercise training. Children must understand why they are performing these exercises and must freely desire to participate. The goal is for children to participate in exercise training because they want to be involved, not just to please an adult.

Setting Realistic Expectations and Goals

Setting realistic expectations of what a resistance training program can accomplish is very important. Proper expectations are based on the understanding of how the body responds at various ages to different training programs. A goal of developing larger muscles in a 10-year-old boy is not consistent with the adaptations that occur in young children. You must help the child develop proper expectations and goals; this requires a basic understanding of what is realistic and possible. Statements such as "you should be about 25 pounds heavier if you want to play" or "anyone can be a world champion" are irresponsible statements that send the wrong signals to children. The results range from losing the trust of the child and lowering his or her self-

esteem to contributing to anabolic substance abuse.

It is important that the child compete against his or her own progress and not against others. Because children mature at different rates and have genetic predispositions for physical characteristics, self-improvement is one of the most important concepts that you can develop. Encourage this viewpoint and you will contribute to each child's self-esteem.

Training methods and goals change as a child grows older. A change in training may be due to a child's changing interests in different sports. Even if the child maintains a long-term interest in a particular sport, his or her exercise prescription will change dramatically to address increased physical maturity and the more rigorous demands of advanced sport competition.

Presenting the Program Philosophy

For formal programs (e.g., those in schools or health clubs), the program philosophy must be expressed in the environment. This means that the signs, wall charts, and handouts need to send the right signals to the child. This is especially important when both adults and children train in the same facility. You can present the program philosophy in the following ways:

- Post age-related instructions for the child next to the adult guidelines.

Training Day Schedule

	Adult
Heavy day:	100% of 3 to 5 RM
Moderate day:	90% of 3 to 5 RM
Light day:	85% of 3 to 5 RM
	Child (15 and under)
Heavy day:	100% of 8 to 10 RM
Moderate day:	90% of 8 to 10 RM
Light day:	85% of 8 to 10 RM

- Use posters and pictures that depict boys and girls and promote proper expectations from resistance training.
- Use charts, contests, and awards to promote the type of principles on which children need to concentrate; these can include
  - training consistency charts and awards,
  - exercise technique contests and awards,
  - total conditioning fitness awards focusing on progress in other components of

physical fitness (e.g., endurance runs, flexibility), and

— fitness preparation awards prior to a sports season and maintenance program awards during a sports season.

Administrative Concerns

The availability of equipment, space, and time for resistance training, and the number of children and their maturity levels, are all factors that have a great impact on the training program. In the initial design of an exercise program, however, you should not consider these administrative concerns but should first design an optimal program. Then you can make needed changes in the program due to administrative concerns. Try to remedy administrative considerations that severely compromise the initial program design as soon as possible. For example, if an exercise in the optimal program cannot be performed because of lack of proper equipment, plan to obtain the equipment.

Equipment Availability

The availability of resistance training equipment is perhaps the greatest obstacle to many programs. This is especially true in elementary, junior high, and high school programs. Some resistance training programs do not require a great deal of equipment; participants use body weight and partner-resisted exercises. However, many exercises do require equipment.

If you are going to purchase equipment for a program, evaluate the equipment based upon safety, cost, construction, and proper fit for children. Establish a plan of equipment purchases so that all the major muscle groups of the body can be trained. Do not buy resistance exercise machines that duplicate your capabilities or equipment for a specific sport or small muscle group until you have equipment to train all the major muscle groups. Obtaining equipment that you can use to train several different muscle groups should be a higher priority than obtaining equipment that can be used to train only one muscle group.

If the available equipment is minimal, find viable alternatives for the muscle groups for which you have no equipment. In these situations consider body weight–resisted and partner-resisted exercises. Dynamic drills (e.g., hill running and stair running) are also viable substitutions.

When you are considering enrolling a child at a spa or health club, evaluate the equipment as described in chapter 5 and consider the factors listed in the following box.

FACTORS TO CONSIDER WHEN PURCHASING A CLUB MEMBERSHIP FOR A CHILD

1. Are the instructors certified by a non-profit, professional organization concerned with knowledge and understanding of resistance training?
2. Are the instructors certified in first aid and cardiopulmonary resuscitation (CPR)?
3. How many children are members of the club?
4. Are there special times or classes for children members?
5. Do the instructors know how to train children?
6. Do parents have to be present for children to use the resistance exercise facilities? How old must the children be to use the facilities alone?
7. Is the resistance exercise room well supervised?
8. Is pre-testing and testing performed, and are results used to help design the program?
9. Is the program individually designed?
10. Is aerobic training monitored by use of a physiological variable (e.g., heart rate)?
11. Does the club have a medical or scientific advisory board?
12. What is the medical emergency plan?
13. Is the equipment maintained in good working condition?
14. Does the equipment properly fit children or can it be modified to do so?

Number of Individuals Training

Many times a training facility has adequate equipment to train all the major muscle groups but the program is inadequate because the facility is too crowded. The number of children

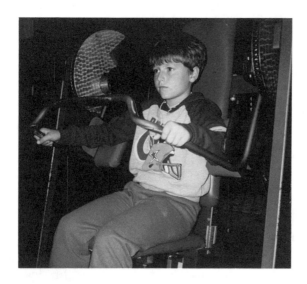

Equipment should fit children properly. Some exercise machines may not fit a child's limb length.

who can be effectively trained at one time depends in part on their maturity (i.e., their abilities to follow directions and their desire to train). These factors in turn may depend upon children's understanding of what they are doing and why. In many instances, a facility is overcrowded only at certain times of the day (e.g., noon or after school).

One solution to alleviate overcrowding is to develop a master schedule of training times for teams or individuals. Accurate information about the facility's use also aids requests for the facility to be open for a greater number of hours, such as before or after school and during free periods, and provides strong support for requests for more equipment and space. The largest numbers of people typically train at noon, after school, and late in the afternoon, when athletic teams are training and children have free time. When attempting to schedule athletic teams, obtain from coaches the times they desire to use the facility and alternate times, such as in the morning before school. Inform all parties using the facility that staying with the established schedule will greatly improve the amount of actual training that takes place because the facility will not be overcrowded and individuals will be training, not waiting to use a piece of equipment. Consider adult supervision when developing the schedule of the facility's open hours. For safety reasons, the number of individuals in the facility needs to be carefully monitored and controlled.

A second solution to overcrowding is to better organize the flow of lifters during their training sessions. To do this, you must know which pieces of equipment are used most often in various training programs and where the lines develop for people waiting to use equipment. Requiring children to wait to use a piece of equipment is an open invitation to horseplay, distraction, and possible injury. Furthermore, excessive delays reduce the effectiveness of timed programs. Several measures can help improve the flow pattern within the training facility:

• *Use timed training sessions* (i.e., specified time to perform an exercise and specified rest periods between exercises), so that lifters must move quickly from one piece of equipment to the next. However, remember to account for the time needed to modify equipment so that it fits the children and the time needed to change the resistance on the equipment.

• *Use predetermined exercise sequences*, so that lines do not form by the group's favorite piece of equipment.

• *Schedule individuals who follow a similar training program at the same time of the day.* This type of scheduling also gives the children an opportunity to have training partners.

• *Schedule individuals who need similar equipment modifications at the same time of the day, if possible.*

• *Have the pads or blocks needed to make equipment modifications available at each exercise station.*

• *Carefully plan programs for groups that use different exercises or time sequences and that need to train at the same time of the day,* so the groups do not interfere with each other's movement through the exercises.

For timed training sessions, you can use a whistle and stopwatch to control rest period length between sets and exercises and length of time to perform a *set*. You can also play a tape recording of the rest and exercise sequence on a facility-wide audio system. For example, play music during the training session and use a voice-over to indicate the rest periods and times to move to the next exercise. In addition, you can indicate the exercise sequence on the floor with color-coded tape, and on work-out sheets lifters can carry to help control the flow pattern. All of these measures free you to assist the children with exercise technique, not act as a traffic cop. These methods may be mandatory when you are training a large group, but they also help you stress the proper exercise sequence and rest periods to be used in an exercise program.

Equipment Modification

Modifying equipment to fit children will create organizational problems. For example, each exercise station must have the pads and/or blocks necessary to modify the equipment to fit the child. Equipment such as *dumbbells* must be available so the child can perform an alternate exercise when a machine does not fit or cannot provide the proper resistance. Each child must also know how to set up the necessary modification for each exercise. Equipment modifications will change as a child grows; thus you will need to check equipment for proper fit as frequently as every month. Prior to the training session, preparation of the resistance training facility is needed to address such equipment modification concerns. If you use timed workouts, you must consider the time needed for equipment modifications. This is especially true when several children are training and modifications are being made for many exercises. One way to solve this problem is to note necessary modifications on each child's workout card. Additionally, an adult can make the modifications for the children. Although effective, this may be somewhat impractical with a large group of children.

To find out how long it takes to make a particular equipment modification, have the child

Each exercise station must have the pads and blocks necessary to modify the equipment to fit the child.

perform a trial training session. Then modify the rest periods to account for the time needed for equipment modifications. Younger children (8 to 10 years old) may require more time to make the modifications themselves, or an adult may have to make the modifications for them. This requires more adult supervision but may be needed to ensure the safety of the children. Although it may be desirable to have 1-minute rest periods in a particular training session, organizational problems such as equipment fit may make this impossible. For example, exercise machines typically require more modifications than free weights due to fixed movement patterns and positions. You must resolve these organizational problems as best as possible without sacrificing the safety of the children or lessening the training session's effectiveness.

Space Availability

Space availability refers to the amount of total floor space in the resistance training facility. Space is needed not only for the resistance training equipment but also for walkways between pieces of equipment. Ideally at least 5 feet should separate each piece of equipment. This space is necessary for lifters to move about safely and to change the resistance on some pieces of equipment and for the *spotters* to perform their exercise monitoring during a lift. When free weights are used, space is needed where the lifter can dump the weight if necessary; this is especially true for *ballistic*-type lifts (e.g., power cleans and snatches). Before you obtain any new equipment for a facility, be sure sufficient space to meet these needs is available.

Time Availability

The best designed training program is of no use if children do not have sufficient time for training. After designing a program, calculate the total amount of time needed to perform a training session including rest periods, time to change the resistance, and time to make equipment modifications. You may do this by having one or two children perform the workout, including any equipment modifications. Modifications to a training program that reduce the total training time must be made carefully. Don't simply drop the last exercise in a session; if an exercise needs to be dropped from the program, it should be the exercise that is least needed, based upon the needs analysis (see chapter 4) of the group or individual. If more than one exercise for a major muscle group is included in the program, it may be possible to drop one of them. Don't decrease rest periods simply to save time. Increased blood lactate levels result when rest periods are reduced and are associated with increased exercise discomfort. Pay close attention to see if the child tolerates more demanding, high lactate workouts. Rest periods should only be reduced when you want to increase high-*intensity* local muscular endurance of the lifters. This may be desirable for children participating in such sports as certain track events (e.g., 400- and 800-m sprints), or wrestling. But if the major goal of the training is to increase strength/power, the rest periods should not be decreased below 2 minutes. Carefully evaluate any changes you make in the training program to meet time constraints. Also evaluate how the changes affect the exercise training stimulus.

Program Evaluation and Testing

You should evaluate the training program to determine whether it meets the goals it was designed for. If it does not meet its goals, the program needs to be altered. Programs are commonly evaluated for the strength gains and changes in motor performance they produce. At least 8 weeks of training should be performed before a program is evaluated. This allows time for adaptations to the program to occur.

Examining a training log is the easiest and quickest way to evaluate strength gains. Simply examine the training logs to see what improvements children have made in repetition maximum resistances. You can do this in a cursory manner, or you can calculate percent gains for individuals or a group. When evaluating gains in strength, remember that during the first 3 to 4 weeks of a training program large gains in strength (up to 20 percent) will occur as the children learn to perform the exercises. In 8 to 14 weeks of training, gains in strength of up to 43 percent have been demonstrated in previously untrained children. Thus, gains in strength of approximately 30 to 40 percent in 8 to 14 weeks indicate a successful program in terms of strength gains. However, gains in strength of this magnitude may not occur if the children have previous resistance training experience.

Testing for strength gains involves determining repetition maximum (RM) resistances for the children. We will discuss how to determine RM resistances later in the chapter. The RM is a resistance that allows the performance of no more than a specific number of repetitions. It is not necessary to test for RMs for all exercises performed in the training program; this is very time-consuming, and in many instances training log data can answer questions concerning strength gains. Normally RMs are determined for two or three multijoint exercises such as the leg press, squat, bench press, or incline press.

Training Log

The child should record in a training log the number of sets, repetitions, and resistances for each exercise in a training session. This information is useful in several ways. It demonstrates the progress of each lifter in terms of resistance used and repetitions performed, information that can be motivational for children. The log will also help you evaluate the success of the training program and determine when the resistance should be increased for a particular exercise. Last, it is a reminder of the order of exercises to be performed, the resistance to be used, and the number of repetitions to be performed during a training session.

Some training logs allow the user to record total body weight prior to each training session. This is useful especially if an individual is attempting to lose or gain weight. Training logs also may have a place for comments concerning the training session, such as whether the session seemed easy or difficult. A training log for children should have a place for notes on necessary equipment modifications (see Figure 3.1).

The child can keep a training log in a notebook, using an abbreviated form of notation (see Figure 3.2). For example, the notation "bench press 3 × 10 RM at 70, 60, 55 (1 min)" means the lifter performed three sets of the bench press with resistances for the first, second, and third sets at 70, 60, and 55 pounds, respectively, and rested 1 minute between the sets. Use this type of notation to record each exercise of a training session.

RM Determination

In children, RMs for six or seven repetitions are sufficient as a measure of strength. You should

Name _____   Age _____

Week _____   Week _____   Week _____

Day _____   Day _____   Day _____

Weight _____ lb   Weight _____ lb   Weight _____ lb

Exercise	Set 1		Set 2		Set 3		Set 1		Set 2		Set 3		Set 1		Set 2		Set 3	
	Weight	Reps	Weight	Reps	Weight	Reps	Weight	Reps	Weight	Reps	Weight	Reps	Weight	Reps	Weight	Reps	Weight	Reps

Comments: _____

_____

_____

_____

Exercise   Modifications

_____   _____

_____   _____

_____   _____

_____   _____

Figure 3.1 Training log that can document three sets of an exercise per training session and three training sessions per week. This log allows the user to record total body weight prior to each training session and to note necessary equipment modifications.

Training Log
Jan 16
Body weight - 101 lb.
Leg press 3 × 12 RM - 100, 95, 90
Bench press 3 × 12 RM - 65, 60, 55
Leg curls 3 × 10 RM - 25
Arm curls 3 × 10 RM - 15
Military press 3 × 8 RM - 50, 45, 40
Leg extensions 3 × 10 RM - 35
Incline sit-ups 3 × 2 - Board at 2nd highest
position
Comments:
1 - 2 min. rest between all exercises. Felt good.
Almost time to increase leg press resistance to
105.

Figure 3.2 Notebook log for one training session.

closely control RM testing, because the length of the rest periods and the number of sets performed will affect the results. An estimation of the RM will help you determine warm-up resistances to be used in RM testing. If the child has weight-training experience, you can get an estimation of the RM from his or her training log. If the child has been tested for RM previously, you can estimate RM from the results of the previous test. The following is a procedure to determine a 6 RM:

1. The child warms up with 5 to 10 repetitions with 50 percent of the estimated 6 RM.
2. After 1 minute of rest and some stretching, the child performs six repetitions at 70 percent of the estimated 6 RM.
3. The child repeats step 2 at 90 percent of the estimated 6 RM.
4. After about 2 minutes of rest, depending upon the effort needed to perform the 90 percent set, the child performs six repetitions with 100 or 105 percent of the estimated 6 RM.
5. If the child successfully completes six repetitions in Step 4, add 2.5 to 5 percent of the resistance used in Step 4 and have the child attempt six repetitions after 2 minutes of rest. If the child does not complete six repetitions in Step 4, subtract 2.5 to 5 percent of the resistance used in Step 4 and have the child attempt six repetitions after 2 minutes of rest.
6. If the first part of Step 5 is successful (the child lifts 2.5 to 5 percent more resistance than used in Step 4), retest the child starting with higher resistances after at least 24 hours of rest, because performance of more sets will be greatly affected by fatigue. If the second part of Step 5 is successful (the child lifts 2.5 to 5 percent less than the resistance used in Step 4), this is the child's 6 RM. If the second part of Step 5 is not successful (the child does not lift 2.5 to 5 percent less resistance used in Step 4), retest the child after at least 24 hours of rest, starting with less resistance.

As an example, a child's estimated 6 RM for the leg press is 100 pounds. The child performs 5 to 10 repetitions with 50 pounds as a warm-up (100 pounds × 0.50 = 50 pounds, Step 1). After 1 minute of rest and stretching, the child performs six repetitions with 70 pounds (100 pounds × 0.70 = 70 pounds, Step 2). After 2 minutes of rest the child performs six repetitions with 90 pounds (100 pounds × 0.90 = 90 pounds, Step 3). This child performs the six repetitions at 90 pounds very easily, so you decide to use 105 percent of the estimated 6-RM resistance. After 2 minutes of rest the child performs six repetitions with 105 pounds, (100 pounds × 1.05 = 105 pounds, Step 4). Performance of the set at 105 pounds appears to be very difficult so you decide to have the child try another set at 108 pounds (105 pounds × 0.025 = 2.6 pounds, 105 pounds + 2.6 pounds = 107.6 pounds. It is impossible to get a resistance of 107.6 pounds on the leg press being used so you have the child use 108 pounds, Step 5.) After 2 minutes of rest the child completes only four repetitions, so this child's 6-RM resistance for the leg press is 105 pounds. It typically will be impossible to get the exact weight needed for RM testing on the bar or machine the child is using, so you will have to use a resistance that's as close as possible to the resistance needed.

When you are using machines for RM testing it is possible to get resistances in between the increments on the weight stack by using small weights (usually 2.5 or 5 pounds) available for some machines that fit on top of the weight stack or by hanging additional small weights off an additional weight stack pin. When using this second method make sure the additional weights do not interfere with the movement of the weight stack.

Correct RM testing does require a relatively long time period, 10 to 15 minutes per child per exercise. However, you can greatly reduce this time by staggering children so that when one child is resting another is performing a set. You can also reduce testing time by having more than one testing station going on at the same time.

It is important that RM testing be performed at least 24 hours after the last training session so that fatigue does not affect the results. Whether machines or free weights are used, body, hand, and foot position must be the same for all testing. If the child's feet are blocked for one test, they should be blocked for the next test. The seat on a machine must be in the same position for all tests. Whether or not the child grows significantly between tests, he or she must attempt to achieve the same relative body position (e.g., same angle at the elbows, shoulders, and knees). Correct exercise technique must be used for all testing and spotters must be present so that an injury does not occur. You must use correct and repeatable procedures for all testing to ensure the safety of the lifters and to ensure reliable test results.

Local Muscular Endurance Test

If increased local muscular endurance is a goal of the training, you may desire to evaluate it. You can perform a simple local muscular endurance test by having the child do as many repetitions as possible at a specified percentage of his or her body weight or of his or her 6-RM resistance. RM testing and local muscular endurance testing should be separated by at least 24 to 48 hours so that fatigue does not affect the results. You can use 60 to 80 percent of the 6 RM to test relative local muscular endurance. Terminate tests of relative local muscular endurance when exercise technique deteriorates to a point that endangers the child's safety. As with RM testing, use spotters and require proper exercise technique for all repetitions performed during testing.

Motor Performance Testing

A goal of some resistance training programs is to improve motor performance. Common motor performance tests are short sprints (30 to 50 yards) and vertical jumping. It is beyond the scope of this text to describe proper procedure for motor performance tests. This information is available from many other sources, such as a text concerning measurement or evaluation in physical education. An example of such a text is T.A. Baumgartner and A.S. Jackson's *Measurement for Evaluation in Physical Education*.

Equipment Maintenance

Resistance training equipment is very durable; however, maintenance of equipment is necessary for safe operation and will increase the life of the equipment. Welds on equipment should be inspected for cracks and bolts checked for tightness at least weekly; a cracked weld or loose bolt can easily cause an injury. Be sure there is adequate air circulation in the training facility so that excessive moisture does not cause machines to rust. The simplest and easiest ways to ensure adequate air ventilation is to keep doors and windows open and to use fans where possible. If needed to keep the moisture level down, install an air conditioner or a dehumidifier. If rust does develop on a piece of equipment, use naval jelly to remove it immediately and touch up the rust spot with a rust-resistant paint.

Lubrication of Equipment

Resistance training equipment has many moving parts, which need to be lubricated to prevent wear. A spray-on silicone lubricant is best for most lubrication needs. Clean and lubricate chains once a week to ensure their smooth operation. Clean and lubricate weight stack rods weekly when they are in heavy use so that the weight plates slide freely and smoothly. Fine steel wool works for removing dirt from weight stack rods. In addition, you should inspect the bushings in weight stack plates for wear and smooth operation and replace them if needed to prevent damage to the weight stack rods.

Cables and Pulleys

Many pieces of equipment have a cable-and-pulley or chain-and-pulley arrangement, which can become worn. The cables, chains, and pulleys should be inspected daily to ensure they are aligned properly and are operating smoothly as a unit. Lubricate the bearings of the pulley regularly; check the pulley for side-to-side wobble and tighten it if needed. A pulley and cable or chain unit that is not operating smoothly will wear out very quickly. For safety reasons, replace worn cables, chains, and pulleys immediately.

Weight Plates

Free-weight plates and weight plates in a weight stack on a machine do crack and break occasionally. The most common cause of this is dropping of the resistance after the lifter completes a repetition. Thus, don't allow dropping of free weights or excessive "banging" of plates of a weight stack. It's possible to weld weight plates after they are cracked or broken, but this is difficult due to the high graphite content of many weight plates. In most instances welding of weight plates does not last, and therefore it is normally best to retire the broken plate and replace it. For exercises in which the plates commonly hit the ground (e.g., dead lift, high pulls), you can buy plates with rubber bumpers (called *bumper plates*), but these are more expensive.

Olympic Bars

Olympic bars are *barbells* 7 feet 2 inches long that are used for Olympic and power lifting. They have revolving sleeves on each end that allow the weights to rotate during a lift. This allows the bar to revolve during the lift and prevents skin from ripping off the hands of the lifter or the wrist being injured (see Figure 3.3). Olympic bars are very durable; however, a few problems can develop. The bar may become bent if the supports holding the bar are very close together and the bar is loaded heavily. This can easily happen if the bar is left loaded overnight or between training sessions; thus the bar should be unloaded when it is not in use. The revolving sleeves on Olympic bars at times become loose; normally you can remedy this by tightening the allen screw at the end of the sleeve. The sleeves should also be lubricated regularly with a light lubricant. After lubrication, wipe the sleeves clean; if lubricant is on the outside of the bar, the plates will easily slide off the bar. This is one reason that the use of collars on all free-weight bars should be mandatory. Olympic bars

come in a wide price range, and typically it is the less expensive bars that develop problems. Therefore, when obtaining Olympic bars make sure they are of quality construction and have good tensile strength.

Upholstery

The benches and seats of resistance training equipment are covered with vinyl or Naugahyde. Disinfectants used to remove moisture, sweat, and dirt from these coverings will over time cause them to crack. Therefore, regular cleaning with a strong disinfectant should be followed by a mild soap rinse, and a vinyl restorant product should be applied to these surfaces regularly. To help prevent the buildup of dirt on these surfaces, make clean clothing mandatory in the facility and require lifters to wear shirts. In addition, lifters should use towels to wipe off sweat after they have finished with a piece of equipment. If the covering becomes excessively cracked or ripped, it can be replaced; most equipment companies sell replacement pads for their equipment. It is also possible to have a local upholsterer recover the pad with a high-grade vinyl or Naugahyde.

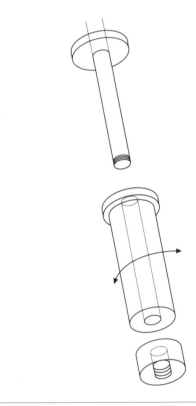

Figure 3.3 Olympic bar revolving sleeve.

Floor Protection

If possible, install a dark rubberized flooring throughout the facility. Place rubber mats where weight plates will most likely be placed on the floor or dropped, especially in the area where such lifts as deadlifts and cleans are performed. Typically, facilities place lifting platforms in the areas where power cleans and variations of the Olympic lifts are performed. An official Olympic lifting platform is a square 13 feet, 1-1/4 inches per side. Constructed of wood, it is designed to protect the floor if the barbell is dropped. You can obtain plans on how to construct a weight-lifting platform from the U.S. Weightlifting Federation, U.S. Olympic Complex, 1750 East Boulder St., Colorado Springs, CO 80909.

Resistance Facility Tool Kit

Many simple equipment repairs require tools, and you should keep the most frequently needed tools in the facility. A training facility tool kit should include the following:

- Complete set of allen wrenches
- Complete set of screw drivers (Phillip's head and regular head)
- Files for smoothing rough spots on equipment
- Staple gun
- Complete socket set
- Paint touch-up equipment
- Bolt cutters
- Measuring tape
- Light silicon lubricant spray
- Naval jelly
- Strong disinfectant, rubber gloves, mild soap, vinyl restorant, sponge, and bucket to clean upholstery

Technique Evaluation

Many young children will want to see how strong they are by trying to lift as much as possible for one repetition. To satisfy the competitiveness of some children, you can hold lifting technique contests. Typically, lifts such as the squat, bench press, power clean, or power snatch, which involve multijoint movements and a higher degree of skill, are used for such contests that stress correct lifting technique rather than the total resistance lifted. The appendix to this chapter contains technique evaluation forms for these lifts. You can develop your own forms for other lifts following these examples. The appendix suggests the amount of resistance you should use for technique evaluation, but you should adjust this to the strength levels of the children in a particular group and for specific exercises. Correct technique for all of these lifts is described in detail in chapter 6.

Summing Up and Looking Ahead

Development and administration of a resistance training program do not end after the program has started. Rather they comprise an ongoing process of many factors, from daily correction of exercise technique and adjustment of a child's resistances to program evaluation and program changes needed to meet the desired goals of the program.

In the next chapter we will discuss some things you should consider when designing a resistance training program for children.

Additional Readings

Baechle, T.R., & Groves, B.R. (1992). *Weight training steps to success*. Champaign, IL: Leisure Press.

Baumgartner, B.A., & Jackson, A.S. (1982). *Measurement for evaluation in physical education*. (2nd ed.). Dubuque, IA: William C. Brown. Co. Pub.

Brown, E.W., & Branta, C.F. (Eds.) (1988). *Competitive sports for children and youth: An overview of research and issues*. Champaign, IL: Human Kinetics.

Coker, E. (1987). Equipment padding and covering. *National Strength and Conditioning Association Journal*, **9**(6), 77-78.

Coker, E. (1987). The Olympic bar. *National Strength and Conditioning Association Journal*, **9**(4), 73-74.

Coker, E. (1988). Broken mirrors. *National Strength and Conditioning Association Journal*, **10**(5), 58-59.

Coker, E. (1988). Broken plates. *National Strength and Conditioning Association Journal*, **10**(3), 58.

Coker, E. (1988). Repairing and inspecting welds. *National Strength and Conditioning Association Journal*, **10**(2), 62-63.

Coker, E. (1989). Weight room flooring. *National*

Strength and Conditioning Association Journal, **11**(1), 26-27.

Coker, E. (1989). Weight room tool kit. *National Strength and Conditioning Association Journal,* **11**(3), 62.

Hurd, J. (1987). Lubricating equipment. *National Strength and Conditioning Association Journal,* **9**(5), 69.

Hurd, J. (1988). Cables: Inspecting and replac-ing. *National Strength and Conditioning Association Journal,* **10**(1), 81.

Martens, R. (1987). *Joy and sadness in children's sports.* Champaign, IL: Human Kinetics.

Pauletto, B. (1991). *Strength Training for Coaches.* Champaign, IL: Leisure Press.

Rotella, R.J., & Bunker, L.K. (1987). *Parenting your superstar.* Champaign, IL: Leisure Press.

Appendix:

Technique Evaluation Forms

The purpose of the resistance used in technique competition is to provide only enough resistance to require the lifter to demonstrate balance, control, and coordinated movement during the lift. Resistance is dependent on strength level.

Front or Back Squat Technique

Resistance Used

Back squat, 60 to 70 percent of body weight; front squat, 50 to 60 percent of body weight.

Starting Position

Feet are shoulder-width apart and pointing forward or slightly out; back is straight; bar is on spines of *scapulae*; hands are slightly wider than shoulder-width for back squat; elbows are rotated up and bar is on upper chest and front of shoulder for front squat; bar is centered and horizontal; head is in neutral position.

Points Available: 0-4   *Points Earned*: _____

Lowering (Eccentric) Phase

Feet stay flat; descent is performed in a controlled manner; back stays straight; no excessive forward lean; bar stays horizontal; descent is to where thighs are parallel to the floor; head stays in line with rest of back.

Points Available: 0-9   *Points Earned*: _____

Up (Concentric) Phase

Feet stay flat; back stays straight; legs (not back) lift weight; no excessive forward lean; bar stays horizontal; head stays in line with rest of back.

Points Available: 0-9   *Points Earned*: _____

Finishing Position

Knee and hip extension is complete; position is same as starting position.

Points Available: 0-3   *Points Earned*: _____

Total Points Available: 0-25   Total Points Earned: ____

Bench Press Technique

Resistance Used

40 to 50 percent of body weight.

Starting Position

Elbows are straight; feet are flat on the floor; buttocks and shoulders touch bench; back is not excessively arched; bar is over upper chest; bar is horizontal.

Points Available: 0-6   *Points Earned*: _____

Lowering (Eccentric) Phase

Descent of bar is controlled; elbows are out to side; bar touches chest at nipple level; there is no bounce on chest touch; bar is horizontal; feet stay flat on floor; back is not excessively arched; head stays still.

Points Available: 0-7   *Points Earned*: _____

Up (Concentric) Phase

Back is not excessively arched; elbows are out to sides; bar is horizontal; both arms straighten at same speed; motion is smooth and continuous; head stays still; feet stay flat on floor.

Points Available: 0-9   *Points Earned*: _____

Finishing Position

Same position as starting position.

Points Available: 0-3   *Points Earned*: _____

Total Points Available: 0-25   Total Points Earned: ____

Power Clean Technique

Resistance Used

40 to 50 percent of body weight.

Starting Position

Bar is over balls of feet; feet are hip width or slightly wider apart; shoulders are over or slightly in front of bar; grip is slightly wider than shoulder-width; head is in neutral position, back is straight.

Points Available: 0-5   *Points Earned*: _____

Pull

Back stays at the same angle to floor as in the starting position until bar is at knee height; shoulders stay over bar; bar stays close to body; bar does not bounce off of thighs during second pull; second pull is explosive; elbows stay above bar; shoulders shrug; lifter rises on toes; elbows do not bend until shoulder shrug and rise on toes is complete; bar is horizontal.

Points Available: 0-9   *Points Earned*: _____

Clean

Elbows rotate under bar quickly; back is straight; knees are bent as bar is caught; bar is horizontal.

Points Available: 0-9   *Points Earned*: _____

Finishing Position

Back is upright; knees are straight; bar is horizontal; elbows are high in front of bar so bar rests on front of shoulders.

Points Available: 0-2   *Points Earned*: _____

Return of Bar to Floor

Elbows rotate down; bar is returned to floor, not dropped.

Points Available: 0-2   *Points Earned*: _____

Total Points Available: 0-27   Total Points Earned: ____

Power Snatch Technique

Resistance Used

30 to 40 percent of body weight.

Starting Position

Bar is over balls of feet; feet are hip width or slightly wider apart; shoulders are over or slightly in front of bar; back is straight; head is in neutral position; grip is at correct width.

Points Available: 0-5   *Points Earned*: _____

Pull

Back stays at same angle to floor as in the starting position until bar is at knee height; shoulders stay over bar; bar stays close to body; bar does not bounce off of thighs during second pull; elbows stay above bar; shoulders shrug; lifter rises on toes; elbows do not bend until shoulders are shrugged and rise on toes is complete; bar is horizontal.

Points Available: 0-9   *Points Earned*: _____

Catch

Elbows rotate under bar quickly; elbows extended quickly; bar is not pressed out; bar is above ears in overhead position; knees are bent as bar is caught; back is straight; bar is horizontal.

Points Available: 0-7   *Points Earned*: _____

Finishing Position

Knees straighten completely; bar is above ears; elbows are straight; back is straight.

Points Available: 0-3   *Points Earned*: _____

Return of Bar to Floor

Bar is returned to floor, not dropped.

Points Available: 0-1   *Points Earned*: _____

Total Points Available: 0-25   Total Points Earned: ____

Chapter 4

Designing Individualized Strength Training Programs for Children

Before beginning a resistance training program, children, like anyone, should be examined by a physician. Any physical problems that are found must be considered in the design of the program; for example, if a child has *Osgood-Schlatter's disease*, exercises involving extreme bending of the knee may be contraindicated. The child should then begin a basic resistance training program that exercises all the major muscle groups around each joint. The program should include warm-up and flexibility exercises before and after each training session. You can add additional sport-specific exercises and exercises based on individu-

al need after the child has learned basic lifting techniques. The key to a successful program is adherence to basic program principles.

Basic Program Principles

When planning weight training programs for children, follow four basic principles:

- Total conditioning of all fitness components (strength, flexibility, cardiovascular endurance, and body composition)

- Balanced choice of exercises for upper and lower body development
- Balanced choice of exercises for muscles around each joint
- Use of body part as well as structural exercises

You don't need to make a major distinction between boys and girls when planning resistance training programs, because general fitness requires training of all major muscle groups and successful performance of a particular sport skill depends upon the strength and power of particular muscle groups, not the participant's gender. However, a program specific for girls may emphasize the strength/power of the upper body and shoulder girdle, because many girls lack strength and power in these areas. Another consideration is differences in maturation and development of boys and girls, which is discussed in chapter 2 and in this chapter.

The Needs Analysis

Before designing the program you should perform a needs analysis, which involves nothing more than determining the child's needs. Then you can determine specific goals for the resistance training program. Some common goals of resistance training programs are listed here:

- Increased strength/power of specific muscle groups
- Increased local muscular endurance of specific muscle groups
- Increased motor performance (i.e., increased ability to jump, run, or throw)
- Increased total body weight (age dependent)
- Increased muscle hypertrophy (age dependent)
- Decreased body fat

It is possible to achieve all of these goals with a well-planned resistance training program. However, the expected changes in these characteristics must be kept within reasonable limits depending upon the age of the child and his or her biological potential for change.

The easiest way to conduct a needs analysis is to answer a series of questions concerning the desired goals of the resistance training program. Progress toward some of these goals is easy to assess. If the trainees are performing specific exercises with more resistance, specific muscle groups are increasing in strength. Progress toward other goals is more difficult to assess; increased muscle hypertrophy, especially in prepubescents, may be difficult to observe.

What Muscle Groups Need to be Strengthened?

A program for general fitness or strength should typically include all the major muscle groups of the body and exercise muscles around each joint (neck, shoulders, upper back, lower back, abdominals, front and back of upper leg, calf, front and back of upper arm, front and back of forearm) (see programs in chapter 7). This type of program is called an agonist-antagonist, or push-pull, program; it increases the strength and/or local muscular endurance in all movements possible at a joint. If the program goal is to increase sprinting ability, the major muscle groups strengthened are the legs, or more specifically the front of the thigh (*quadriceps*), back of the thigh (*hamstrings*), calf (*gastrocnemius*), and buttocks (*gluteals*). For a program to improve sprint running, you would choose exercises training these muscle groups.

What Type of Muscular Contraction Does the Sport Use?

The three major types of muscle actions are *isometric*, *dynamic concentric*, and *dynamic eccentric*. During an isometric contraction the muscle contracts but no movement takes place, as when a lifter attempts to perform a leg press with a resistance that he or she cannot lift. A dynamic concentric contraction takes place when the muscle contracts and shortens and movement occurs. For example, a dynamic concentric contraction of the quadriceps occurs when the front of the thigh contracts and the knee joint extends. A dynamic eccentric contraction takes place when the muscle contracts and lengthens and movement occurs. Lowering a weight from the extended knee position is a dynamic eccentric contraction of the quadriceps. When a lifter performs the exercise called knee extensions, the quadriceps performs a dynamic concentric contraction to lift the weight and a dynamic eccentric contraction to lower the weight. Descending a flight of stairs or slowing down after sprinting requires dynamic eccentric contractions of the quadriceps. Dynamic concentric and eccentric contractions occur in most daily and sport-

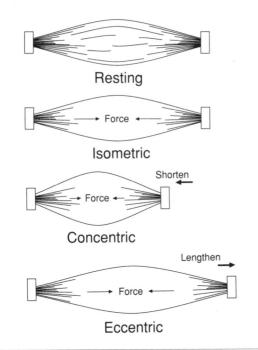

Figure 4.1 Basic types of muscle actions.

ing activities. Figure 4.1 depicts the three major types of muscle actions.

Should the lifter practice isometric contractions to be successful in the activity in question? For a sport like wrestling, yes; for swimming, no. If performing the sport requires isometric contractions, then you should include some specific isometric training in the resistance training program for that activity. Dynamic concentric and eccentric contractions are needed for virtually all recreational activities and sports. Be sure the equipment your lifters use can exercise the eccentric as well as the concentric phases of movement. Some pieces of equipment provide no resistance as the movement returns to the starting position; on such equipment the lifter must pull the bar back into the starting position, and this does not have an eccentric contraction. If your lifters are training for sports in which direction must be changed quickly and often, include some specific eccentric exercises for the muscles involved in these movements. Exercises can be performed in a typical manner where a resistance can be moved in a concentric motion and lowered in an eccentric manner. Eccentric only training involves just the lowering of the weight with loads greater than can be lifted concentrically. Care must be taken when performing eccentric loaded exercises due to the heavy resistances (105-120 percent of maximum 1 RM

concentric strength), which create an increased possibility of injury and require advanced supervision. Heavy eccentric only training should not be taught to inexperienced resistance trainers or performed by prepubescent children.

However, recent data shows that using both concentric and eccentric motions in a repetition is superior to using only one type of movement. By controlling both the concentric and eccentric movements of an exercise, training benefits (strength) will be observed. Children can gain eccentric benefits in training by lowering, in a controlled manner, the normal concentric loads used in training.

What Energy Source Is Needed for the Sport?

Consider the time needed to perform the sport activity and the intensity of the activity. A sport like marathon running requires a long time to perform (2-3 hours) and is performed with submaximal muscular contractions.

Shot putting takes a very short time to complete (1-2 seconds) and is performed with maximal muscular contractions. Many sports are between these two extremes, such as the 400-meter run, which takes 1 to 2 minutes to complete and requires near-maximal contractions. The duration and intensity of muscular contractions used in the activity determine whether the energy source of the activity is aerobic or anaerobic (see Table 4.1). Long-duration events performed with submaximal contractions are *aerobic*, which means the majority of energy used to perform the event is derived from the body's use of oxygen to break down carbohydrates and fats. Very short duration events performed with maximal muscular contractions are *anaerobic*, which means the body uses energy already stored in the muscle in the form of high-energy molecules. Activities of moderate duration that require near-maximal contractions are also anaerobic. However, their major energy source is not the stored energy molecules in muscle but the breakdown of stored carbohydrates (i.e., *glycogen*) without the use of oxygen, which produces *lactic acid*. Lactic acid is a substance associated with fatigue that gives the athlete's muscles a tired and heavy feeling after he or she completes an event like a 400-meter sprint. Although one energy source may be predominant for a particular activity, all three sources always contribute some energy for the performance of any activity.

Table 4.1

**Guidelines for Primary Energy Sources
for an Activity**

Energy Source	Muscular Contractions	Duration of Activity
Anaerobic: stored energy molecules	Maximal	Very short (seconds)
Lactic acid	Near maximal	Short to moderate (15 s to 6 min)
Aerobic	Submaximal	Long (4 min to hours)

Note. Although one energy source may predominate in an activity, any activity uses all three energy sources to some extent.

What Injuries Will the Sport Most Likely Cause?

When designing a resistance training program, consider sites of common injury in a particular sport or activity and sites of previous injury to an individual and incorporate exercises to strengthen these areas. Common sites of injury in many activities are the knees, elbows, shoulders, neck, and ankles.

Special Considerations

Due to their immature skeletal and muscular systems, children are more prone than adults to certain types of injury (e.g., growth cartilage injury). In addition, certain muscle groups in many children are chronically weak (e.g., upper body). Include in the program exercises to strengthen chronically weak muscle groups. Carefully consider the health and functional ability of the joints involved so that no injury results to prepubescent or pubescent children.

Growth Cartilage

Growth cartilage, a type of connective tissue, is located at three major sites: the growth plate or *epiphyseal plate* of long bones; the site of tendon insertion onto bone, or *apophyseal insertion*; and cartilage on the joint surfaces, or *articular cartilage* (see Figure 4.2). Long bones of the body grow

in length from the epiphyseal plates located at their ends. Severe damage to epiphyseal plates before they ossify, which happens late in puberty, can result in no further growth in the length of the bone. Growth cartilage at the apophyseal insertions ensures a solid connection between the tendon and bone. Damage to growth cartilage at the apophyseal insertions may cause pain upon movement and may increase the chance of separation of the tendon from the bone. Articular cartilage acts as a shock absorber between the bones of a joint. Damage to this cartilage may lead to rough surfaces between the bones of a joint and ensuing pain upon movement of the joint.

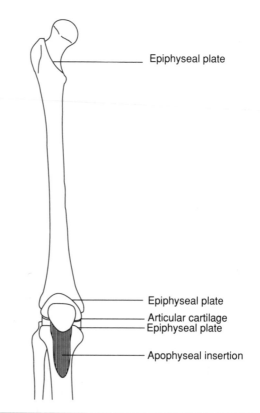

Figure 4.2 Locations of growth cartilage at the knee.

Damage to all three sites of growth cartilage may occur either due to a single incident, or an acute injury, or due to repeated microtraumas, which result in an overuse injury. Damage to the epiphyseal plate is the most common acute injury to growth cartilage. Epiphyseal plate fractures in prepubescents caused by resistance training have been reported. The majority of these injuries occurred during unsupervised performance of overhead lifts (i.e., overhead press, jerk press) with near-maximal resistances. Children should take two precautions to minimize the chance of epiphyseal plate fracture. They should not perform overhead lifts with near-maximal or maximal resistance, and they should use proper form during any lift. Also, when prepubescents perform overhead lifts use lighter weights and constantly stress proper lifting technique.

Repeated microtraumas can cause overuse injuries. Researchers have proposed that early heavy physical exercise by children can cause epiphyseal plate damage resulting in bone deformation. Pain in the shoulder associated with the throwing movement in prepubescents is often called "Little League shoulder." One of its causes is damage to the epiphyseal plate of the upper arm bone, the *humerus*, caused by repeated throwing. However, it is also likely that the *rotator cuff* muscles of the shoulder are also weak or out of balance, that is, one of the muscles is substantially stronger than the muscle that causes the opposite movement; this sets the stage for shoulder pain and injury. Resistance training can be used to increase rotator cuff strength to avoid shoulder pain and injury in throwing sports. Exercises designed to strengthen the rotator cuff muscles of the shoulder are presented in chapter 6, pp. 67-72. You should incorporate these exercises into resistance training programs designed for a throwing sport. In general, most athletes can benefit from these exercises.

Articular cartilage can also be damaged by repeated microtrauma. This is one of the factors responsible for *osteochondritis dissecans*, separation of a portion of the articular cartilage from the joint surface. This can occur at the elbows of Little League pitchers and at the ankles of young distance runners. Damage to the growth cartilage at the apophyseal insertions may be in part responsible for the pain associated with Osgood-Schlatter's disease, which is degeneration of the bone at the site where the patellar tendon attaches to the tibia.

Damage to growth cartilage is not a necessary outcome of resistance training. However, you must consider the potential to damage these areas when you are designing a program for children and must take appropriate precautions. Overuse injuries are a result of microtraumas caused by all activities performed. Thus, an overuse injury in a child performing resistance training may not be due to the resistance training but to other activities he or she is involved in. In addition, resistance training does help prevent overuse injuries such as Little League shoulder, tennis elbow, pain in the knee due to running, and swim-

mer's shoulder. Use of proper techniques in exercise training can eliminate possible overuse or microtrauma problems related to resistance training.

Lower Back Problems

The musculature and vertebral column of a prepubescent's lower back are not well developed; therefore children may be at greater risk of lower back pain and injury than adults. During the growth spurt many children develop *lumbar lordosis*. This condition involves an anterior (forward) bending of the spine, many times accompanied by a forward tilting of the top of the pelvis (see Figure 4.3). Factors contributing to lordosis include tight hamstrings, as well as growth of the front portion of the vertebrae to a greater extent than growth of the back portion of vertebrae.

Lower back problems in children and adults can be a result of an acute injury. Lower back problems due to resistance training are primarily caused by improper lifting technique, which can result in strains and sprains of the muscles and ligaments of the lower back. In many cases, attempting to lift maximal or near-maximal resistance is a contributing factor to improper technique. This is especially true for exercises that place stress on the lower back region, such as dead lifts and squats. When performing these types of exercises, the child must keep the back straight and as upright as possible and must use the legs to lift the weight. This keeps the torque on the lower back as small as possible and keeps the resistance over the child's feet, protecting the lower back from injury. Leg press machines can also cause back problems, because the seat may remove the normal curve in the back. Thus, injuries can result if a child uses improperly designed machines or uses incorrect technique while performing the exercises. If lower back pain persists, the child should see a physician.

You can help your lifters prevent lower back problems by assigning strengthening exercises for the lower back and abdominal musculature and flexibility exercises for the lower back area and hamstrings. Use exercises such as back extensions and sit-ups to strengthen the lower back and abdominal regions, respectively. When a child performs exercises for the lower back, the resistance should be light to moderate, thus allowing at least eight repetitions to be performed. Flexibility exercises for the lower back and hamstrings area to prevent lower back problems are presented in chapter 6, pp. 98-103.

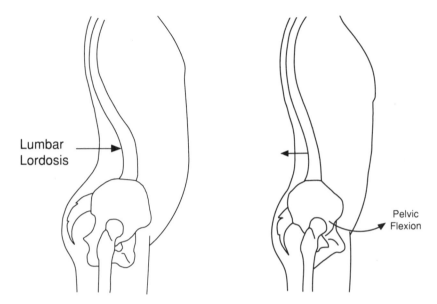

Figure 4.3 Lumbar lordosis is an increased bending of the lower spine many times accompanied by a forward tilt of the pelvis. This condition is often reversible with exercise of the lower back and abdominals.

Abdominal Strength

The American Alliance of Health, Physical Education, Recreation and Dance (1980) measures abdominal muscular strength and endurance by the number of sit-ups a person can perform in 1 minute. The mean number of sit-ups in 1 minute for girls shows little improvement from age 10 to 17 (27 to 31 sit-ups). The President's Council on Physical Fitness and Sports test shows no increase in the number of sit-ups beginning at age 14 and an actual decrease after age 16 for both boys and girls. Due to the important role abdominal muscles play in many sport skills, weak abdominals can limit an athlete's proficiency in many sports. Therefore, a resistance training program for children must emphasize the abdominal area.

Upper Body Strength and Local Muscular Endurance

Upper body strength is often assessed by the number of pull-ups boys can perform and by the amount of time girls can maintain a flexed arm hang. Sixty percent of girls from ages 6 to 17 years cannot perform one pull-up. The President's Council on Physical Fitness and Sports has concluded that upper arm and shoulder girdle strength and endurance for both boys and girls are poor and represent significant weaknesses in children (Reiff et al., 1985). Upper body strength does limit many sport-specific tasks even at the

recreational level. Due to the general lack of strength in the upper body of many prepubescent and pubescent children, resistance training programs for these groups should emphasize exercises for the upper body.

Program Variation

Once you have designed one training session, should the children perform the same training session again and again? For a program to bring about continual increases in strength/power and local muscular endurance, training sessions must vary. Changes in the exercise sessions keep them from becoming boring and therefore keep the trainee's interest high. In addition, changing the program brings about continual increases in strength/power and local muscular endurance, whereas a nonchanging program eventually results in *plateaus*, long periods when no progress is made. All programs should be varied in the ways discussed next.

Cycling or Periodization

Cycling or *periodization* is a popular way of varying the training *volume* and intensity of an adult's workout. Normally in a periodized training format, major changes in the training sessions are made every 2 to 4 weeks; many times these changes are only made in the multiple-joint exercises (i.e., bench press, squats, leg press) but they can be made in all exercises. The periodization model presented in Table 4.2 is for an adult strength/power athlete (e.g., shot putter or weight lifter). The start of a training cycle is characterized by high volume, or a large number of repetitions, and low intensity, or light resistances. As the cycle progresses the volume of training decreases but the intensity increases. In the model presented for strength/power training, the goals of the base phase are to prepare the individual for the heavier exercise to be performed in the latter phases and to cause an increase in muscle size. The major goals of the strength and power phases are to cause increases in maximal strength and power. The peaking phase is designed to maximize strength/power for a short-term high-intensity activity. This type of periodization increases maximal strength/power to a greater extent than nonperiodized resistance training.

Table 4.2

Traditional Periodization for an Adult Strength/Power Athlete

Training Phase	Sets	Reps	Intensity
Base	3-5	8-15	Low
Strength	3-5	2-6	High
Power	3-5	2-3	High
Peaking	1-3	1-3	Very high
Active rest	Physical activity (not necessarily resistance training)		

Note. From "A Theoretical Model for Strength Training" by M.H. Stone, H. O'Bryant, J.G. Garhammer, J. McMillian, and R. Rozenek, 1982, *National Strength and Conditioning Journal*, **4**, pp. 36-38.

The use of periodization with children or young adults and its effects on them have received little study. However, research has demonstrated that use of the traditional periodization model with a high school football team leads to greater gains in 1-RM strength and vertical jumping ability than nonperiodized resistance training. However, the traditional periodization model requires the performance of exercises with near-maximal and maximal resistances and, therefore, may not be applicable for prepubescent individuals. However, a variation of such a resistance training program can be accomplished within the guidelines of a program for prepubescent individuals.

Varying Resistance, Repetitions, Sets, and Rest Periods

Changing the resistance used for a particular exercise is the easiest and most common way to change a program. The use of RMs ensures progression as the trainee becomes stronger. If a child can perform eight but not nine repetitions of the bench press with 50 pounds, then 50 pounds is an 8-RM resistance for that child. As the child becomes stronger 60 pounds may become his or her 8-RM resistance for the bench press. If you design the program so that the child uses 8 RMs for 3 weeks, as the child becomes stronger the resistance will increase so that he or she is still training at the desired 8 RM. Changes in resistance may be difficult to accomplish and to monitor in some body weight exercises such as push-ups and self- or partner-resisted exercises.

You can also change resistances from one training session to the next on a weekly basis to provide heavy, moderate, and light exercise sessions. Some athletes and coaches believe this is important to ensure continual gains in strength/power and local muscular endurance. For example, a heavy training day may involve a 10-RM load. On moderate and light training days the lifter may use 90 and 80 percent of that 10-RM load, respectively. Therefore, if a child's 10 RM for the leg press is 100 pounds, a heavy training day will include sets of 10 at 100 pounds. A moderate training day will include sets of 10 at 90 pounds (0.90 × 100 pounds) and a light training day sets of 10 at 80 pounds (0.80 × 100 pounds).

A normal sequence for this type of load *variation* for three training sessions per week is Monday, light; Wednesday, heavy; and Friday, moderate. Three training sessions per week are normally considered sufficient to cause maximal gains in strength/power. This arrangement provides for recovery before and after the heavy training day, which allows the trainees to perform up to their potential on the heavy training days. Heavy, moderate, and light training days also minimize the possibility of fatigue buildup during training; such a buildup of fatigue prevents further gains in strength/power or local muscular endurance.

You may also vary RM loads every 2 to 4 weeks so that training emphasizes either strength/power or local muscular endurance. The concept of a repetition continuum is that at certain RM resistances, training emphasizes either strength/power or local muscular endurance. Using this concept you can design resistance training programs similar to the traditional periodization model for an adult strength/power athlete and still remain within the guidelines of resistances for prepubescents. The RM resistances for a prepubescent equivalent to the normal phases of a traditional periodization format are presented in Table 4.3. Sets can be varied between one and three per exercise: within these guidelines, a considerable amount of variation in volume is possible.

Table 4.3

Periodization Model for a Prepubescent

Training Phase	Sets	Repetitions (repetition maximum range)
Base	3	10-15
Strength	3	6-10
Power	2-3	6-8
Peaking	1-2	6-8
Active rest	Physical activity (not necessarily resistance training)	

There are other ways to vary resistance and sets and still remain within the guidelines for prepubescents. A training session designed to predominantly increase local muscular endurance may consist of three sets of each exercise of 15 repetitions per set at a 15-RM resistance. A session designed to predominantly increase strength/power may consist of three sets of each exercise of 10 repetitions per set at a 10-RM resistance. A session designed to maintain increases in strength/power and local muscular endurance may consist of only one set of each exercise of 12 repetitions at a 12-RM resistance. You may use this type of program for in-season sport maintenance for a group of athletes.

The length of the rest periods between exercises and sets should vary based upon the goal of the resistance training session. Length of rest periods should also vary depending upon the major goals of the training during a particular phase of the training cycle. For example, in a session designed to predominantly increase strength/power, include rest periods of 2 to 3

minutes or more. Another training session designed to maintain gains in strength/power and local muscular endurance may include rest periods of 1 minute or less. Short rest periods will lead to buildup of lactic acid in the blood, resulting in a general weakness in the fingers and toes and general weakness in the limbs, which is normally associated with fatigue. If a child begins a resistance training program that includes short rest periods before he or she is physically ready for this type of stress, feelings of light-headedness and nausea can result.

Varying the Exercises

Empirical evidence suggests that variation in exercises for the same muscle group causes greater increases in strength/power than no variation in exercises. This does not mean that every training session should include different exercises or that all exercises must be changed when one change is made. However, you may introduce new exercises every 2 to 3 weeks or vary some exercises every other training session. For example, initially include the bench press for the arms and shoulder and change to the incline press or a bench press with dumbbells after 2 to 3 weeks. Or, have children perform the bench press on Monday and Friday and the incline press on Wednesday. However, remember that some major muscle group exercises need to be maintained throughout the training program, in order to see training adaptations in primary movement. Some possible training variations follow:

- Increased resistance for a particular RM
- Variation in the RM used (6 to 20 RM)
- Variation in the number of sets (one to three, and more in some exercises)
- Heavy, moderate, and light training days during a week
- Variation in exercises for the same muscle groups

Considering the Child When Designing the Program

Always consider the child first when designing the exercise program. Be aware of the child's total activity pattern when you develop an exercise training program. Some young athletes are involved with many different sport and recreational activities, in addition to school; you need to evaluate these activities so the child can avoid various types of burnout, overuse injuries, or overtraining syndromes.

- Ask the child what sports and/or recreational activities he or she is really interested in, and develop possible schedules.
- Consider adopting physical preparation periods for sports to help reduce or prevent injuries and improve sport performance. This may mean reducing the number of sport and recreational activities in which the child participates and/or reducing the time spent in each activity.
- Avoid overscheduling sport and recreational activities.
- Balance conditioning programs so they train both muscular strength and endurance and improve cardiovascular endurance.
- Develop realistic sport training and activity schedules so that the child has free time for play and individual development.

A key factor of resistance training is recovery. If the child needs a crane to get out of bed in the morning, the previous exercise session was too intense and the program needs to be modified. Some soreness or stiffness may be present the day after a workout, which is called *delayed-onset muscle soreness*, but this should not be extreme and should not severely limit normal activities or range of motion. Furthermore, this muscle stiffness or soreness should disappear after a few days. If soreness persists, reduce the intensity or volume of exercise, or both, for the next exercise session. Gradual progression and variation in training play important roles in a resistance training program.

Consider the Child's Feelings

Recovery is not only physical but mental, too. How the young athlete feels about his or her training is important! Proper progression, goals, and a basic understanding of training can help the young athlete explore this new-found physical expression and potential. Don't force the young athlete to do anything he or she is unsure about. Never underestimate the importance of the child's feelings, and take time to explain even the most obvious concept. Be sure the child knows the following:

- The expected stress and fatigue of the exercises performed and the purpose of the exercise program should be discussed with the child.
- It is normal to experience some fatigue, but no pain, excessive discomfort, or excessive fatigue should be present during or following an exercise session.
- It is OK for the child to tell you how he or she feels about an exercise session or the training program, and more importantly, the child can expect you to make appropriate modifications.
- The child should feel adequately recovered before starting a workout.
- You are working with the child to develop a resistance training program he or she is comfortable with and feels excited about, and it is up to the child if he or she wants to participate in it.

Assuring Proper Progression

''No pain, no gain'' is but one message that sends the wrong signal to many young athletes. Research has shown that a painful resistance training workout does not necessarily mean optimal gains in strength. Thus, it is important to think about the signals we and the rest of the world communicate to young people. Take time to explain basic principles of resistance training, correct misconceptions, and state realistic expectations.

A number of steps can help you establish proper progression:

1. Show the child how to perform each exercise using little or no resistance. Do not rush this period of orientation and physical interaction with the exercise.
2. For the first workout, start the child with only one set of relatively light resistance (i.e., 12-15 RM).
3. Plan for a 3- to 4-week learning period. Start out with the simpler body-part exercises and then very slowly add specific multijoint structural exercises based upon individual needs.
4. Gradually increase the number of sets and the resistance used so that after 4 to 5 weeks the child reaches the starting point for a program.
5. Carefully monitor the recovery of the child and don't overshoot his or her physical or mental abilities to recover; cut back if needed.

As the child gains muscular strength and endurance, the resistances lifted and the number of repetitions performed can increase. Do not allow the child to become obsessed with performance in each exercise session; this places undue stress on a child and discourages participation in an activity that can produce positive health and fitness benefits. Look for improvement, but be positive and allow for normal ups and downs in training. Don't ever let the young athlete become self-critical because of performance in an exercise training session. The designed workout is only a goal or guide, and you must be realistic and sensitive in your approach to training progression.

Because every child matures at a different rate, children must value the improvements they make and must not compare themselves to other children. You play a vital role in developing the child's self-esteem and helping the child to focus on his or her own training gains. Provide rewards and support for individual improvement. Furthermore, help children understand that improvement can slow down in one area but can be made in other areas. A child cannot expect constant improvement in all areas.

Proper Perspectives for Training

It is important that the child develop realistic goals and expectations. Each individual has a genetic potential for growth and performance. The purpose of training is to enhance each child's genetic potential for fitness, health, and performance. Parents, teachers, and coaches are important influences on the way young children think about training and performance and thus need to send out the right signals. Let young athletes know that the rewards of sport participation come from self-improvement, not just from winning. For example, a football coach may tell a young athlete that he must gain 30 pounds to play on the team. This is not a realistic training goal, and the methods required to achieve it are not ethically acceptable. You and the athletes themselves need to be patient and realize that making true physical gains takes time; there is no quick fix. Only through commitment to a developmental conditioning program including exercise, good nutrition, and skill practice can the athlete safely make gains.

At the beginning of any training program, strength and endurance gains are made quickly, typically because the individual starts at a low level of fitness. Then as training continues the magnitude of the gains slows down until the individual reaches a plateau. In reality changes are taking place but are so slight that our measures (e.g., training resistance) cannot pick up the small day-to-day changes. For example, in the first 3 months of training, the weight a child lifts

for 10 repetitions may increase 50 pounds in a leg press. Then, over the next 3 months, the improvement may be only 10 pounds. The child cannot expect large constant increases during training because the physiological adaptations slow down once initial adaptations are made.

Children's potentials for strength at a given age can be dramatically different depending on their maturation status. For example, during a growth spurt a young boy will increase muscle size and strength without any training at all. Keep this in mind as strength changes during all periods of the child's maturation. Only long-term training will increase the child's strength beyond growth-related changes.

Scheduling in a Total Conditioning Program

It is important for children to participate in a total conditioning program. Resistance training should not be the only training activity. The major components of a total conditioning program include the following:

- Resistance training for development of muscular strength and local muscular endurance
- Aerobic training to enhance cardiovascular endurance fitness
- Flexibility training
- Supplemental training where needed for agility, coordination, balance, and speed for sport-related skills
- An appropriate nutritional program for optimal development of body composition and health

You must develop a realistic schedule when planning such an integrated training program so as not to overstress the child. For example, some activity schedules may look like the following:

A = aerobic training, R = resistance training

Mon.	Tue.	Wed.	Thurs.	Fri.	Sat.	Sun.
A		A		A		
R		R		R		

According to this schedule, the athlete trains 3 days per week, performing both aerobic and resistance exercises on the same day. Flexibility training is part of the warm-up and cool-down. Both aerobic and resistance training can be performed in the same training session or in different training sessions (e.g., aerobic in the morning and resistance in the afternoon). If the athlete wishes to split the two training sessions in order to spend more time on a particular activity, several hours must be allowed between workouts. This schedule allows 4 days for sports and other activities.

Mon.	Tue.	Wed.	Thurs.	Fri.	Sat.	Sun.
R	A	R	A	R	A	

This schedule splits up the aerobic and resistance training sessions, and the flexibility program is part of the warm-up and cool-down. This type of schedule can allow the athlete to spend more time on a particular training activity but is demanding and typically is not needed until the athlete has gained considerable training experience. Still, this schedule accommodates an athlete who does not have large blocks of time available on 3 days.

Limitless variations in the training schedule are possible. The previous two schedules may work well for a high school athlete or someone very dedicated to staying physically fit, but for children involved in numerous activities these schedules may be too restrictive. Use your imagination when designing schedules for children. For example, a young child can resistance train on Monday and Wednesday and perform aerobic training on Tuesday and Thursday. Although sessions are less frequent and gains are made more slowly, this is one viable scheduling alternative. Remember, training must be fun, not frightening, if children are to perform it willingly and establish good fitness habits.

Again, it is important that the child recovers from exercise stress. Without recovery, positive physical changes will not occur. Training is more than physical, and you need to be sensitive to its mental aspects as well. Start with a low frequency of training in the beginning, or use heavy, moderate, and light days of training. This will allow the child to progress into the training program with greater ease.

It is typically recommended that adults train three times per week so that the exercise stress will bring about physiological changes. The optimal exercise frequency for children is unknown, but three days per week appears to be an appropriate starting point for children as well. A child may need to alter this frequency due to schedule constraints, but a frequency of less than three days per week is not optimal. The body should have enough exposure to exercise stress to stimulate change. Too much exercise stress can cause ''distress'' or overtraining; too little can make a program ineffective. This is why

you must observe how the child is handling the physical and emotional stress of a training program and make immediate changes if the child is not tolerating the exercise session physically or emotionally.

Summing Up and Looking Ahead

No one type of training (e.g., resistance training) can effect all of the changes needed to promote cardiovascular endurance, muscular strength, fitness, and improved sport performance. A varied training schedule also exposes the young athlete to various types of exercise, such as lifting, running, and skiing.

The status of youth fitness is poor in the United States. Many children are not involved in any type of exercise training. Therefore, the stress a child experiences during sport participation increases the possibility of injury. Athletes cannot play themselves into shape; they must be physically and mentally prepared to play the game.

Although a child's chosen sport may require only one type of conditioning, encourage the child to participate in a total conditioning program and not become a specialist at a young age. Total conditioning will lead to a better overall physical development and will thereby enhance health and fitness.

In chapter 5 we examine the various factors involved in teaching exercise techniques, which is a very important part of the program implementation process.

Additional Readings

Adams, J.E. (1965). Injuries to the throwing arm: A study of traumatic changes in the elbow of boy baseball players. *California Medicine*, **102**, 127-132.

Amateur Athletic Union House. (1981). *Amateur Athletic Union Physical Fitness Program*. Indianapolis: Author.

American Alliance for Health, Physical Education, Recreation and Dance. (1980). *Health related physical fitness test manual*. Reston, VA: Author.

Baker, S., & Winterstein, A. (1984, Fall.). Rotator cuff injuries: The need for specific exercises in a prevention and treatment program. *Athletic Training*, pp. 214-217.

Baratta, R., Solomonow, M., Zhou, B.H., Letson, D., Chuinard, R., & Ambrosia, R. (1988). Muscular coactivation. The role of the antagonist musculature in maintaining knee stability. *The American Journal of Sports Medicine*, **16**, 113-122.

Barnett, L.S. (1985). Little League shoulder syndrome: Proximal humeral epiphyseolysis in adolescent baseball pitchers. *The Journal of Bone and Joint Surgery*, **7-A**, 495-496.

Bennett, J.G., & Stauber, W.T. (1986). Evaluation and treatment of anterior knee pain using eccentric exercise. *Medicine and Science in Sports and Exercise*, **8**, 526-530.

Chandler, J., & Stone, M.H. (1991). The squat exercise in athletic conditioning: A position statement and review of the literature. *National Strength and Conditioning Association Journal*, **13**(5), 51-58.

Conale, S.T., & Belding, R.H. (1980). Osteochondral lesions of the talus. *The Journal of Bone and Joint Surgery*, **62-A**, 97-102.

Cooney, W.P. (1988). Addendum: A comparative electromyographic analysis of the shoulder during pitching-professional versus amateur pitchers. *American Journal of Sports Medicine*, **15**, 588-590.

Dominguez, R.H. (1978). Shoulder pain in age group swimmers. In B. Ericksson & B. Furong (Eds.), *Swimming medicine IV* (pp. 105-109). Baltimore: University Park Press.

Gowan, I.D., Jobe, F.W., Tibone, J.E., Perry, J., & Moynes, D.R. (1988). A comparative electromyographic analysis of the shoulder during pitching-professional versus amateur pitchers. *American Journal of Sports Medicine*, **15**, 586-589.

Gruchow, W., & Pelleiter, P. (1979). An epidemiologic study of tennis elbow. *American Journal of Sports Medicine*, **7**, 234-238.

Grumps, V.L., Seagal, D., Halligan, J.B., & Lower, G. (1982). Bilateral radius and ulnar fractures in adolescent weight lifters. *American Journal of Sports Medicine*, **10**, 375-379.

Hawkins, R.J., & Kennedy, J.C. (1980). Impingement syndrome in athletes. *American Journal of Sports Medicine*, **8**, 151-158.

Karpovich, P.V., Singh, M., & Tipton, C. (1970). Effect of deep knee bends on knee stability. *Teorie a Praxe Telesne Vchovy*, **18**, 112-115.

Kato, S., & Ishiko, T. (1976). Obstructed growth of children's bones due to excessive labor in remote corners of the world. In K. Kato (Ed.), *Proceedings of the International Congress of Sports Sciences*. Tokyo: Japanese Union of Sport Sciences, 476.

Kraemer, W.J., & Baechle, T.R. (1989). Development of a strength training program. In A.J. Ryan & F.L. Allman (Eds.), *Sports Medicine* (2nd ed., pp. 113-127). San Diego: Academic Press.

Kuland, D.N.M., McCue, F.C., Rockwell, D.A., & Geick, J.A. (1979). Tennis injuries: Prevention and treatment. *American Journal of Sports Medicine*, **7**, 249-253.

Lipscomb, A.B. (1975). Baseball pitching in growing athletes. *Journal of Sports Medicine*, **3**, 25-34.

Micheli, L.J. (1983). Overuse injuries in children's sports: The growth factor. *The Orthopedic Clinics of North America*, **14**, 337-360.

Priest, J.P., & Nagel, P.A. (1976). Tennis shoulder. *American Journal of Sports Medicine*, **4**, 28-42.

Reiff, G.G., Dixon, W.R., Jacoby, D., Ye, X.G., Spain, C.G., & Hunsicker, P.A. (1985). President's Council on Physical Fitness and Sports, *National School Population Fitness Survey* (Research Project 282-84-0086). Ann Arbor, MI: The University of Michigan.

Ross, J.G., Dotson, O., Gilbert, G.G., & Katz, S.J. (1985). The national children and youth fitness study: New standards for fitness measurement. *Journal of Physical Education, Recreation and Dance*, **56**, 20-24.

Rovere, G.D. (1988). Low back pain in athletes. *The Physician and Sportsmedicine*, **15**, 105-117.

Rowe, T.A. (1979). Cartilage fracture due to weight lifting. *British Journal of Sports Medicine*, **13**, 130-131.

Ryan, J.R., & Salciccioli, G.G. (1976). Fractures of the distal radial epiphysis in adolescent weight lifters. *Sports Medicine*, **4**, 26-27.

Stone, M.H., O'Bryant, H., Garhammer, J.D., McMillian, J., & Rozenek, R. (1982). A theoretical model for strength training. *National Strength and Conditioning Association Journal*, **4**, 36-39.

Tipton, C.M., Matthes, R.D., Maynard, J.A., & Carey, R.A. (1975). The influence of physical activity on ligaments and tendons. *Medicine and Science in Sports*, **7**, 165-175.

Torg, J.S., Pollack, H., & Sweterlitsch, P. (1972). The effect of competitive pitching on the shoulders and elbows of preadolescent baseball pitchers. *Pediatrics*, **49**, 267-272.

Chapter 5

Teaching Exercise
Techniques

The two most important characteristics needed to teach any activity, including resistance training exercise techniques, are patience with the trainees and knowledge of the material being taught. Improper lifting and spotting techniques can lead to injury of the lifter. Therefore, knowing and teaching correct exercise techniques are very important for a safe and effective program.

Know Proper Exercise Technique

You must completely understand the technique of an exercise before attempting to teach it to others. This is especially true for multijoint exercises such as the squat. Chapter 6 includes proper techniques for many commonly performed resistance training exercises. Study and practice the lifts that you plan to teach. When trying to learn a new exercise start with a very light resistance. Critique the exercise technique yourself by watching yourself in a mirror, or have an experienced individual (perhaps a training partner or strength coach) critique it.

In using proper technique, the lifter performs the exercise with the fullest range of motion possible as dictated by the body position of the exercise and uses only those muscles that are supposed to be involved in the exercise. Using full range of motion means lowering and lifting the resistance as far as possible during each repetition. Using muscles that are not supposed to be trained by the exercise compromises the training effect for the muscles that are supposed to be trained by the exercise.

Improper exercise technique may also place undue stress on a body part, resulting in injury. This is especially true in exercises involving the lower back and the use of heavy resistances, such as squats or dead lifts. A lifter can also injure the lower back while performing arm curls or shoulder presses if he or she uses a rocking motion of the back to initiate movement of the resistance. When children use improper exercise technique, it's usually because they either are trying to lift too much weight or they lose concentration on proper form. Improper progression in resistance can also cause improper technique and possible injury. Improper progression in resistance many times is due to the increases in resistance being too great or occurring too soon in the training program.

Know Proper Spotting Technique

Good spotting technique is vital for a safe resistance training program. The following box provides a checklist that spotters should use at all times.

SPOTTING CHECKLIST

1. Know proper exercise technique.
2. Know proper spotting technique.
3. Be sure you are strong enough to assist the lifter with the resistance he or she is using.
4. Know how many repetitions the lifter intends to do.
5. Be attentive to the lifter at all times.
6. Stop the exercise if technique is wrong. Have the lifter practice the exercise with little or no resistance.
7. Know the plan of action if a serious injury occurs.

The goal of correct spotting is to prevent injury. A lifter should always have access to a spotter. You and the children should know correct exercise and spotting techniques for all exercises performed in the training program, and when possible, children should spot each other on exercises that require spotting. If the children cannot spot each other, as may be the case in some situations (special education classes, classes of individuals with handicaps, or classes in which training pairs are unequal with regard to strength), enlist the help of other adults or reduce the number of children.

Provide Spotting and Exercise Technique Practice

When you teach a new exercise, demonstrate proper exercise and spotting techniques and discuss the major points of the techniques. Then allow each child to try the exercise using a very light resistance. For free-weight exercises a light resistance may be a barbell or dumbbell with no weight plates on it, or even a broomstick. For an exercise performed with a machine, using a light resistance may mean removing all weight from the machine or taking the pin out of the weight stack. After a child attempts to perform the exercise, point out any flaws in technique. Then continue further technique practice with light resistances, which will minimize the effects of fatigue during the learning stage. In addition to practicing the exercise, all children should demonstrate proper spotting techniques for the exercises.

You will usually need more time to teach proper exercise and spotting techniques for free-weight exercises than for exercises on machines. This is because free weights require the lifter to balance the resistance in all directions (left, right, forward, backward, up, down). Machines "groove" the exercises into one plane of movement and require little if any balancing. Still, both free weight and machine exercises are important to a well-rounded program. Additional time may be needed to teach proper exercise techniques for multijoint exercises. This is especially true for free-weight multijoint exercises, such as squats, because coordination of movement at several joints is needed to balance the resistance.

Attempting to teach techniques for too many exercises at once, especially multijoint exercises, will slow down the learning process. How many exercise techniques a child can learn at one time will vary. A good starting point is seven to eight exercises, of which one to three may be multijoint exercises.

Increase Resistance Slowly

Increasing the resistance too quickly when a child is attempting to learn proper technique will slow down the learning process and can result in injury. If an increase of resistance results in poor technique, the increase is too great. This is true for both beginning and experienced lifters.

During the initial 3 to 4 weeks of a strength training program, the resistance that the child can lift typically increases greatly. If the child has previously performed the exercise, increases in resistance are smaller. These initial increases are not due to true increases in strength or power but rather to the child's learning to perform the exercise correctly. Keep this in mind as you formulate goals concerning increases in strength. If you are planning to use testing to evaluate a child's strength or power, do not conduct the test until the child can properly perform the exercise.

Teach Proper Breathing Technique

The lifter should inhale just before and during the lowering phase of the repetition and exhale during the lifting phase. During isometric training, the lifter should not hold the breath during the muscular contraction. Some breath holding will occur during the last repetition of a set or during heavy lifts (e.g., 1 to 6 RM) but don't allow breath holding throughout a complete repetition. When a lifter holds his or her breath, blood pressure rises drastically. This makes it very difficult for the heart to pump blood and reduces blood flow to the heart from the rest of the body. When the breath is released, blood flow to the head and brain is reduced. This can cause light-headedness after completion of a set and even fainting, which can result in loss of control of the resistance and possible injury. Because lifting maximal or near-maximal resistances is not the object of a child's training session, there is no need for excessive breath holding.

Provide Constant Feedback

Children should receive constant feedback on their exercise and spotting techniques. You must provide this feedback in language they can understand. Feedback is as important after weeks or even months of training as it is at the start of a program. Without feedback concerning proper technique, it is easy for a child to gradually develop a flaw in lifting technique as resistances increase.

Encourage Symmetrical Muscular Development

Symmetrical muscular development depends upon the use of single-arm and single-leg exercises, called *unilateral exercises*. If only double-arm or double-leg exercises are used, called *bilateral exercises*, the stronger limb can compensate for the weaker one. This is especially true on most resistance training machines. Although it is natural for one arm or leg to be stronger,

the difference in strength between limbs should be less than 10%. Proper exercise programming and use of unilateral exercises can reduce any drastic differences. This may reduce possibilities of injury and will promote good physical development. Although bilateral exercises are important to a program, you should also include appropriate unilateral exercises.

Examples of unilateral exercises are single-leg knee extensions, single-leg knee curls, and one-arm shoulder presses with dumbbells. A leg press or bench press for which the lifter uses both legs or both arms at the same time is a bilateral exercise.

Muscle balance around a joint is also very important. Thus, if a lifter does a quadriceps exercise during a workout, then he or she should also do a hamstring exercise. Balance of the muscles around a joint may reduce the potential for injury.

Have an Emergency Plan Prepared

Safety considerations and proper supervision are concerns of all conditioning programs for adolescents. Injuries due to a properly supervised resistance training program are rare, with the most common type of injury being muscle strains. The following are some possible causes of injury during resistance training:

- The lifter attempts to lift too much weight.
- The lifter uses improper lifting technique.
- The lifter improperly places feet or hands on a resistance training machine so they slide off of the pedals or handles.
- The lifter places hands on the chain or pulley system of a resistance training machine.
- The lifter places hands between the weight plates of a resistance training machine.
- The lifter drops free weights or the weight stack of a resistance training machine after completion of a repetition.
- Spotters are inattentive.
- There is improper behavior in the facility.
- A bench or piece of equipment slides during the exercise.
- Worn out equipment breaks during lifting (e.g., machine cables or pulleys).
- The lifter does not use collars on free weights.
- The lifter accidentally drops free weight plates while loading or unloading a bar.

Even though injuries are rare, a resistance training facility should have an emergency plan to deal with a serious injury that requires medical attention. The plan should be posted in the weight room, and all supervisors should be familiar with it.

An emergency plan should include the following:

- Phone number of the nearest ambulance service and/or hospital
- Location of the nearest hospital or emergency room
- Training facility address and any pertinent information emergency personnel need to locate the weight room
- Alphabetical card catalog of children, including parents' or guardians' home and business phone numbers and addresses

A phone should be located in the weight room. If not, all supervisors should know the location of the nearest phone. In addition, all supervisors should have basic first aid and cardiopulmonary resuscitation (CPR) skills.

Make Equipment Decisions Carefully

Most advanced forms of resistance training require some type of equipment. Either this equipment must be purchased, or a membership in a club must be purchased, neither of which is inexpensive. So equipment needs must be carefully and thoroughly considered.

Should Machines or Free Weights Be Used?

Machines allow movement only in a predetermined plane and path of movement, so balancing the resistance in all directions is not necessary. Balancing the resistance requires the use of muscles not involved in the movement as prime movers. For example, prime movers in the military press are the outside of the shoulder area, or the *deltoid*, and the back of the upper arm, or the *triceps*. However, the muscles of the upper and lower back, smaller muscles around the shoulder area, and even the abdominals are involved in balancing the resistance. The

involvement of these secondary or balancing muscles is greater with *free weights* than machines. Advocates of free weights point out that a sporting event or a daily life activity requires the balancing of any resistance moved; thus balancing is an important part of resistance training. Conversely, machine advocates claim that the lack of a need to balance the resistance allows greater isolation of the prime movers. In addition, machine advocates claim, because movement is allowed only in one plane and direction, proper exercise technique is easier to achieve. Both sides in this controversy use the same facts but interpret them differently. This can lead to confusion when you are trying to make decisions regarding equipment.

In reality, you can use both machines and free weights to your advantage in a resistance training program. Machines allowing movement in only one plane and direction, thus providing isolation of a muscle group, are very useful when the goal of the program is to increase strength/power or local muscular endurance of a specific muscle group. Because machines allow the isolation of a muscle group, they are ideal for rehabilitation programs after an injury. Machines are also ideal for programs aimed at increasing strength or local muscular endurance of a particular muscle group or joint that is prone to injury or of a muscle group that is the weak link in performance of a certain sporting activity. Free weight exercises, which require the lifter to balance the resistance in all directions, are a good choice if the goal of the program is to strengthen total body movements and provide coordination between various muscle groups. Thus, both machine and free-weight, also called *fixed-form* and *free-form* exercises, respectively, have a place in a well-designed resistance training program.

We need to address two other factors concerning free weights and machine exercises. First, although the research is not conclusive, it appears that for adults free-weight exercises such as squats result in greater increases in vertical jumping ability than do machine leg-press exercises. This is probably due to a greater mechanical similarity of squat exercises to the jumping motion. However, both squat and leg-press exercises can cause an increase in vertical jumping ability. Second, due to the need for balancing the weight during the performance of free-weight exercises, proper technique is more difficult to learn for free weights than for machines. Thus, allow for more time when teaching free-weight exercise techniques.

What Types of Machines Are Most Beneficial?

Although many types of machines have been developed, the two most common are variable resistance and *isokinetic* machines.

Variable Resistance Machines. Variable resistance machines have a cam or some other mechanical device that is supposed to vary the resistance to match the strength curve of the exercise. Proponents of variable resistance machines believe that if the resistance matches the strength curve of an exercise, the muscles involved in the exercise will contract near-maximally throughout the range of motion and this will cause greater gains in strength. For a machine to match the strength curve of a movement, the machine must account for limb lengths, muscle lengths, point of attachment of muscles to bones, and body position. It has been shown that variable resistance machines are far from perfect in matching the strength curves of adults in the exercises for which the machines were designed. It is even more unlikely that the machines match the strength curves of children.

Isokinetic Machines. Isokinetic machines normally have an electrically braked, mechanically braked, or hydraulic system that attempts to make the velocity of the movement constant. Theoretically, because this machine controls the speed of movement, it allows the performance of a maximal voluntary muscular contraction throughout the full range of motion of a movement. Due to the need for acceleration and deceleration during the movement, a true isokinetic contraction probably only occurs in approximately the middle third of the movement. Isokinetic machines are popular because they cause less muscular soreness than other forms of resistance training, at least during the initial training sessions. Various isokinetic machines allow for no eccentric phase (muscle lengthening) of muscular contraction as one gets when lowering a weight. This lack of an eccentric contraction is in part responsible for less muscle soreness with isokinetic training. How-

ever, eccentric strength is important in many athletic events and daily living activities; simply walking down steps involves eccentric contractions of the quadriceps. In addition, eccentric contractions may be a vital part of the stimulus to promote strength gains and muscle growth.

Can Equipment Be Adjusted to Fit Children?

When you are training prepubescents or pubescents, the most important equipment consideration is that the resistance training equipment fits the child. When you use free weights, body weight exercises, or exercises for which a partner supplies the resistance, this is typically not a critical concern. However, with resistance training machines *equipment fit* can be a very critical concern, because most resistance training machines are made to fit an adult male. Most prepubescents' limbs are too short to properly fit many resistance training machines, which makes correct technique and full range of motion of the exercise virtually impossible. Most critical, a body part may slip off of its point of contact with the machine, such as a footpad or an arm pad, resulting in injury to the child.

With some machines you can make simple alterations that allow a child to safely use the machine; for example, you can use additional seat pads on a knee extension machine or raise up a bench with blocks. Simply adjusting seat height often is not enough to make a machine fit the child. You may also need to adjust for proper positioning of the arms and legs on the contact points of the machine. In addition, raising the seat height may make it impossible for the child's feet to reach the floor. In many exercises the feet need to touch the floor to aid in balance. Therefore, if you raise the seat you may also need to place blocks under the child's feet.

Altering a piece of equipment to fit one child does not guarantee that the equipment will fit another child. Check each child for proper fit before the equipment is used. Ensure that additional padding or blocks do not slide during performance of the exercise, which could result in injury. You can avoid this in some alterations by attaching rubber mats to the top and bottom of blocks and to the back of additional pads.

Remember that safety is the major issue. If you cannot safely adapt a piece of equipment to properly fit a child, that piece of equipment should not be used.

Does Equipment Allow Appropriate Resistance Increases for Children?

Another potential problem with certain resistance machines is that the resistance increases in increments that are too large to allow a smooth progression in resistance as the child becomes stronger. Many machines' weight stacks increase in increments of 10 to 20 pounds. If a child is bench pressing 30 pounds on a machine whose stack increases in increments of 10 pounds, an increase of one increment is a 33 percent increase in resistance. This is too large for a safe and smooth progression. You can remedy this problem on some machines by purchasing specially designed weights that can be easily added and removed from the weight stack. Such weights are usually available in 2-1/2 and 5 pounds.

On some machines the starting resistance is too great for a child to perform even one repetition. In this case the child will have to perform free-weight, body-weight, or partner-resisted exercises until he or she is strong enough to use the machine. We hope that in the future more resistance machines will be manufactured that accommodate children.

Making a Choice

Despite all the claims made by equipment manufacturers, research on adults and children shows that virtually all resistance training equipment causes essentially equal gains in strength/ power and motor performance. One interpretation of this is that gains in strength/power and motor performance most likely depend more upon the design of the training program and the effort the individual puts into the program than upon the type of equipment used.

Still, you must decide whether to purchase or use various pieces of equipment, and you need a basis upon which to make these decisions. We have addressed proper fit and weight stack increments of the resistance training equipment. Other factors that you should consider are presented in the following box. You may find that one manufacturer may best suit your needs for the bench press, whereas another manufacturer's leg press is best. It is not necessary that all your equipment be made by the same company.

FACTORS TO CONSIDER WHEN EXAMINING RESISTANCE EQUIPMENT

1. If the equipment does not fit children, can it be safely altered to do so?
2. If you are purchasing the equipment, what is its cost per exercise station?
3. If you are purchasing the equipment, how much will it cost to purchase sufficient equipment to exercise all major muscle groups of the body?
4. If you are purchasing the equipment, how long is its warranty?
5. If you are purchasing the equipment, what does its warranty cover?
6. Is the equipment made from heavy-gauge steel?
7. Is the equipment sturdily constructed (e.g., are the welds solid)?
8. How easy is it to adjust the resistance?
9. Does the resistance increase in increments suitable for children?

Use of Strength Training Accessories

The three most commonly used strength training accessories are a weight training belt, gloves, and shoes. Although not absolutely necessary for a safe and effective strength training program, all three do offer some benefits.

Weight training belts, gloves, and shoes are helpful accessories for a safe program.

Weight Training Belt

A weight training belt has a wide back and is designed to help support the lower back. Although weight training belts come in many sizes, a belt small enough to fit small children is not commonly available. A belt is not necessary for resistance training but is merely an aid to counteract a lack of strong abdominal and lower back musculature.

Weight training belts do help support the lower spine but not from the back as is commonly thought. The belt gives the abdominal muscles an object to push against, allowing a buildup of pressure in the abdomen, which pushes against the lower spine from the front.

Wearing a tightly cinched belt during activity causes a higher blood pressure than if the activity is performed without a belt. This makes the pumping of blood by the heart more difficult and may cause undue cardiovascular stress. Thus, wearing a belt during resistance exercises in which the lower back is not heavily involved is not recommended. A belt can be worn during lifts involving the lower back, but it should not be used to alleviate technique problems due to weak lower back and abdominal muscles. Rather than allowing a lifter to rely on a belt, incorporate into the program exercises to strengthen the abdominal and lower back muscles. This can help eliminate chronic lower back weakness, which can lead to poor exercise technique. In addition, strong abdominals and lower back muscles can help prevent injury to the lower back during all physical activity.

Weight Training Gloves

Specially designed for resistance training, these gloves do not cover the fingers but only the palms. They protect the palms somewhat from such things as the knurling on many barbells, dumbbells, and equipment handles, and they may help prevent the formation of blisters or the ripping of calluses on the hands. However, gloves are typically not necessary for safe resistance training.

Weight Training Shoes

Weight training shoes are mainly designed to provide good arch support, a tight fit, and a nonslip surface on the sole. In addition, weight training shoes offer little or no shock absorbance in the soles; thus any force or power that the lifter develops by extending the leg or hip is not used to compress the sole of the shoe and is available to lift the weight in such exercises as the squat or clean. A lifter should wear a shoe with a nonslip surface on the sole and good arch support, but it does not have to be a shoe specifically designed for power or Olympic weight lifting.

Summing Up and Looking Ahead

Teaching proper resistance training exercise technique requires a knowledge not only of correct technique but also of how to select resistance training equipment, properly fit children to equipment, and ensure smooth progression in the resistance used. You must consider all these factors when teaching technique for one exercise, when implementing a program for general total body strength, or when implementing a program to improve performance in a particular sport. The following box is a checklist of requirements for teaching resistance training exercise techniques.

EXERCISE TEACHING CHECKLIST

_____ 1. Know correct exercise technique.

_____ 2. Know proper spotting technique.

_____ 3. If a child uses a resistance training machine, be sure the machine properly fits the child.

_____ 4. Be sure equipment is in good working condition (i.e., pulleys and cables are not worn; weight stack moves freely).

_____ 5. Be sure benches or other equipment will not slide during the exercise; bolt equipment securely to the floor or wall, if appropriate.

_____ 6. If a child uses free weights, be sure collars are fastened securely.

_____ 7. Demonstrate and discuss proper exercise and spotting techniques to the children.

_____ 8. Allow all children to perform the exercise and spotting techniques, giving feedback to them concerning their performances.

_____ 9. Do not increase resistances too rapidly when children are learning exercise technique.

Next, we describe proper technique for many popular exercises.

Additional Readings

Baechle T.R., & Groves, B.R. (1992). *Weight Training Steps to Success*. Champaign, IL: Leisure Press.

Garhammer, J. (1987). *Sports Illustrated: Strength Training*, New York: Winner's Circle Books.

National Strength and Conditioning Association (1991). *How to Teach* [Video Series 1, 2, & 3]. Lincoln, NE.

Stone, M., & O'Bryant, H. (1987). *Weight Training: A Scientific Approach*. Minneapolis, MN: Burgess International Group, Inc.

Chapter 6

Strength Training

Exercises

Proper exercise technique and spotting are necessary to ensure the safety and optimal physical improvement of children. This chapter describes the major points of proper lifting and spotting techniques for common resistance training exercises. The majority of exercises are described for use with free weights, because some exercises cannot be performed with machines (e.g., squats, power cleans) and because in many instances free-weight lifting technique is very close to the technique required for machines. Remember that exercise technique may vary slightly from one manufacturer's equipment to another's. Consult the manufacturer's description of proper lifting technique for a particular piece of equipment before using any resistance training machine. This will ensure that lifters use proper exercise technique on all resistance training equipment.

Use common sense when selecting and teaching resistance training exercises for children. If a child fears a particular exercise, assign an alternate exercise. If the children cannot safely spot each other, due to immaturity or any other reason, avoid exercises that require spotting until the children can safely spot each other. Or, provide sufficient adult supervision so the adults can act as spotters. Some exercises that place stress on the lower back (e.g., dead lifts, squats) should not be performed with heavy resistances (less than 6 RM), and you must constantly emphasize proper lifting technique when children perform these lifts.

Partner Exercises

During a partner exercise, another person supplies the resistance. These exercises are valuable to an in-season maintenance program because they can easily be performed on a playing field or in a gym. Partner exercises are also useful with small children who do not fit resistance machines. In addition, if these exercises are done correctly, the resistance is adjusted to match the strength curve of the movement and is adjusted as the trainee fatigues during a set of the exercise. The major disadvantage is that determining the effort the trainee exerts is difficult; thus, keeping motivation high and ensuring adherence to such programs may be difficult. This is why partner exercises are typically used in a starter program or in situations where equipment is limited.

Following are descriptions of several partner exercises. This section does not describe all partner exercises possible but introduces the concept of partner exercise. With some thought you can devise many more partner exercises.

Proper Technique.   Both the person performing the exercise and the individual supplying the resistance must act in a mature manner. The partner and the trainee must communicate well so that the resistance provided is of the correct magnitude and is applied in a constant manner. The partner must allow the movement of the exercise to occur in a smooth fashion but must also supply sufficient resistance so that performance of the movement is difficult for the trainee. The partner's role is to help train the lifter, not impress him or her.

PARTNER-RESISTED BACK SQUAT

Starting Position.   The trainee stands with the back straight, eyes looking forward, feet flat on the ground approximately shoulder-width apart, and toes pointing directly forward or slightly to the outside. A partner is on the trainee's back, and the trainee grasps the partner's thighs (Figure 6.1a).

Movement.   In a controlled manner, the trainee slowly bends at the knees and hips until the thighs are parallel to the floor (Figure 6.1b). The trainee then returns to the starting position by straightening the knees and hips. The feet should remain flat on the floor, and the entire back should stay as upright as possible throughout the exercise. Bending at the lower back places undue stress on the lower back. Some forward lean of the back will occur, but this should be kept to a minimum. The head should be kept upright, and the neck should be in line with the rest of the spine throughout the exercise.

Spotting and Safety.   Spotting is not needed, because the trainee can simply release the partner and the partner can then assume a standing position. However, the trainee should warn the partner before releasing him or her.

Muscles Strengthened.   Quadriceps, hamstrings, gluteals, lower back (*back extensors*), and to some extent the upper back (*trapezius, levator scapulae*), shoulder girdle, and elbow flexors of the upper arm (biceps and *brachialis*).

a

b

Figure 6.1 (a) Starting and finishing position for partner squat. (b) Bottom position for partner squat; note that the thighs are parallel to the floor.

PARTNER-RESISTED ELBOW CURL

Starting Position. The trainee stands erect with feet approximately shoulder-width apart and the knees slightly bent and grasps a towel in the middle with an underhand grip. The arms are straight, the head is upright, and the back is straight. A partner kneels, grasps both ends of the towel, and places his or her hands slightly behind and below the trainee's hands (Figure 6.2a). As an alternate position, the trainee can sit on a preacher curl bench with the upper arm supported as shown in Figure 6.2b. Adjust the height of the angled padding for the arm so the back of the upper arm rests comfortably on the padding at approximately a 45-degree angle to the torso.

Movement. In the standing position, the trainee keeps the elbows close to the body and flexes at the elbow until the arms are completely flexed and the hands are touching or almost touching the chest (Figure 6.2c). In the sitting position, the trainee must keep the elbows properly positioned on the preacher curl bench. The partner supplies resistance by pulling on the towel. The partner should allow the trainee to complete the movement in approximately 6 seconds. Either the trainee and the partner assume the starting position and repeat the exercise (concentric only movement), or they perform the motion in reverse with the trainee resisting and the partner supplying force (eccentric, lowering phase). When they reach the starting position, they repeat the exercise.

Spotting and Safety. No spotting is needed. However, the partner should give the trainee feedback concerning proper body position during the exercise. Make sure the towel used is sturdy enough to withstand the forces it must tolerate during the exercise.

Muscles Strengthened. Elbow flexors located on the front of the upper arm (biceps brachii, and brachialis) and some of the muscles on the palm side of the forearm.

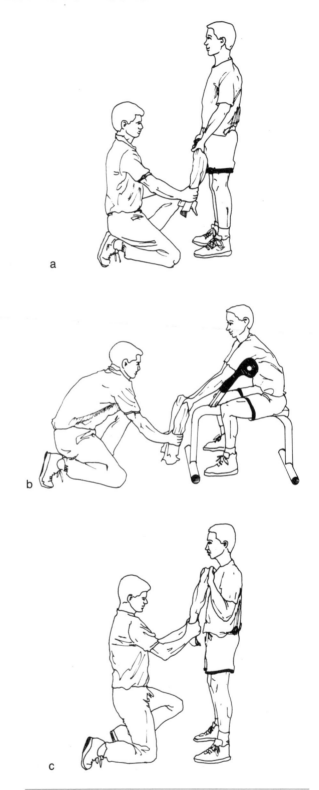

a

b

c

Figure 6.2 (a) Starting position for partner-resisted elbow curl. (b) Starting position for partner-resisted elbow curl performed with a preacher bench. (c) Finishing position of partner-resisted elbow curl.

PARTNER-RESISTED LATERAL ARM RAISE

Starting Position.   The trainee stands erect, head up and arms at the sides. A partner stands either behind or in front of the trainee and places his or her hands just above the trainee's elbows (Figure 6.3a).

Movement.   The trainee raises the arms laterally until they are parallel to the floor (Figure 6.3b). The partner supplies resistance so that the trainee can complete this motion in approximately 6 seconds. The motion is then done in reverse, with the trainee resisting and the partner supplying force. Returning to the starting position should also take about 6 seconds. The back and head of the trainee should remain erect and upright throughout the exercise.

Spotting and Safety.   No spotting is needed. The partner should give the trainee feedback concerning proper exercise technique.

Muscles Strengthened.   The lateral portion of the shoulder (deltoid).

a

b

Figure 6.3 (a) Starting and finishing position for partner-resisted lateral arm raise. (b) Top position for partner-resisted lateral arm raise is with trainee's arms parallel to the floor.

PARTNER-RESISTED TRICEPS EXTENSION

Starting Position. The trainee stands erect with the feet approximately shoulder-width apart, the back straight, and the head upright. The arms are overhead with the lower arms parallel to the floor and the elbows flexed. The trainee grasps the middle of a towel, which hangs behind the trainee's head. A partner grasps the towel at both ends (Figure 6.4a).

Movement.   Keeping the upper arms perpendicular to the floor, the trainee straightens the elbows. The partner supplies resistance by pulling on the towel but allows the trainee's elbows to become completely straight in approximately 6 seconds (Figure 6.4b). The motion is then reversed, with the trainee resisting movement and the partner supplying resistance so that the starting position is reassumed in approximately 6 seconds.

Spotting and Safety.   No spotting is needed. The towel needs to be strong enough to withstand the forces encountered in the exercise.

Muscles Strengthened.   Extensors of the elbow (triceps) located on the back of the upper arm.

a

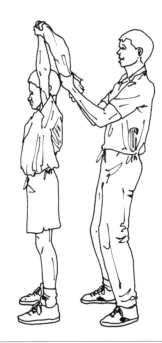

b

Figure 6.4 (a) Starting and finishing position for partner-resisted triceps extension. (b) Top position for partner-resisted triceps extension.

PARTNER-RESISTED KNEE CURL

Starting Position.   The trainee lies on the floor on his or her stomach, with knees flexed at about a 45-degree angle. A partner kneels facing the soles of the trainee's feet, grasping the lower leg just below the heels of the trainee (Figure 6.5a).

Movement.   The trainee flexes at the knees until the heels touch the buttocks (Figure 6.5b). The partner resists the trainee but allows completion of the movement in approximately 6 seconds. The trainee and partner reassume the starting position and perform the next repetition.

Spotting and Safety.   No spotting is needed. The partner must have a secure grip on the trainee's ankles in order to supply sufficient resistance.

Muscles Strengthened.   The hamstrings group located on the back of the upper leg.

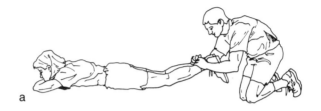

Figure 6.5   (a) Starting position for partner-resisted knee curl; trainee's knees are flexed at a 45-degree angle to the floor. (b) Finishing position for partner-resisted knee curls; heels touch the buttocks.

Rubber Cord Exercises

To teach this type of resistance training, you need a thick rubber cord resembling surgical tubing, which can be purchased from some sporting good stores. The rubber cord is available in varying thicknesses; the thicker the tubing the greater the resistance it will provide. Handles can be made by tying one end of the cord to the cord, thus making a loop at the end. Rubber cord exercises have several advantages and disadvantages, as summarized here:

ADVANTAGES

- The equipment needed in minimal.
- The equipment is relatively inexpensive.
- Exercises are safe, so no spotting is normally needed.
- The trainee can perform both single- and multijoint exercises.

DISADVANTAGES

- No visible movement of a weight takes place, and this can lead to a motivational problem with some children.
- It can be difficult to judge the trainee's effort.

When a person performs a rubber cord exercise, the resistance is the greatest as the movement nears completion. This is opposite of what occurs in most sport movements, daily activities, and typical resistance exercise, and therefore it may be of concern in regard to training *specificity*. Many rubber cord exercises are possible but only two are described here.

Proper Technique.   During an exercise, either the cord is securely attached to an immovable object or the trainee stands on the cord to hold it stationary. The resistance is adjusted by the amount of prestretch on the cord or by the thickness of the cord itself.

RUBBER CORD ELBOW CURL

Starting Position. The trainee stands on top of the cord, keeping the back straight, holding the head upright, and grasping the handles on both ends of the cord (Figure 6.6a). Equal lengths of the cord should extend from beneath each foot.

Movement. Moving only the forearms, the trainee pulls the handles upward until the elbows are completely flexed (Figure 6.6b). Then in a controlled manner, the trainee returns the arms to the starting position. The back, legs, and upper arms should remain stationary throughout the entire exercise.

Spotting and Safety. No spotting is needed. The trainee should not step off of the rubber cord unless the arms are in the starting position and no tension is in the rubber cord.

Muscles Strengthened. Elbow flexors located on the front of the upper arm (*biceps brachii*, brachialis) and some of the muscles located on the front of the forearm.

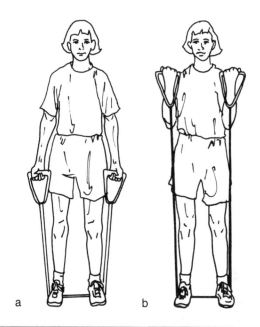

Figure 6.6 (a) Starting and finishing position for rubber cord elbow curl. (b) Top position for rubber cord elbow curl.

RUBBER CORD SEATED ROW

Starting Position. Attach the rubber cord to an immovable object, such as a pole or wall. The trainee sits with feet against the immovable object, with the back and legs straight. The trainee grasps the handles on the ends of the cord, one in each hand (Figure 6.7a).

Movement. The trainee pulls the arms back until the handles are even with or slightly past the chest (Figure 6.7b). Then, in a controlled manner, the trainee returns the arms to the starting position. The back should remain stationary during the entire exercise.

Spotting and Safety. No spotting is needed. Make certain the rubber cord is securely fastened to the immovable object.

Muscles Strengthened. Upper back (trapezius, *rhomboids*), shoulder extensor (*latissimus dorsi*), back of the shoulder area (posterior deltoid), and elbow flexors to some degree (biceps brachii, brachialis).

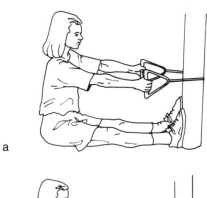

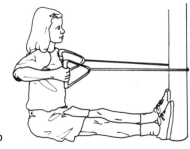

Figure 6.7 (a) Starting and finishing position for rubber cord seated row. (b) End of the pulling phase in rubber cord seated row.

Shoulder Area Exercises

Many common resistance training exercises such as the bench and military press train the shoulder area concurrently with other muscle groups. The following shoulder area exercises, however, are designed to isolate and train specific portions of the shoulder musculature.

Example Activities Muscles Are Used For.   Passing a football, using the crawl stroke in swimming, shot putting, batting a baseball, performing a handstand, and performing virtually all movements of the shoulder joint.

Proper Technique.   The lifter should perform the movements in a controlled manner and with a resistance that allows movement through the full range of motion.

SIDE (LATERAL) SHOULDER RAISE

Starting Position. The lifter stands erect with the feet approximately shoulder-width apart and holds a dumbbell in each hand. The arms hang at the sides of the body with the elbows slightly bent (Figure 6.8a). (Some resistance training machines allow the lifter to perform a variation of a side lateral raise.)

Movement. In a controlled manner the lifter raises both dumbbells until the arms are parallel to the floor and holds this position for 1 to 2 seconds (Figure 6.8b). Then the arms slowly return to the starting position and stop there for 1 to 2 seconds. The elbows should remain slightly bent throughout the entire motion. The exercise can also be performed with one arm at a time.

Spotting and Safety. No spotting or safety precautions are needed.

Muscles Strengthened. Muscles of the shoulder joint that raise the arm to the side, that is, abduct the shoulder; the major muscle used is the deltoid, which covers the front, back, and side of the shoulder.

a

b

Figure 6.8 (a) Starting and finishing position for side lateral shoulder raise. (b) Top position for side lateral shoulder raise performed with dumbbells. The arms do not have to be raised any higher than parallel to the floor.

FRONT (ANTERIOR) SHOULDER RAISE

Starting Position.   The lifter stands erect with the feet approximately shoulder-width apart and holds a dumbbell in each hand. The elbows are slightly bent (Figure 6.9a).

Movement.   The lifter raises the dumbbells forward in a controlled manner by moving the arms at the shoulders until the arms are parallel to the floor. The arms stop for 1 to 2 seconds when they are parallel to the floor. Then they slowly return to the starting position. The elbows should be slightly bent throughout the entire exercise. Some individuals may prefer to perform this exercise alternating arms (Figure 6.9b). For variation, perform this exercise with palms facing down.

Spotting and Safety.   No spotting or safety precautions are needed.

Muscles Strengthened.   The muscles of the shoulder joint that raise the arm forward, mainly the anterior deltoid.

a

b

Figure 6.9   (a) Starting and finishing position for front (anterior) shoulder raise. (b) Top position for front shoulder raise with the right arm. The exercise is being performed with alternating arms.

BACK (POSTERIOR) SHOULDER RAISE

Starting Position.   The lifter stands erect with the feet approximately shoulder-width apart and holds a dumbbell in each hand. The elbows are slightly bent (Figure 6.10a).

Movement.   In a controlled manner the lifter raises both dumbbells backward by moving the arms at the shoulders until the arms are parallel to the floor. The arms stop for 1 to 2 seconds when they are parallel to the floor or as near to that position as possible. Then they slowly return to the starting position. The elbows should remain slightly bent throughout the entire exercise. The lifter can also perform the exercise alternating arms (Figure 6.10b).

Spotting and Safety.   No spotting or safety precautions are needed.

Muscles Strengthened.   Muscles of the shoulder joint that raise the arm posteriorly, mainly the posterior deltoid.

a

b

Figure 6.10   (a) Starting and finishing position for back (posterior) shoulder raise. (b) Top position for back shoulder raise. The exercise is being performed with alternating arms.

SHOULDER SHRUG

Starting Position. The lifter stands erect with the feet approximately shoulder-width apart and holds a barbell at waist level with an overhand grip. The elbows are straight and the shoulders are in a natural position (Figure 6.11a). Some resistance training machines allow the lifter to perform a shoulder shrug. Many bench press machines can also be used for this exercise.

Movement. Without bending the elbows, the lifter raises or shrugs the shoulders, attempting to touch the shoulders to the ears (Figure 6.11b). Then in a controlled manner the lifter returns to the starting position. To vary the exercise, the lifter can pull the shoulders back as far as possible, attempt to touch the ears with the shoulders, bring the shoulders as far forward as possible, and then lower them back to the starting position. This motion should be slow, continuous, and rolling.

Spotting and Safety. No spotting or safety precautions are needed.

Muscles Strengthened. The trapezius, which connects the shoulder and shoulder blade to the neck and spine.

Variation: Dumbbell Shoulder Shrug. The lifter holds a dumbbell in each hand and performs the exercise in the same manner as the shoulder shrug (Figure 6.12).

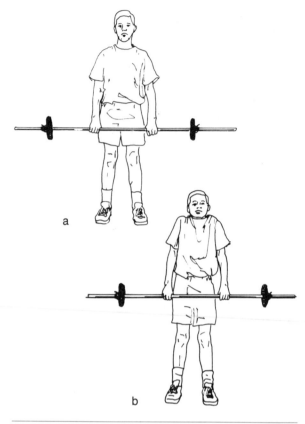

a

b

Figure 6.11 (a) Starting and finishing position for shoulder shrug with a barbell. (b) Top position for shoulder shrug performed with a barbell. The elbows are straight; therefore the lifter did not bend the elbows to lift the weight.

Figure 6.12 Top position of shoulder shrug performed with dumbbells.

Shoulder Rotator Cuff Exercises

The rotator cuff is a group of muscles that rotate the upper arm in the shoulder joint and stabilize the humerus in the shoulder joint. The rotator cuff and surrounding muscles are frequently the source of pain in common shoulder overuse injuries such as Little League shoulder or swimmer's shoulder. You can use these exercises to treat a rotator cuff injury or to prevent such injury.

Example Activities Muscles Are Used For. Virtually all throwing activities, tennis strokes, and swimming.

Proper Technique. The lifter should perform the exercises with both arms, using light weights (initially as light as 1-1/2 pounds) and relatively high numbers of repetitions per set (10 to 15). All exercises should be performed in a controlled manner. The resistance should be increased very gradually and in small increments.

SHOULDER INTERNAL ROTATION

Starting Position.   The lifter lies on the floor on his or her back, grasping a light dumbbell in one hand. The elbow is at a 90-degree angle, the upper arm is at the side, and the back of the forearm is touching the floor (Figure 6.13a).

Movement.   The lifter raises the dumbbell until the forearm is pointing directly at the ceiling (Figure 6.13b). Then in a controlled manner the lifter lowers the dumbbell back to the starting position.

Spotting and Safety.   No spotting or safety precautions are needed. Do not perform this exercise if you have rotator cuff pain.

Muscles Strengthened.   Muscles of the rotator cuff, especially the *subscapularis*.

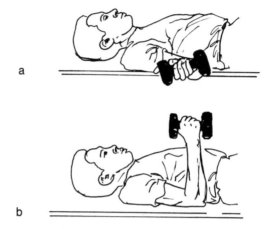

a

b

Figure 6.13   (a) Starting and finishing position for shoulder internal rotation. (b) Top position for shoulder internal rotation. Motion only at the shoulder should occur during this exercise; the elbow is stationary. Avoid this exercise if you experience rotator cuff pain.

SHOULDER EXTERNAL ROTATION

Starting Position.   The lifter lies on the floor on his or her side, grasping a dumbbell in one hand and keeping the upper arm alongside the body. The elbow is at approximately 90 degrees and the dumbbell almost touches the ground (Figure 6.14a).

Movement.   The lifter slowly raises the forearm by rotating the arm at the shoulder as far as he or she is comfortably able (Figure 6.14b). The arm then slowly returns to the starting position.

Spotting and Safety.   No spotting or safety precautions are needed.

Muscles Strengthened.   Muscles of the rotator cuff, in particular the *infraspinatus* and *teres minor*.

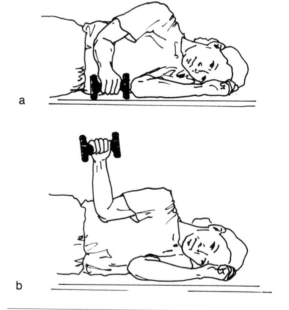

a

b

Figure 6.14   (a) Starting and finishing position for shoulder external rotation. (b) Top position for shoulder external rotation. The elbow should remain at a 90-degree angle throughout this exercise.

SHOULDER HORIZONTAL ABDUCTION

Starting Position. The lifter lies on his or her stomach on a bench or table, grasping a dumbbell in one hand. The arm of the hand grasping the dumbbell hangs over the edge of the bench or table, pointing directly at the floor (Figure 6.15a).

Movement. The lifter slowly moves the arm directly out to the side until the arm is parallel to the floor and then slowly returns it to the starting position. The elbow should remain straight, but not locked, throughout the entire motion (Figure 6.15b).

Spotting and Safety. No spotting is needed. Be certain the table or bench used is sturdy enough to hold the trainee's body weight.

Muscles Strengthened. Muscles of the rotator cuff; the major and minor rhomboids; in addition, the posterior deltoid.

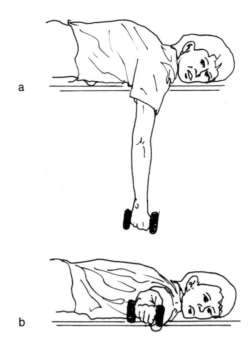

Figure 6.15 (a) Starting and finishing position for shoulder horizontal abduction. (b) Top position for shoulder horizontal abduction. The arm is raised directly out to the side of the body until the arm is parallel to the ground.

SHOULDER ABDUCTION

Starting Position.   The lifter stands erect grasping a dumbbell in one hand. The hand grasping the dumbbell hangs beside the body with the palm facing the side of the body (Figure 6.16a).

Movement.   The lifter slowly raises the dumbbell directly out to the side until the arm is parallel to the floor and then slowly returns the arm to the starting position. The elbow should remain straight but not locked throughout the entire movement (Figure 6.16b).

Spotting and Safety.   No spotting or safety precautions are needed.

Muscles Strengthened.   The middle portion of the deltoid and all rotator cuff muscles that stabilize the humerus in the shoulder joint.

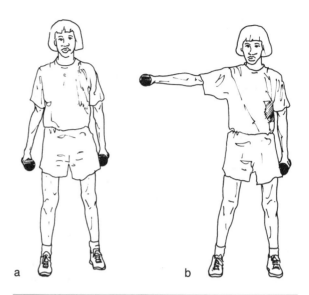

Figure 6.16   (a) Starting and finishing position for shoulder abduction. (b) Top position for shoulder abduction. The arm is raised directly out to the side of the body until it is parallel to the ground.

SHOULDER FLEXION

Starting Position.   The lifter stands erect grasping a dumbbell in one hand. The hand grasping the dumbbell hangs beside the body with the palm facing the side of the body (Figure 6.17a).

Movement.   The lifter slowly lifts the dumbbell forward until the arm is parallel to the floor and then slowly returns the arm to the starting position. The elbow should remain straight but not locked during the movement (Figure 6.17b).

Spotting and Safety.   No spotting or safety precautions are needed.

Muscles Strengthened.   Anterior deltoid.

Figure 6.17   (a) Starting and finishing position for shoulder flexion. (b) Top position for shoulder flexion. The arm is raised directly forward until it is parallel to the ground.

30-DEGREE SHOULDER FORWARD FLEXION

Starting Position. The lifter stands erect holding a dumbbell in each hand. The elbows are not quite straight, and the palms face backward (Figure 6.18a).

Movement. The trainer lifts both dumbbells until the arms are parallel to the floor. However, the arms are not raised straight out to the sides but at angles 30 degrees forward of the sides. The lifter then returns the arms to the starting position. The elbows should not lock, and the palms should remain facing backward throughout the motion (Figure 6.18b).

Spotting and Safety. No spotting or safety precautions are needed.

Muscles Strengthened. Back of the upper shoulder (supraspinatus).

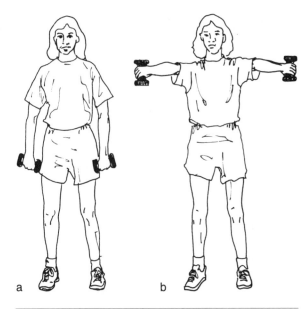

Figure 6.18 (a) Starting and finishing position for 30-degree shoulder forward flexion. (b) Top position for 30-degree shoulder forward flexion. The arms are not directly out to the sides but 30 degrees forward of the sides.

SHOULDER EXTENSION

Starting Position. The lifter lies on his or her stomach on a bench or table, grasping a dumbbell in one hand. The arm grasping the dumbbell hangs over the edge of the bench or table, pointing directly at the floor (Figure 6.19a).

Movement. Keeping the elbow straight but not locked and the arm close to the body, the lifter slowly raises the arm backward until it is parallel to the floor (Figure 6.19b). The arm then returns to the starting position.

Spotting and Safety. No spotting is needed. Be certain the bench or table will hold the lifter's body weight.

Muscles Strengthened. Posterior deltoid, latissismus dorsi, and lower trapezius.

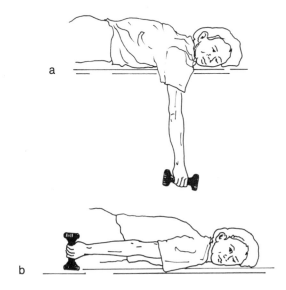

Figure 6.19 (a) Starting and finishing position for shoulder extension. (b) Top position for shoulder extension. The arm is parallel to the ground at the end of the lifting phase.

STABILIZATION EXERCISE

Starting Position.   The lifter lies on his or her back on the floor with one arm extended straight upward (Figure 6.20).

Movement.   A partner applies pressure to the trainee's arm randomly in all four directions. The pressure should be applied just below the wrist. The trainee resists the pressure, and as soon as the partner feels the trainee resist, the partner applies pressure in another direction. The exercise is performed in bouts of 30 seconds.

Spotting and Safety.   No spotting is needed. This exercise requires the partner to be very attentive and to react quickly when the trainee responds to the applied pressure. The pressure applied should not be excessive.

Muscles Strengthened.   Muscles of the rotator cuff.

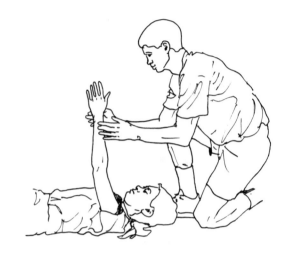

Figure 6.20   Body position for shoulder stabilization exercise.

Back of Upper Arm (Triceps) Exercises

The major muscle on the back of the upper arm, the triceps, is trained along with other upper body muscle groups by many of the upper body multijoint exercises such as the bench and military press. The exercises described in this section, however, are designed to train predominantly the triceps and not other muscle groups.

Example Activities Muscles Are Used For.   Pushing off in pole vaulting, passing a football or basketball, shot putting, and all pushing or extending movements of the elbow.

Proper Technique.   During all variations of these body part isolation exercises, the elbow is the only joint that should move. The lifter should straighten and flex the elbow in a controlled manner during performance of all of the exercises in this group.

STANDING BARBELL TRICEPS EXTENSION (FRENCH PRESS)

Starting Position. The lifter holds a barbell overhead with the arms fully extended. The hands should be 6 inches apart or less. The lifter stands erect with the feet approximately shoulder-width apart (Figure 6.21a).

Movement. Keeping the shoulders and upper arms stationary, the lifter slowly lowers the barbell by bending the arms at the elbows until the barbell touches the back of the neck (Figure 6.21b). Keeping the upper arms stationary the lifter raises the barbell to the starting position by straightening the elbows. The lifter should not use the legs or back to start the barbell moving back to the starting position. The elbows should remain close to the head during the entire movement and the upper arms should remain stationary.

Spotting and Safety. One spotter may spot this exercise by standing behind the lifter. From this position the spotter can help the lifter complete a repetition or take the barbell away from the lifter if necessary. Make sure the collars holding the weight plates on the bar are tight. Because the barbell is held overhead, the weight plates may fall on the trainee if they come off of the bar. Small children may find it especially difficult to balance the barbell in this exercise.

Muscles Strengthened. Back of upper arm (triceps).

Variation: Standing Dumbbell Triceps Extension. Substitute a dumbbell for the barbell. The lifter grasps one end of the dumbbell with both hands and performs the exercise in a fashion similar to the standing barbell triceps extension (Figure 6.22 a and b). Be sure that the collars on the dumbbell are tight so the weight plates don't fall on the lifter.

a   b

Figure 6.21 (a) Starting and finishing position for standing barbell triceps extension or French press. (b) Bottom position for standing barbell triceps extension. The upper arms should remain stationary during the entire exercise.

a   b

Figure 6.22 (a) Starting and finishing position for standing dumbbell triceps extension. (b) Bottom position for standing dumbbell triceps extension. Be certain that the collars of the dumbbell are tight.

DUMBBELL KICKBACK

Starting Position. With the feet shoulder-width apart and slightly staggered, the lifter bends over at the waist until the upper torso is parallel to the floor. The lifter holds a dumbbell in one hand with the palm facing the body and keeps the upper arm parallel to the floor. The elbow is bent at a 90-degree angle so that the forearm is perpendicular to the floor. The lifter can place the opposite hand on top of a chair or bench to aid in balance and provide support (Figure 6.23a).

Movement. The lifter slowly straightens the elbow until the arm is completely straight, then slowly bends the elbow back to the starting position. Only the elbow should move; the legs or back should not assist in moving the dumbbell during any portion of the movement (Figure 6.23b).

Spotting and Safety. No spotting or safety precautions are needed.

Muscles Strengthened. Back of upper arm (triceps).

a

b

Figure 6.23 (a) Starting and finishing position for dumbbell kickback. The right hand is placed on a bench to help keep the upper body stationary. (b) Top position for dumbbell kickback.

LYING BARBELL TRICEPS EXTENSION

Starting Position.   The lifter lies on his or her back on a flat bench (bench for performing the bench press) and holds a barbell at arm's length above the chest. The feet are flat on the floor, and the hands are approximately 6 inches apart (Figure 6.24a).

Movement.   Moving only at the elbows, the lifter lowers the barbell until it touches the forehead or passes over the top of the head (Figure 6.24b). Again moving only at the elbows, the lifter returns to the starting position. The upper arm remains stationary throughout this exercise.

Spotting and Safety.   A spotter stands behind the lifter's head. Due to the movement of the barbell toward the head, the spotter must pay careful attention at all times. If you assign another child to spot, be sure the spotter is mature and strong enough to spot the lifter. Be sure that the resistance used is light enough that the exercise can be performed safely.

Muscles Strengthened.   Back of upper arm (triceps).

Variation: Dumbbell and EZ Curl Bar Triceps Extension.   Substitute a dumbbell for the barbell. The lifter grasps one end of the dumbbell (Figure 6.25a). The exercise is performed in the same manner except the lifter lowers the dumbbell until it is even with the back of the head (Figure 6.25b). Instead of a normal barbell, the lifter can use an *EZ curl bar*, a specially designed bar with bends in it. Many people find the wrist and hand positions used with this type of bar more comfortable for many exercises than positions used with a conventional straight barbell. The exercise is performed in the same manner as with a normal barbell.

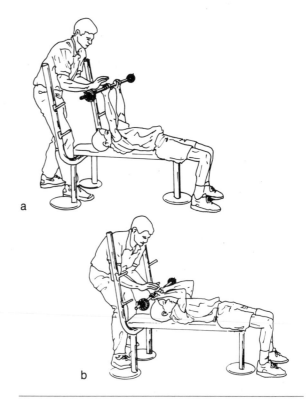

Figure 6.24   (a) Starting and finishing position for the lying barbell triceps extension. A spotter should be used for this exercise, because the weight is over the lifter's head during the exercise. (b) Bottom position of the lying barbell triceps extension. The upper arms should remain stationary throughout this exercise.

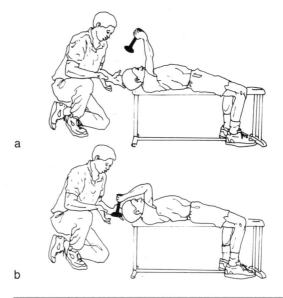

Figure 6.25   (a) Starting and finishing position for dumbbell triceps extension. (b) Bottom position for dumbbell triceps extension. The dumbbell passes over the head during the exercise, so the lifter must make sure that the dumbbell collars are tight.

STANDING HIGH PULLEY TRICEPS EXTENSION (TRICEPS PRESS-DOWN)

Starting Position.   The lifter stands erect facing the handle of a lat pull-down machine or high pulley. The lifter grasps the handle with both hands and pulls it down until it is at shoulder level. The elbows touch the sides of the ribs and the hands are approximately 6 inches apart (Figure 6.26a).

Movement.   The lifter slowly straightens the elbows completely. This should move the handle down to below waist level (Figure 6.26b). The arms then slowly return to the starting position. The elbows should touch the sides of the body at all times, and movement should occur only at the elbows.

Spotting and Safety.   No spotting is necessary. The lifter must keep his or her head out of the way of the machine's cable and must control the movement when returning the handle to its original position to avoid being hit in the chin.

Muscles Strengthened.   Back of upper arm (triceps).

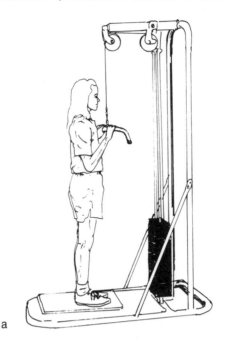

a

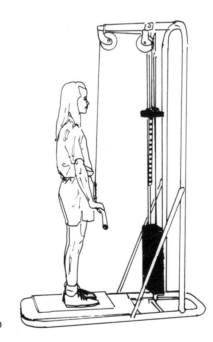

b

Figure 6.26   (a) Starting and finishing position of the standing high pulley triceps extension or triceps press-down. (b) Bottom position of the triceps press-down. During the exercise the upper arms remain stationary and against the sides of the body. During the exercise movement should take place only at the elbows.

Elbow Flexor Exercises

The muscles that flex the elbow are used to some extent in all multi-joint exercises of the upper body that involve a pulling motion. The goal of these exercises is to isolate the elbow flexors for a greater training effect.

Example Activities Muscles Are Used For.   Rope climbing, wrestling, pole vaulting, backstroke in swimming, rebounding in basketball, and most pulling motions performed with the upper body.

Proper Technique.   The lifter should move the resistance only by bending the elbows. Swinging or rocking the legs or back to move the resistance will reduce the training stimulus on the elbow flexors and may cause injury to the lower back. The lifter should raise and lower the resistance in a controlled manner.

STANDING BARBELL ELBOW (ARM) CURL

Starting Position. The lifter stands erect with the feet about shoulder-width apart and the knees slightly bent. The lifter grasps a barbell with an underhand grip so that the hands are shoulder-width or slightly farther apart. The bar rests on the thighs, the head is up, and the back is straight (Figure 6.27a). The lifter can also perform the exercise while standing with the back against a wall. This helps eliminate the urge to cheat by rocking with the lower back.

Movement. Keeping the elbows close to the body, the lifter raises the barbell until the elbows are completely flexed and the barbell touches the chest area. The lifter briefly holds the bar in the top position (Figure 6.27b), then lowers the barbell in a controlled manner to the starting position.

Spotting and Safety. Spotting is not needed. Don't allow the lifter to use the lower back to move the resistance. Extreme use of the lower back for this purpose may result in injury to the lower back area.

Muscles Strengthened. Front of upper arm (biceps brachii and brachialis) and some of the muscles on the palm side of the forearm.

Variation: Dumbbell and EZ Curl Bar Elbow Curl. The lifter holds two dumbbells (Figure 6.28a) and performs a curl in the same manner as the standing barbell elbow curl. The lifter can lift a dumbbell in one hand while lowering the dumbbell in the other hand (Figure 6.28b), or both arms can lift and lower at the same time. An EZ curl bar can be used for this exercise, as can a low pulley and other types of resistance training machines.

Figure 6.27 (a) Starting and finishing position for the standing barbell elbow (arm) curl using an EZ curl bar. The lower back and legs should not be used to start the barbell moving from the starting position. (b) Top position of the standing barbell elbow curl. Movement should occur only at the elbow during this exercise.

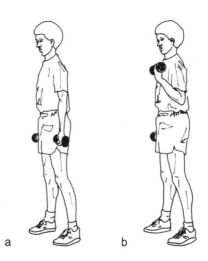

Figure 6.28 (a) Starting and finishing position for standing dumbbell elbow curl. (b) The top position in standing dumbbell elbow curl with the left arm when the standing dumbbell elbow curl is performed with alternating arms.

SELF-RESISTED ELBOW CURL

Starting Position.   The lifter stands erect with the feet shoulder-width apart. The arm to be exercised is fully extended in front of the body with the palm facing forward. The hand of the opposite arm grasps the hand of the exercising arm (Figure 6.29a).

Movement.   The lifter contracts the elbow flexors of the exercising arm and resists with the opposite arm, allowing the exercising arm to reach a fully flexed position in approximately 6 seconds (Figure 6.29b). The lifter returns the arms to the starting position in approximately 6 seconds, pushing with the opposite arm and resisting with the exercising arm, thus performing an eccentric contraction with the elbow flexors of the exercising arm.

Spotting and Safety.   No spotting or safety precautions are needed.

Muscles Strengthened.   Front of upper arm (biceps brachii and brachialis) and some of the muscles on the palm side of the forearm.

a

b

Figure 6.29   (a) Starting and finishing position for self-resisted elbow curl. (b) Top position of self-resisted elbow curl. Moving from the starting position to the top position should take approximately 6 seconds.

PREACHER BENCH CURL

Starting Position.   A preacher bench is a piece of resistance training equipment that allows the trainee to be seated with the upper arm supported away from the body. Adjust the height of the angled padding for the arms so the backs of the upper arms rest comfortably on the padding at approximately a 45-degree angle to the torso. The lifter grasps a barbell with an underhand grip, keeping the hands about shoulder-width apart (Figure 6.30a).

Movement.   The lifter bends the elbows until the bar touches the shoulder area, briefly holding the bar at the top position (Figure 6.30b), and then returns to the starting position in a controlled manner.

Spotting and Safety.   A spotter may assist the lifter if needed. The spotter for this exercise normally stands facing the lifter. If the preacher curl bench does not have a rack for the barbell, the spotter may have to hand the barbell to the lifter and take the barbell from the lifter after completion of a set.

Muscles Strengthened.   Front of upper arm (biceps brachii and brachialis) and some of the muscles on the palm side of the forearm.

Variation: EZ Curl Bar Preacher Bench Curl.   The lifter uses an EZ curl bar instead of a normal barbell.

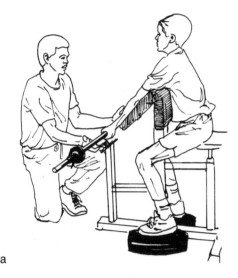

a

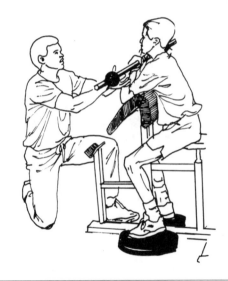

b

Figure 6.30 (a) Starting and finishing position for preacher bench curl. (b) Top position of a preacher bench curl. The preacher bench in the figure has a rack for the barbell. Feet should be flat on the floor. If not, use blocks as shown here.

STANDING REVERSE ELBOW CURL

Starting Position.   The lifter stands erect with the feet about shoulder-width apart and the knees slightly bent and grasps a barbell with an overhand grip, positioning the hands shoulder-width or slightly farther apart. The barbell rests on the thighs, the head is up, and the back is straight (Figure 6.31a). The lifter can also perform the exercise while standing with the back against a wall. This helps eliminate the urge to cheat by rocking with the lower back.

Movement.   The lifter raises the barbell until it touches the chest area (Figure 6.31b), then in a controlled manner returns it to the starting position. Movement should take place only at the elbows.

Spotting and Safety.   Spotting is not needed. The lifter must not use the back or legs to get the weight moving, because this can injure the lower back.

Muscles Strengthened.   Front of upper arm (biceps brachii and brachialis) and some of the muscles on the front and back of the forearm.

Variation: EZ Curl Bar Reverse Elbow Curl.   The lifter uses an EZ curl bar instead of a normal barbell.

a

b

Figure 6.31   (a) Starting and finishing position for standing reverse elbow curl. The lifter must not use the lower back and legs to get the weight moving from the starting position, because this can injure the lower back. (b) Top position of the standing reverse elbow curl.

DUMBBELL CONCENTRATION CURL

Starting Position. While seated on a bench, the lifter grasps a dumbbell with the right hand using a palm-up grip. The right elbow is straight and rests on the inside of the right thigh. The lifter places the left hand on the top of the left thigh for support or behind the right arm and on top of the right thigh to help stabilize the right arm (Figure 6.32a).

Movement. Keeping the back as upright as possible, the lifter flexes the right elbow until the dumbbells touch the right shoulder area (Figure 6.32b). In a controlled manner, the lifter lowers the dumbbell back to the starting position. After the desired number of repetitions have been completed, the lifter performs the exercise with the left arm.

Spotting and Safety. No spotting is needed, because the lifter can place the dumbbell on the floor during the exercise if necessary. No safety precautions are necessary.

Muscles Strengthened. Front of upper arm (biceps brachii and brachialis) and some of the muscles on the palm side of the forearm.

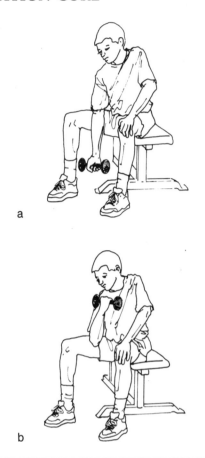

a

b

Figure 6.32 (a) Starting and finishing position for dumbbell concentration curl. The hand not grasping the dumbbell is used to help stabilize the torso. (b) Top position of the dumbbell concentration curl.

INCLINE BENCH DUMBBELL ELBOW CURL

Starting Position.   The lifter lies on his or her back on an incline bench and grasps a dumbbell with each hand with a palms-up grip. The elbows are straight, and the arms hang down from the shoulders, the head and back are flat against the incline bench, and the feet are flat on the floor (Figure 6.33a).

Movement.   The lifter flexes at the elbows until the dumbbells are at shoulder level (Figure 6.33b). Then in a controlled manner the lifter lowers the dumbbells back to the starting position. The back and head should remain flat against the incline bench at all times. The feet should remain flat on the floor at all times, and the lifter should not use a jerk of the shoulder to get the dumbbells moving when starting a repetition.

Spotting and Safety.   Spotters can hand the dumbbells to the lifter, assist with completion of a repetition, and take the dumbbells from the lifter after completion of a set.

Muscles Strengthened.   Elbow flexors on the front of the upper arms (biceps brachii and brachialis) and some of the muscles on the palm side of the forearm.

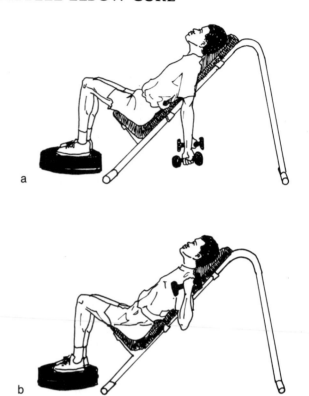

Figure 6.33   (a) Starting and finishing position for incline bench dumbbell elbow curl. (b) Top position of incline bench dumbbell curl. Movement should take place only at the elbow during this exercise. This lifter's feet would not be flat on the floor, so blocks are used to allow the lifter to use his legs for balance during the exercise.

Chest Exercises

Many equipment companies manufacture resistance training machines designed to develop the chest area. One type of these machines is commonly referred to as a *pec deck*, referring to the major muscle group of the chest, the *pectoralis* group. Proper technique for the use of these machines varies and is not described here. You should learn proper technique from a qualified resistance training instructor or from written material concerning the equipment before teaching exercises using these machines.

Example Activities Muscles Are Used For. Pushing off in pole vaulting, using breaststroke and butterfly stroke in swimming, shot putting, chest passing in basketball, discus throwing, and pass blocking in football.

Proper Technique. These exercises when performed correctly place a great training stress on the chest area. If dumbbells are used, they should not accelerate on the way down, because when the lifter attempts to slow the dumbbells, injury may result to the chest.

DUMBBELL FLY

Starting Position.   The lifter lies with the back flat on a bench and the feet flat on the floor. With arms up, the lifter holds a dumbbell in each hand directly above the chest. The elbow is not locked but slightly bent (Figure 6.34a).

Movement.   Keeping the arms directly out to the sides of the body at all times, the lifter lowers the dumbbells toward the floor. Movement should take place only at the shoulder joint and should be a sideward motion. The lifter lowers the dumbbells until they are slightly below chest level (Figure 6.34b) and then returns them to the starting position. The elbow is slightly bent, but little movement of the elbow joint should occur during this exercise.

Spotting and Safety.   A spotter can assist the lifter by handing him or her the dumbbells after the lifter lies on the bench. The spotter can also place his or her hands underneath the lifter's elbows and help the lifter complete a repetition. If only one spotter is used, the spotter must be able to reach both of the lifter's elbows and both dumbbells at one time and must be strong enough to assist both of the lifter's arms at the same time if needed. If two spotters are available, each spotter can assist one arm or grasp one dumbbell if needed. Inform the lifter that bending the elbows makes the exercise significantly easier. The lifter can use this technique to complete the last repetition of a set when the chest muscles are fatigued.

Muscles Strengthened.   The chest area (pectoralis muscle group) and the anterior shoulder area (anterior deltoid).

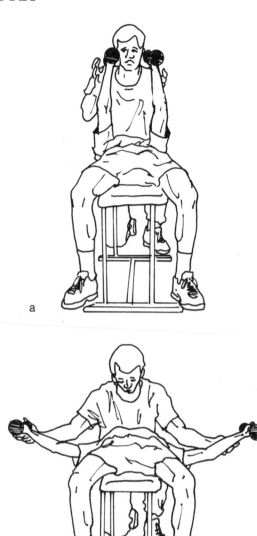

a

b

Figure 6.34 (a) Starting and finishing position for dumbbell fly. (b) Bottom position of dumbbell fly. Having a slight bend in the elbows can make raising the dumbbells to the finish position significantly easier.

Forearm Exercises

The forearm musculature is important to many daily and sporting activities. However, exercises for the forearm are frequently overlooked in many resistance training programs.

Example Activities Muscles Are Used For.   Batting a baseball, using the forehand in tennis, passing a football, swinging a golf club, gripping in wrestling, essentially all throwing and gripping tasks.

Proper Technique.   During all wrist exercises, the wrist joint must move through the full range of motion. Both the concentric and eccentric portion of the exercise should be performed in a controlled manner.

BARBELL WRIST CURL

Starting Position.   The lifter sits on the end of a flat bench with the feet flat on the floor and grasps a barbell in both hands with a palms-up grip. The backs of the forearms are supported on the thighs so that the wrists just hang over the knees. The lifter holds the barbell while extending the fingers as much as possible, putting the barbell in a position as close to the floor as possible and still holding it by the fingertips (Figure 6.35a).

Movement.   The lifter flexes the fingers and then wrists in a controlled manner, raising the barbell as high as possible while still keeping the forearms flat on the thighs (Figure 6.35b). The lifter then slowly returns to the starting position. Only movement at the finger and wrist joints should occur.

Spotting and Safety.   The spotter should be especially attentive when the fingers are in their most extended position, because it is possible that the child will lose his or her grip and the barbell will fall to the floor.

Muscles Strengthened.   Flexors of the wrist and fingers (palm side of forearm).

Variation: Dumbbell Wrist Curl.   The lifter performs a dumbbell wrist curl in a manner similar to a barbell wrist curl, except a dumbbell is held in each hand (Figure 6.36a). The movement is the same as for the barbell wrist curl (Figure 6.36b). This exercise can be performed with both arms at once or with only one arm at a time.

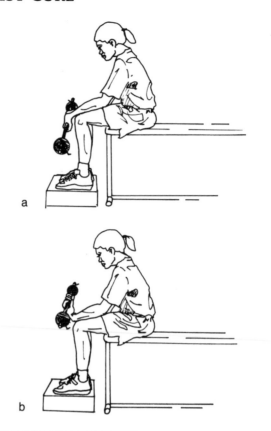

Figure 6.35   (a) Starting and finishing position for barbell wrist curl; the fingers are extended as much as possible while still holding the barbell; (b) Top position for barbell wrist curl; the wrist is flexed as much as possible.

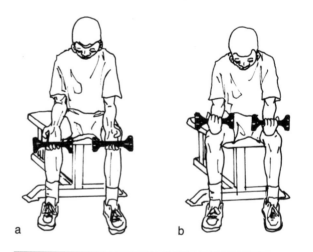

Figure 6.36   (a) Starting and finishing position for dumbbell wrist curl; position is similar to the barbell wrist curl except a dumbbell is held in each hand. (b) Top position for dumbbell wrist curl; wrists are flexed as much as possible and forearms remain flat on the thighs.

WRIST ROLLER

Some resistance training equipment companies manufacture a wrist roller training station. If you do not have access to such equipment, you can make a simple wrist roller. Drill a hole in the middle of a piece of round wood (e.g., a broomstick handle), insert a piece of cord approximately 3 to 5 feet long into the hole, and tie the cord. Attach the resistance you plan to use—a weight plate works well—to the other end of the cord. This inexpensive piece of equipment works very well in developing the wrist extensors and flexors.

Starting Position.   The lifter grasps the handle of the wrist roller in both hands with a palms-down grip. The upper arms are at the sides of the body and the elbows are bent at approximately a 90-degree angle. The lifter stands erect with the feet about shoulder-width apart (Figure 6.37a).

Movement.   The lifter alternately grasps the handle and moves the wrists so that the cord is wrapped around the handle. When the cord is completely wound around the handle, the lifter reverses the movement and unwinds the cord from the handle. Clockwise rotation of the handle develops the wrist flexors and counterclockwise rotation develops the wrist extensors (Figure 6.37b).

Spotting and Safety.   No spotting is needed. If your lifter uses a homemade wrist roller, make sure the handle is sturdy, the rope is securely fastened to the handle, and the weight is securely fastened to the rope.

Muscles Strengthened.   Clockwise rotation develops the wrist flexors located on the palm sides of the forearms. Counterclockwise rotation develops the wrist extensors located on the backs of the forearms.

a

b

Figure 6.37   (a) Starting position for wrist roller. (b) Wrapping the cord around the wooden handle in the wrist roller in a clockwise and counterclockwise direction develops the wrist flexors and extensors, respectively.

GRIPPING EXERCISE

Starting Position.   The lifter sits or stands, holding a tennis ball in the palm of each hand. The lifter can also use resistance equipment designed to develop the finger flexors. Only the wrist flexors are involved in this exercise, so arm position makes no difference.

Movement.   The lifter squeezes the tennis ball as hard as possible with the fingers and holds the squeeze for 2 to 3 seconds. The lifter relaxes the grip for 2 to 3 seconds and repeats (Figure 6.38).

Spotting and Safety.   No spotting or safety precautions are needed.

Muscles Strengthened.   Wrist and finger flexors located on the palm sides of the forearms.

Figure 6.38   Gripping exercise; squeezing tennis balls is a good exercise to develop the wrist flexors.

REVERSE WRIST CURL

Starting Position.   The lifter sits on the end of a flat bench with feet flat on the floor. The lifter grasps a barbell with a palms-down grip and holds the barbell with the fingers flexed so the bar touches the palms. The palm side of the forearm rests on the tops of the thighs. The wrists are relaxed so that the hands are as close to the floor as possible (Figure 6.39a).

Movement.   Using only the wrist extensors, the lifter slowly raises the barbell as high as possible from the floor (Figure 6.39b), then returns the barbell to the starting position. The entire forearms should remain in contact with the thighs throughout this exercise.

Spotting and Safety.   The wrist extensors are a relatively weak muscle group. Therefore, you may need to use a completely unloaded barbell or a small piece of metal pipe as the resistance when starting this exercise with young children. One spotter can stand in front of the lifter for this exercise.

Muscles Strengthened.   Wrist extensors located on the backs of the forearms.

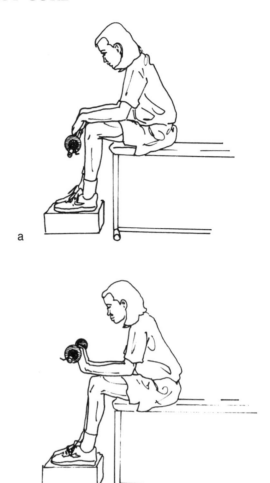

Figure 6.39 (a) Starting and finishing position for reverse wrist curl. The lifter holds the barbell with the fingers flexed as if making a fist. (b) Top position of reverse wrist curl; the lifter raises the barbell as far as possible by pulling the backs of the hands toward the backs of the forearms while keeping the forearms on the thighs.

Lower Back Exercises

The exercises in this group are traditional resistance training exercises to strengthen the lower back muscles. The lower back musculature, called the *lumbar region*, is important because along with the abdominal region the lower back is the link between the leg muscles and the upper body. If the muscles of the lower back are weak, a person cannot transfer the force developed by the legs and hips to the upper body, which is necessary for many sporting and daily life activities. A lifter who has a history of lower back pain should see a physician before starting a program to strengthen the lumbar region.

Example Activities Muscles Are Used For. Rowing, blocking in football, tennis swing, start in swimming, and virtually all lifting tasks using the legs.

Proper Technique. Due to the possibility of straining the lower back region, the lifter must use great caution when increasing resistance and must pay a great deal of attention to correct exercise technique when performing these exercises.

LYING BACK EXTENSION

Starting Position.   The lifter lies on his or her stomach on the floor with the arms lying at the sides. To make the exercise more difficult, the lifter can clasp the hands behind the head or hold a weight plate behind the head. A partner may need to hold down the lower body by pushing down on the legs just above the knees (Figure 6.40a).

Movement.   The lifter slowly raises the head, shoulders, and chest off the floor (Figure 6.40b), then slowly returns to the starting position.

Spotting and Safety.   No spotting or safety precautions are needed.

Muscles Strengthened.   *Spinal erectors* of the lumbar region predominantly.

Variation: Superhero.   This exercise is a more difficult version of the lying back extensions. The lifter lies on his or her stomach on the floor with the arms out in front of the body (Figure 6.41a). A partner is not needed to hold down the legs. The lifter slowly raises the head, shoulders, chest, and legs off the ground at the same time. With the arms in the air and out in front of the body the exerciser looks like a superhero flying (Figure 6.41b). The starting position is then slowly reassumed.

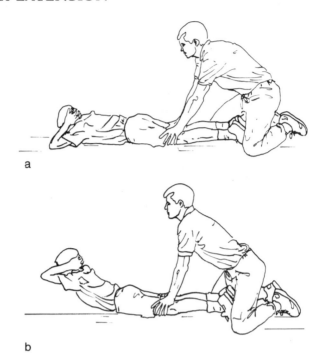

a

b

Figure 6.40   (a) Starting and finishing position for lying back extension. A partner holds the legs down by grasping them just above the knees. (b) Top position for lying back extension. The lifter can hold a weight plate behind the head to make the exercise more difficult.

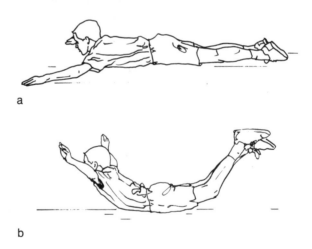

a

b

Figure 6.41   (a) Starting and finishing position for superhero. (b) Top position for superhero; the exerciser looks like he is flying.

BACK EXTENSION

Starting Position.   This exercise is more difficult than the two previous exercises because it involves a greater *range of motion*. Back extensions require a benchlike piece of equipment specifically designed for this exercise, or a tall bench or table and a partner. The lifter lies on the bench so that the hips are just over the edge and free movement is possible in the lumbar spine hip region. If using a specially designed bench, the lifter hooks the ankles under the pads provided (Figure 6.42a). If using a tall table or bench, the partner holds down the lifter's legs just above the knees. The lifter starts with the torso hanging down toward the floor as far as possible (a 90-degree angle between the torso and legs) and the hands clasped behind the head.

a

Movement.   The lifter slowly raises the head and shoulders until they are parallel to the floor (Figure 6.42b), then slowly returns to the starting position. The lifter should not rock back and forth to start the movement. The lifter can add resistance by holding a weight plate behind the head but should not increase the resistance too rapidly.

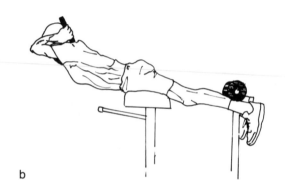

b

Spotting and Safety.   No spotting is needed. Resistance should be increased slowly and carefully. If you are using a tall bench or table for this exercise, many children will find the exercise more comfortable if you place some padding on the edge of the bench or table so that the pelvic area in contact with the edge is padded. The manufactured back extension equipment will not properly fit many children.

Figure 6.42   (a) Starting and finishing position for back extensions performed with specially designed equipment. (b) Top position of back extension. The back is parallel to the floor. The lifter can hold a weight plate behind the head to make the exercise more difficult.

Muscles Strengthened.   Muscles of the lumbar region (spinal erectors) predominantly.

STRAIGHT-BACK GOOD MORNING EXERCISE

Starting Position. The lifter stands erect with feet shoulder-width apart and a barbell resting on the spines of the shoulder blades (the bony ridges running horizontally across the shoulder blades). Spotters can place the barbell into position, the lifter can take the barbell off of a rack, or the lifter can power clean and then lift the barbell over the head and into position. The knees are slightly bent and the head is upright (Figure 6.43a).

Movement. The lifter slowly bends at the waist until the torso is slightly below parallel to the ground (Figure 6.43b), then slowly returns to the starting position. The back should remain straight from the hips to the shoulders during the entire exercise. Due to the straight back, the spinal erectors perform a predominantly isometric contraction, and the gluteals and hamstrings are responsible for the actual movement.

Spotting and Safety. When the lifter uses a barbell, two spotters, one at each end of the bar, can assist the lifter if needed. The lifter must not increase the resistance too rapidly or by increments that are too great. Initially the lifter may perform this exercise with the hands clasped behind the head and not using a barbell. The lifter may also hold a single weight plate behind the head instead of using a barbell.

Muscles Strengthened. Gluteals, hamstrings, and spinal erectors of the entire back, including the lumbar region.

(continued)

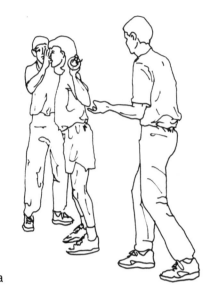

a

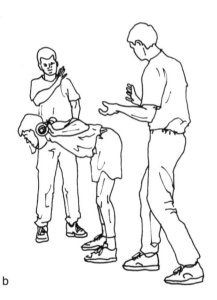

b

Figure 6.43 (a) The starting and finishing position for the straight-back good morning exercise; the knees are slightly bent throughout the movement. (b) Bottom position for straight-back good morning exercise; the entire back remains straight throughout the exercise.

Variation: Rounded-Back Good Morning Exercise. For this exercise the back is rounded during the movement. Because the back begins straight and is then rounded, the spinal erectors are used dynamically as well as isometrically. The starting and finishing position for this exercise is the same as for the straight back good morning exercise (Figure 6.44a). At the start of the movement the back is rounded and stays rounded throughout the lowering phase of the movement until the lifter reaches the bottom position (Figure 6.44b). The back gradually straightens until the lifter reaches the finishing position. The lifter will use much less weight with this exercise as compared to the straight back good morning exercise.

a

b

Figure 6.44 (a) Starting and finishing position for rounded-back good morning exercise. (b) Bottom position for rounded-back good morning exercise. The back is rounded and the knees slightly bent during the movement in this exercise.

STRAIGHT-BACK STIFF-LEGGED DEAD LIFT

Starting Position.   The lifter stands erect with feet approximately shoulder-width apart and the head upright. The lifter bends over and grasps a barbell with an overhand grip, with the hands slightly wider than shoulder-width apart. The entire back is straight and the knees are slightly bent (Figure 6.45a).

Movement.   The lifter slowly lifts the barbell to waist level by extending the lower back (Figure 6.45b), then slowly returns to the starting position. The spinal erectors perform predominantly an isometric contraction, and the movement is actually performed by the gluteals and hamstrings. The back should remain straight during the entire movement.

Spotting and Safety.   Spotting is not needed because the lifter can return the bar to the floor if a repetition cannot be completed. No safety precautions are needed.

Muscles Strengthened.   Gluteals, hamstrings, and spinal erectors of the entire back, including the lumbar region.

Variation: Rounded-Back Stiff-Legged Dead Lift.   The rounded-back dead lift allows the spinal erectors to perform more dynamically. The starting and finishing position for the rounded-back stiff-legged dead lift is the same as for the straight-back stiff-legged dead lift except the back is rounded (Figure 6.46a). The movement is the same as for the straight-back stiff-legged dead lift except the back stays rounded until the end of the lifting phase and reassumes a rounded position at the start of the lowering phase (Figure 6.46b). However, the lifter does assume a full upright position with the back straight, as in the straight-back stiff-legged dead lift, at the very end of the lifting phase (Figure 6.45b). The knees should be slightly bent throughout the exercise. Much less weight should be used for the rounded-back stiff-legged dead lift than for the straight-back stiff-legged dead lift.

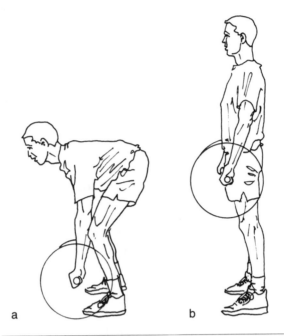

Figure 6.45 (a) Starting and finishing position for straight-back stiff-legged dead lift. The back should stay straight and rigid during the entire exercise. (b) Top position for straight-back stiff-legged dead lift; the barbell is about midthigh level and the lifter stands erect.

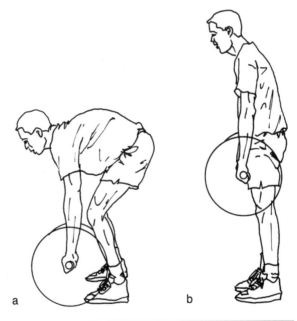

Figure 6.46 (a) Starting position for rounded-back stiff-legged dead lift; starting position is the same as for the straight-back stiff-legged dead lift except the back is rounded. (b) The back stays rounded until just before the lifting phase is over and reassumes a rounded position at the start of the lowering phase. The finishing position is the same as for the straight-back stiff-legged dead lift.

Exercises to Prevent Lower Back Pain

Many individuals including adolescents complain of lower back pain. Common causes of lower back pain are weak abdominal muscles, weak lower back muscles, and tight hamstrings. The exercises in this section are designed to remedy these causes of lower back pain. These exercises can be part of the warm-up for individuals who do not suffer from lower back pain or as part of the actual training session for children and adolescents who do suffer from lower back pain. If lower back pain is consistent or severe, the lifter should consult a physician.

Example Activities Muscles Are Used For.   Virtually all lifting tasks involving the legs, as well as all running and jumping activities.

Proper Technique.   Initially, the lifter should perform, in a controlled manner, one set of 10 repetitions of each of the exercises per training session.

KNEE TO SHOULDER

Starting Position.   The lifter lies on his or her back on the floor with knees bent, arms at the side, and feet flat on the floor (Figure 6.47a).

Movement.   The lifter grasps the right knee with both hands and gently pulls it toward the right shoulder (Figure 6.47b). The lifter holds this position for 5 seconds, then returns to the starting position and repeats with the opposite leg.

Spotting and Safety.   No spotting or safety precautions are needed.

Muscles Strengthened.   Increased flexibility of the hamstrings and lower back.

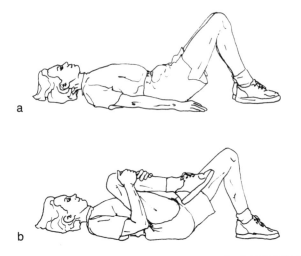

Figure 6.47   (a) Starting and finishing position for knee to shoulder. (b) The lifter pulls the right knee toward the right shoulder.

PELVIC TILT

Starting Position.   The lifter lies on his or her back on the floor with knees bent, arms at the side, and feet flat on the floor (Figure 6.48a).

Movement.   The lifter tightens the abdominal muscles and presses the lower back against the floor (Figure 6.48b). The lifter holds this position for 5 seconds and then slowly relaxes. The lifter should rest for 15 seconds before repeating.

Spotting and Safety.   No spotting or safety precautions are needed.

Muscles Strengthened.   Abdominals.

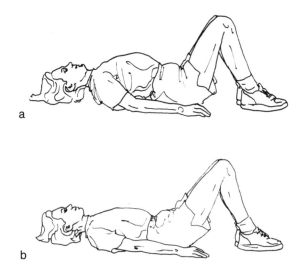

Figure 6.48   (a) Starting and finishing position for pelvic tilt. (b) The lifter flattens the lower back to the floor.

DOUBLE KNEE TO CHEST

Starting Position.   The lifter lies on his or her back on the floor with knees bent, arms at the side, and feet flat on the floor (Figure 6.49a).

Movement.   The lifter grasps the right knee and pulls it to the chest (Figure 6.49b). Leaving the right knee close to the chest, the lifter grasps the left knee and pulls it to the chest, then grasps both knees and pulls them both to the chest (Figure 6.49c). The lifter holds this position for 5 seconds, relaxes, and returns to the starting position to repeat the exercise.

Spotting and Safety.   No spotting or safety precautions are needed.

Muscles Strengthened.   Increased flexibility of the hamstrings and lower back.

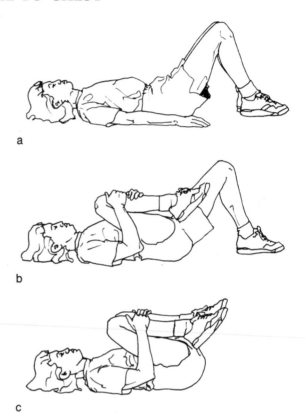

Figure 6.49   (a) Starting and finishing position for double knee to chest. (b) The lifter pulls one knee to the chest, then the other knee, and then (c) pulls both knees to the chest.

PARTIAL SIT-UP

Starting Position.   The lifter lies on his or her back on the floor with knees bent, arms at the side, feet flat on the floor, and the lower back pressed against the floor (Figure 6.50a).

Movement.   The lifter curls the head and shoulders up and forward until the shoulder blades are off of the floor and the hands touch the knees (Figure 6.50b). The lifter holds this position for 2 to 3 seconds and then returns to the starting position.

Spotting and Safety.   No spotting or safety precautions are needed.

Muscles Strengthened.   Abdominals.

Figure 6.50   (a) Starting and finishing position for partial sit-up. (b) Top position of partial sit-up with the shoulder blades off the floor and hands touching knees.

ROTATIONAL SIT-UP

Starting Position.   The lifter lies on his or her back on the floor with knees bent, arms at the side, feet flat on the floor, and the lower back pressed against the floor (Figure 6.51a).

Movement.   Keeping the hips flat on the floor, the lifter rotates the upper body so the left shoulder touches the floor and the right shoulder is higher than the left shoulder (Figure 6.51b). Both hands touch or almost touch the left knee. The lifter holds this position for 2 to 3 seconds and then relaxes and returns to the starting position. The lifter then performs the exercise rotating to the right.

Spotting and Safety.   No spotting or safety precautions are needed.

Muscles Strengthened.   Abdominals.

Figure 6.51   (a) Starting and finishing position for rotational sit-up. (b) In the top position, the body rotates so the left shoulder touches the floor and the right shoulder is higher.

TRUNK FLEXION KNEELING

Starting Position.   The lifter kneels on hands and knees on the floor. The lifter tucks the chin to the chest and arches the back upward (Figure 6.52a).

Movement.   Keeping the back arched, the lifter slowly sits back until the heels touch the buttocks, letting the shoulders drop toward the floor (Figure 6.52b). The lifter returns to the hands and knees position while keeping the back arched, then relaxes and returns to starting position.

Spotting and Safety.   No spotting or safety precautions are needed.

Muscles Strengthened.   Abdominals and lower back muscles.

Figure 6.52   (a) Hands and knee position for trunk flexion kneeling. Chin is tucked to the chest and the back is arched. (b) Heels-to-buttocks position for trunk flexion kneeling.

TRUNK FLEXION SITTING

Starting Position.   The lifter sits on the edge of a chair with the legs spread, feet flat on the floor, and arms crossed over the chest (Figure 6.53a).

Movement.   The lifter tucks the chin to the chest and slowly bends forward and downward as far as possible (Figure 6.53b). The lifter holds this position for 5 seconds, relaxes, and slowly returns to the starting position.

Spotting and Safety.   No spotting is needed. Make certain the chair will not slip during performance of the exercise.

Muscles Strengthened.   Flexibility of the hamstrings and lower back.

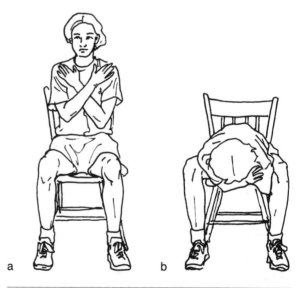

Figure 6.53   (a) Starting and finishing position for trunk flexion sitting. (b) Body position after the lifter slowly bends forward and downward.

BACK ARCH

Starting Position.   The lifter kneels on hands and knees on the floor, letting the stomach sag toward the floor (Figure 6.54a).

Movement.   The lifter tightens the stomach and arches the back as far as possible (Figure 6.54b), then relaxes.

Spotting and Safety.   No spotting or safety precautions are needed.

Muscles Strengthened.   Abdominals and lower back.

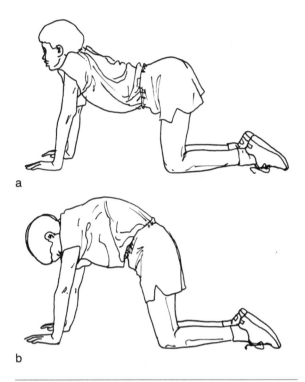

a

b

Figure 6.54   (a) Starting and finishing position for back arch. (b) The back arch position.

Abdominal Exercises

A common misconception concerning training of the abdominal area is that hip flexion (moving the legs toward the torso) involves predominantly the abdominal muscles. Common exercises that involve hip flexion predominantly are leg lifts and the straight-leg sit-up. These exercises involve the abdominals to a much smaller extent than is commonly believed. In reality these exercises train the hip flexors, muscles that attach to the lower back or hip area and to the upper thigh area. Exercises that predominantly train the hip flexors can exacerbate back problems such as lumbar lordosis. If you want to train the hip flexors, then you can use leg lifts and straight-leg sit-ups, but if you want to train the abdominals, then other exercises are a better choice.

Example Activities Muscles Are Used For.   These muscles are important for virtually all sports and activities, because they stabilize the torso during movements of the arms and legs. They are also involved in the twisting motion at the hip area for throwing activities.

Proper Technique.   Legs should be bent throughout the exercise movements so the training effect is predominantly on the abdominals. Pelvic tilt, partial sit-up, and rotational sit-up are described in the section entitled "Exercises to Prevent Lower Back Pain." These exercises, however, also strengthen the abdominal muscles. Please refer to that section for a description of these exercises.

BENT-LEG SIT-UP

Starting Position.   The lifter can perform this exercise on the floor or on an inclined sit-up board. On the floor, the lifter lies on the back with the knees bent at approximately 70 degrees and with the hands crossed over the chest. A partner can hold down the lifter's feet (Figure 6.55a). If the exercise is performed on an inclined sit-up board, the lifter assumes the same position with the feet hooked under the pads provided.

Movement.   The lifter raises the upper back off the floor or board until the elbows or forearms touch the knees or thighs. The lifter tries to curl the trunk toward the knees rather than raise the trunk toward the knees stiffly (Figure 6.55b). The lifter then lowers the trunk back to the floor. The lifter can increase resistance by holding a weight plate on the chest or by increasing the angle of the incline board.

Spotting and Safety.   Spotting is not needed. However, if the exercise is performed on the floor a partner may be needed to hold the lifter's feet on the floor.

Muscles Strengthened.   Abdominals.

a

b

Figure 6.55   (a) Starting and finishing position for bent-leg sit-up performed on the floor, with a partner holding the lifter's feet. (b) Top position for bent-leg sit-up. The lifter should try to curl the upper body toward the knees rather than lift the upper body stiffly.

BENT-LEG SIT-UP WITH A TWIST

Starting Position.   The lifter can perform this exercise on the floor or on an inclined sit-up board. On the floor, the lifter lies on the back with the knees bent at approximately 70 degrees and with the hands crossed over the chest. A partner can hold down the lifter's feet. If the exercise is performed on an inclined sit-up board, the lifter assumes the same position with the feet hooked under the pads provided (Figure 6.56a).

Movement.   The lifter raises the upper back off the floor or board and twists so that the right elbow touches the left knee on one repetition; on the next repetition the left elbow touches the right knee (Figure 6.56b).

Spotting and Safety.   Spotting is not needed. However, if the exercise is performed on the floor a partner may hold the lifter's feet on the floor.

Muscles Strengthened.   The sides of the abdominal area, called *obliques*, which are important for twisting motions such as throwing; also the front of the abdominal area.

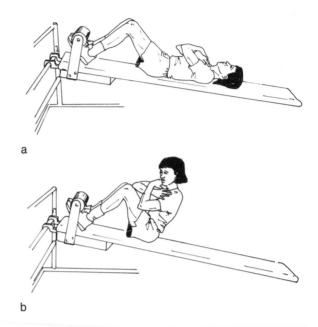

a

b

Figure 6.56   (a) Starting and finishing position for bent-leg sit-up with a twist, performed on an incline sit-up board. (b) Top position of bent-leg sit-up with a twist; right elbow touches left knee.

CRUNCH

Starting Position.   The lifter lies on his or her back on the floor with the lower legs on top of a bench so that the upper legs and the torso form approximately a 90-degree angle. The hands are crossed on the chest, and the back and hips touch the floor (Figure 6.57a).

Movement.   Keeping the hips flat on the floor, the lifter slowly raises the torso until the elbows or forearms almost touch the knees (Figure 6.57b), then slowly returns to the starting position. The lifter should try to curl the torso toward the knees rather than raise it stiffly. The lifter can add resistance by holding a weight plate on the chest.

Spotting and Safety.   Spotting is not needed. A partner may be needed to hold the child's lower legs on top of the bench.

Muscles Strengthened.   Abdominals.

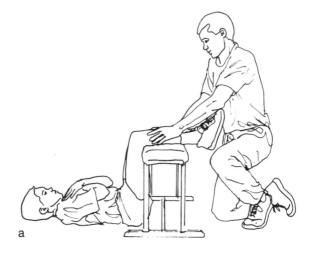

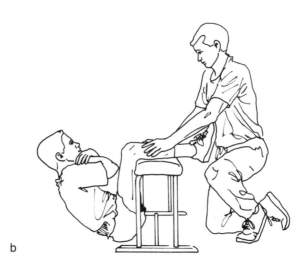

Figure 6.57 (a) Starting and finishing position for crunch; the lower legs lie on top of a bench so the upper legs and torso form approximately a 90-degree angle. (b) Top position for crunch; the elbows should almost touch the knees.

Multijoint Upper Body Pushing Exercises

These exercises strengthen muscles around the shoulder and elbow joints. The muscles of the upper back, torso, and wrists are also involved as stabilizers. Each of the exercises in this group has a different movement pattern and starting position; therefore each exercise emphasizes a slightly different area around the shoulder joint. Many equipment companies manufacture resistance training machines for this group of exercises; make sure the machine properly fits the child.

Example Activities Muscles Are Used For.   Shot putting, performing a handstand, shooting a basketball, pushing off the pole in pole vaulting, all throwing activities and activities that involve pushing an object away from the body.

Proper Technique.   Multijoint or structural exercises involve the coordinated movement of several joints; therefore technique is more difficult to learn than for single-joint or single–body part exercises. You must therefore constantly stress proper technique to beginning lifters. If a lifter uses a resistance machine for any of these exercises, be sure positioning of the child on the machine is correct, because without proper positioning correct technique will not be possible.

BARBELL BENCH PRESS

Starting Position.   The lifter lies on his or her back on a flat bench with the feet flat on the floor, the shoulder blades and buttocks touching the bench, and the back slightly arched. The width of the lifter's grip affects how much the chest and backs of the arms are used in the exercise. The wider the grip, the more the chest is involved; the narrower the grip, the more the backs of the arms are involved. Initially most individuals use a grip slightly wider than shoulder-width. The lifter grips the bar with the palms facing toward the feet. The barbell is held at arm's length and should be above the upper chest area (Figure 6.58a).

Movement.   In a controlled manner the lifter lowers the bar to the middle of the chest area and touches the chest with the bar. The contact point with the chest will vary among individuals, but a good initial contact point is directly on top of the nipples (Figure 6.58b). The bar should travel in an arc from over the upper chest to the point where the bar touches the chest. As the lifter presses the barbell back to the starting position, the barbell should travel in an arc from the contact point on the chest back to a position over the upper chest. During both the lowering and pressing motions the upper arms should not be parallel to the torso, nor should they point directly out to the sides; rather, the upper arms should be somewhere between these two extremes, at an angle to the torso of about 45 degrees.

Spotting and Safety.   The barbell should not be bounced off the chest because this may injure the chest area. Bouncing the barbell is cheating, because the bounce helps start the barbell's movement. The back should not be excessively arched or the buttocks raised off of the bench during the pressing motion back to the starting position; these incorrect actions can place excessive stress on the lower back and cause injury. Because the barbell is always over the head, neck, and chest, spotting is required for this exercise at all times. One spotter may properly spot this exercise by standing behind the lifter's head, grasping the bar, and assisting with completion of a repetition if needed. The spotter can also help the lifter get the bar off the rack and into the starting position and back onto the rack after completion

of the set. A rack to hold the barbell is part of most flat benches. Two spotters may be needed as the lifter increases the weight. Each spotter stands at one end of the barbell, facing each other. Both spotters can then grasp the bar at the ends and assist the lifter as needed. Communication between the spotters and the lifter is very important; when two spotters are used for any lift they must act in unison. The spotters should not rest their hands on the rack, because if the lifter suddenly returns the barbell to the rack the spotters' hands could be injured.

Muscles Strengthened.   Back of upper arm (triceps), front of shoulder (anterior deltoid), and chest (pectoralis group) area.

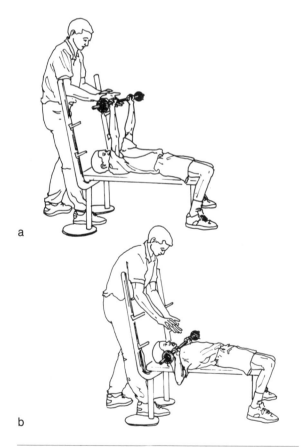

a

b

Figure 6.58 (a) Starting and finishing position for barbell bench press, one person spotting. (b) Bottom position for barbell bench press. The bar should travel in an arc from the starting position to the bar on the chest position and in an arc from the chest position to the finishing position.

NARROW-GRIP BARBELL BENCH PRESS

Starting Position.   The lifter lies on his or her back on a flat bench with the feet flat on the floor, the shoulder blades and buttocks touching the bench, and the back slightly arched. The lifter grips the bar with the palms facing toward the feet, the hands between shoulder-width and 6 inches apart. The barbell is held at arm's length and should be above the upper chest (Figure 6.59a).

Movement.   In a controlled manner the lifter lowers the bar to the middle of the chest area and touches the chest with the bar. The contact point with the chest will vary among individuals, but a good initial contact point is directly on top of the nipples (Figure 6.59b). The bar should travel in an arc from over the upper chest to the point where the bar touches the chest. As the lifter presses the barbell back to the starting position, the barbell should travel in an arc from the contact point on the chest back to a position over the upper chest area. During both the lowering and pressing motions the upper arms should be at an angle to the torso of about 45 degrees.

Spotting and Safety.   The back should not be excessively arched or the buttocks raised off the bench during the pressing motion back to the starting position. These actions can place excessive stress on the lower back and may cause injury.

Due to the narrow grip, some children may have problems balancing the barbell. Thus, the spotter or spotters must be very attentive, and the resistance must be light while the child is learning to perform the exercise. Because the barbell is always over the head, neck, and chest, spotting is required for this exercise at all times. One spotter may properly spot this exercise by standing behind the lifter's head, grasping the bar, and assisting with completion of a repetition if needed. The spotter can also help the lifter get the bar off the rack and into the starting position and back onto the rack after completion of the set. Two spotters may be needed as the lifter increases the weight. Each spotter stands at one end of the barbell, facing each other. Both spotters can then grasp the bar at the ends and assist the lifter as needed. Communication between the spotters and the lifter is very important; when two spot-

ters are used for any lift they must act in unison. The spotters should not rest their hands on the rack, because if the lifter suddenly returns the barbell to the rack the spotter's hands could be injured.

Muscles Strengthened.   Back of upper arm (triceps) and front of shoulder (anterior deltoid) to a greater extent than with the normal barbell bench press, and the chest (pectoralis group) area to a lesser extent than with the normal barbell bench press.

a

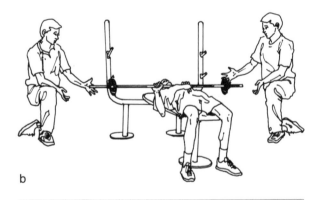

b

Figure 6.59 (a) Starting and finishing position for narrow-grip barbell bench press, two people spotting. (b) Bottom position for narrow-grip barbell bench press. The elbows will be closer to the body for this exercise than for the normal barbell bench press.

DUMBBELL BENCH PRESS

Starting Position. The lifter lies on his or her back on a flat bench with the feet flat on the floor, the shoulder blades and buttocks touching the bench, and the back slightly arched. The dumbbells are held at arm's length above the lower neck and upper chest area with the palms facing toward the feet (Figure 6.60a). To get into the starting position the lifter can grasp the dumbbells while sitting upright on the bench and slowly lie back, or a spotter can hand the dumbbells to the lifter one at a time while the lifter lies in the starting position.

Movement. In a controlled manner the lifter lowers the dumbbells to the middle of the chest area and touches the outer chest area (Figure 6.60b), then presses the dumbbells back to the starting position. The contact point with the chest will vary among individuals, but a good initial contact point is just to the outside of the nipples. The dumbbells should travel in an arc from over the upper chest and lower neck to the point where the dumbbells touch the chest, and they should travel in an arc from the contact point on the chest back to the finishing position over the upper chest. During the lowering and pressing motions the upper arms should not be parallel to the torso, nor should they point directly out to the sides; rather, the upper arms should be somewhere between these two extremes, at an angle to the torso of about 45 degrees.

The movement will seem a little more difficult than a barbell bench press because the arms act independently in terms of position and balance of the dumbbells, that is, unilaterally. The lifter can perform this exercise with alternating arms, although some children will find it very difficult to balance themselves when performing dumbbell bench presses with alternating arms.

Spotting and Safety. The best way to spot this exercise is for two spotters to stand facing each other from the sides of the lifter. If only one spotter is used, the spotter may place his or her hands underneath each elbow of the lifter and help the lifter complete a repetition by pushing upward on the elbows. This spotting

technique should only be used with experienced spotters and lifters. In addition, if only one spotter is used, he or she must have long enough arms to reach both dumbbells at once.

Muscles Strengthened. Back of upper arm (triceps), front of shoulder (anterior deltoid), and chest (pectoralis group) area.

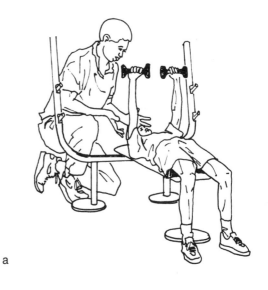

a

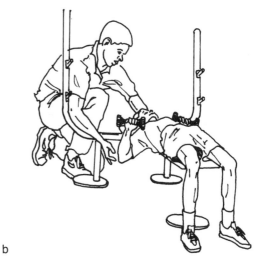

b

Figure 6.60 (a) Starting and finishing position for dumbbell bench press, one person spotting. (b) Bottom position for dumbbell bench press; the dumbbells should touch the chest.

BARBELL INCLINE PRESS

Starting Position.   The lifter lies on his or her back on an incline bench with the shoulder blades and buttocks touching the bench and the feet flat on the floor. The bench should be inclined approximately 45 degrees. The lifter holds the barbell over the chest with the arms perpendicular to the floor. The grip width is normally slightly wider than shoulder-width, although a narrower grip will cause the back of the arms to be used more in the exercise. The lifter should experiment to find the most comfortable grip (Figure 6.61a).

Movement.   In a controlled manner the lifter lowers the barbell in a straight line to the upper chest area and touches the upper chest and collar bones, or *clavicles*, with the barbell (Figure 6.61b). The lifter then presses the barbell in a straight line back to the starting position. The lifter should not bounce the barbell off the upper chest or raise the buttocks off the bench, because either of these may cause injury. The barbell should not move toward the feet during the lowering or lifting motion; this may cause the lifter to lose control of the barbell and drop it on the stomach.

Spotting and Safety.   It is difficult to balance the barbell in this exercise; therefore the initial resistance should be light, and increases in resistance should be carefully controlled. This exercise may be spotted by either one or two spotters. Many incline benches have a platform behind the lifter's head where a single spotter can stand and spot the exercise. The spotter can place his or her hands beneath the lifter's elbows and help the lifter by pushing upward. Or the spotter can simply help balance the barbell. If two spotters are used, they stand facing each other at opposite ends of the bar.

Muscles Strengthened.   Back of upper arm (triceps), front part of the shoulder (anterior deltoid), and upper chest area (pectoralis group).

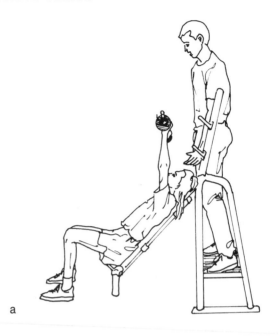

a

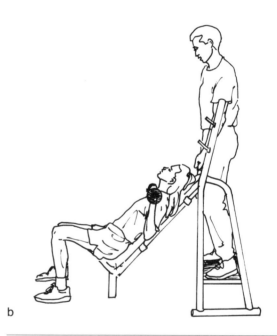

b

Figure 6.61   (a) Starting and finishing position for barbell incline press. The bench is equipped with a platform where a spotter can stand. (b) Upper chest position for barbell incline bench press. The bar should not go forward as it is pressed back to the starting position.

DUMBBELL INCLINE PRESS

Starting Position. The lifter lies on his or her back on an incline bench with the shoulder blades and buttocks touching the bench and the feet flat on the floor. The bench should be inclined approximately 45 degrees. The lifter holds a dumbbell in each hand with the palms facing forward (Figure 6.62a). The dumbbells are held over the chest with arms perpendicular to the floor, which allows for the best control of the dumbbells during the exercise.

Movement. The dumbbells are lowered in a controlled manner until they touch the upper chest area or are even with the upper chest area (Figure 6.62b). The dumbbells are then pressed back to the starting position. The buttocks should stay in contact with the bench and the back should not arch excessively when the lifter presses the dumbbells back to the starting position. The lifter can lower and raise one dumbbell at a time or lower and raise both dumbbells at the same time. Control of the movement may seem more difficult than for a press performed with a barbell, because each arm acts independently, especially when the lifter uses alternating arms.

Spotting and Safety. If two spotters are used, they stand facing each other on opposite sides of the incline bench. Each spotter is responsible for spotting the dumbbell on his or her side of the incline bench. If one spotter is used, he or she stands behind the lifter's head and places the hands beneath the lifter's elbows, helping the lifter push upward. The spotter must have arms long enough to reach both dumbbells at once and must be strong enough to assist with both dumbbells if needed. The one-spotter method is not recommended except with experienced spotters and trainees.

Muscles Strengthened. Back of upper arm (triceps), front part of the shoulder (anterior deltoid), and upper chest area (pectoralis group).

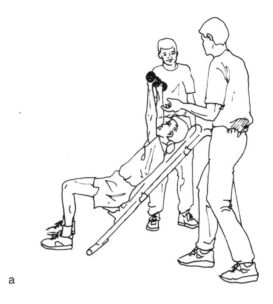

a

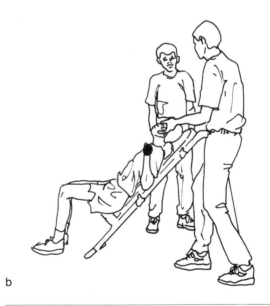

b

Figure 6.62 (a) Starting and finishing position for dumbbell incline press. Two spotters, one on each side of the incline bench, are recommended for this exercise. (b) Bottom position for dumbbell incline press. Controlling the dumbbells may be more difficult than controlling a barbell.

STANDING BARBELL OVERHEAD (MILITARY) PRESS

Starting Position.   The lifter stands erect with the back straight, the head upright, and the eyes looking forward, not up or down. Either the lifter can take the barbell from an approximately shoulder-height rack, lift the barbell with a power clean, or spotters can place the barbell in position. The lifter grasps the barbell so it rests on the clavicles and upper chest area. The hands grasp the bar slightly wider than shoulder-width apart and the palms face forward. The feet are flat on the floor, shoulder-width or slightly wider apart, and are staggered slightly front to back for better balance (Figure 6.63a).

Movement. Keeping the back and legs straight, but with the knees not locked, the lifter presses the barbell straight up to arm's length (Figure 6.63b). The lifter may have to tilt the head slightly backward at the start of movement to avoid hitting the chin with the barbell. The lifter should not push the barbell forward to avoid hitting the chin, because this will put the barbell out in front of the lifter, making it difficult to control. The lifter then slowly lowers the barbell back to the starting position. When the barbell touches the collar bones the knees may be bent slightly to cushion the stopping of the movement of the barbell. The knees should then be straightened and the legs should not be used to help lift the resistance, because the legs are not supposed to be trained during this lift. The lifter must not arch the back during any portion of the exercise as this will place undue stress on the lower back.

Spotting and Safety.   Two spotters are recommended for this exercise. The spotters should stand facing each other at opposite ends of the barbell. From this position they can grasp the ends of the barbell and assist the lifter as needed.

Muscles Strengthened.   Back of upper arm (triceps), anterior shoulder area (anterior deltoid), and upper back musculature.

a

b

Figure 6.63   (a) Starting and finishing position for standing barbell overhead (military) press. The legs and lower back should not help move the bar to the overhead position. (b) Overhead position for standing barbell overhead (military) press.

STANDING DUMBBELL OVERHEAD (MILITARY) PRESS

Starting Position. The lifter stands erect with the back straight, the head upright, and the eyes looking forward, not up or down. The lifter holds a dumbbell in each hand with the palms either facing forward or facing each other. The lifter can pick up the dumbbells from the floor using a power-clean movement to get them into the starting position. The feet are flat on the floor, shoulder-width or slightly wider apart, and are slightly staggered front to back for better balance (Figure 6.64a).

Movement. The dumbbells may be more difficult to control than a barbell because each arm must act independently. Keeping the back and the legs straight, but the knees not locked, the lifter presses the dumbbells straight up to arm's length. The lifter should not push the dumbbells toward the front, back, or sides, because this will make them difficult to control. Then in a controlled manner the lifter lowers the dumbbells back to the starting position. The knees may be bent slightly when the dumbbells reach the starting position, which will cushion the stopping of the movement of the dumbbells, but the knees should be straightened before the next repetition. The lifter must not arch the lower back excessively during any portion of the exercise, because this will place undue stress on the lower back. This exercise can be performed with alternating arms (Figure 6.64b) or with both arms at once.

Spotting and Safety. This exercise should be spotted with two spotters, who stand facing each other on either side of the lifter. Each spotter is responsible for the dumbbell on his or her side.

Muscles Strengthened. Back of upper arm (triceps), anterior shoulder area (anterior deltoid), and upper back musculature.

a

b

Figure 6.64 (a) Starting and finishing position for dumbbell standing overhead (military) press. (b) Right arm in the overhead position and the left in the starting and finishing position for dumbbell standing overhead (military) press. The exercise is being performed with alternating arms.

BARBELL BEHIND-THE-NECK PRESS

Starting Position.   The lifter stands erect with the feet approximately shoulder-width apart and slightly staggered front to back. The barbell is behind the head and resting on the backs of the shoulders, not on the neck. The grip is slightly wider than shoulder-width and the head is upright (Figure 6.65a). To get into starting position, the lifter may power clean the barbell and then slowly raise it over the head and lower it behind the head onto the shoulders. The lifter may also take the barbell from a rack, as if going to do a back squat, or spotters can place the barbell on the shoulders.

Movement.   Keeping the elbows below the barbell, the lifter presses it to arm's length overhead (Figure 6.65b). The legs and back remain stationary and are not used to help lift the barbell. The lifter then lowers the barbell in a controlled manner back to the starting position. It may be easier to finish the exercise if during the last repetition the barbell is lowered to the front of the shoulders. The lifter then returns the barbell to a rack or to the floor, or it is removed by spotters.

Spotting and Safety.   Two spotters are recommended for this exercise. The spotters should stand facing each other at opposite ends of the barbell. From this position they can grasp the ends of the barbell and assist the lifter as needed. The lifter must take care when lowering the barbell so it does not hit and injure the neck.

Muscles Strengthened.   Back of upper arm (triceps), front of shoulder (anterior deltoid), and increased involvement of the upper back (trapezius) compared to the other overhead presses.

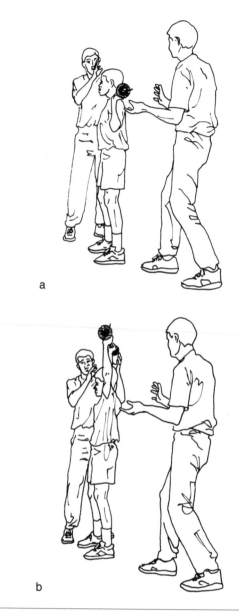

a

b

Figure 6.65   (a) Starting and finishing position for barbell behind-the-neck press. This is similar to the standing overhead (military) press except the barbell rests on the back of the shoulders. (b) Overhead position for behind-the-neck press. This is the same as for the standing overhead (military) press.

BAR DIP

Starting Position.   The lifter grasps the bars of a bar dip or parallel bars and lifts his or her body off the ground. The arms are fully extended, the head is upright, and the palms face each other (Figure 6.66a).

Movement.   The lifter lowers the body by bending the arms at the elbows in a controlled manner until the upper arms are parallel or slightly lower than parallel to the floor (Figure 6.66b). Many lifters find it more comfortable to cross their lower legs. The lifter then returns to the starting position by straightening the arms. The lifter can add additional resistance by hanging weights from a belt designed for this purpose.

Spotting and Safety.   A spotter can help the lifter into the starting position by standing behind the lifter, placing his or her arms underneath the lifter's armpits, and lifting up. To spot this exercise safely for an inexperienced lifter, the spotter must be able to lift the child's body weight. With experienced lifters, the spotter can place his or her hands underneath the lifter's lower legs and assist with completion of a repetition by lifting up on the lower legs if needed. This spotting technique should only be used with experienced lifters who can perform at least several bar dips. As with all body weight exercises the lifter must be relatively strong because the total body weight is the resistance lifted. Care must be used when getting on and off of the dip bars.

Muscles Strengthened.   Back of upper arm (triceps), chest area (pectoralis group), front shoulder area (anterior deltoid), and upper back (trapezius, rhomboids, *serrates anterior*).

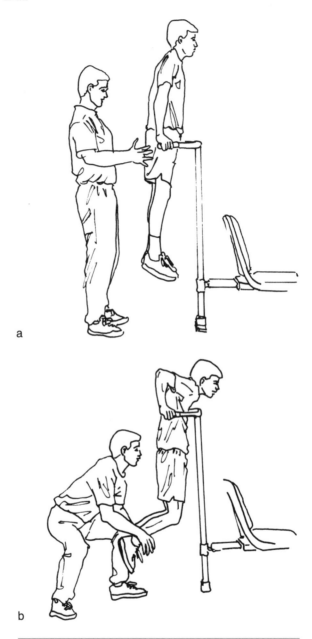

a

b

Figure 6.66 (a) Starting and finishing position for bar dip. A child must be relatively strong to perform this exercise, because the arms lift the body's weight. (b) Bottom position of bar dip. The lower leg spotting technique is shown, which should be used only with experienced lifters who can perform several bar dips.

BENCH DIP

Starting Position.   The lifter places the hands on the edge of a bench and then places the feet one at a time on top of a second bench. The elbows are bent and the buttocks touch the floor, or blocks, if they are used (Figure 6.67a).

Movement.   The lifter raises the body by completely straightening the elbows (Figure 6.67b), then slowly lowers the body back to the starting position by bending the elbows. The lifter can add resistance by placing a weight plate on top of the upper thighs.

Spotting and Safety.   Spotting is normally not needed. If spotting is desired, the spotter stands behind the lifter's head, places the hands under the lifter's armpits, and lifts upward. Make sure the benches are sturdy and will not slide or tip during the exercise. This is a body weight exercise; therefore, the lifter must be able to lift his or her own body weight.

Muscles Strengthened.   Back of upper arm (triceps), front part of shoulder (anterior deltoid) and chest (pectoralis), and upper back.

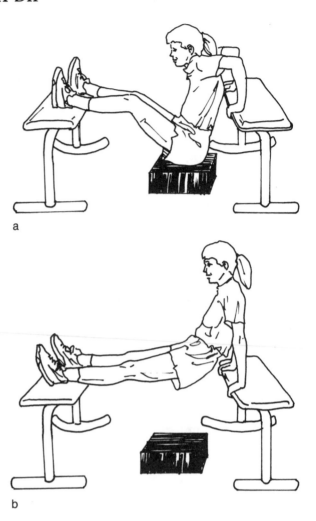

a

b

Figure 6.67   (a) Starting and finishing position for bench dip. The benches must be sturdy and must not slide during performance of the exercise. A block has been placed under the lifter's buttocks because the benches are too high for the lifter. (b) Top position for bench dip; elbows are completely straight.

PUSH-UP

Starting Position. The lifter lies on his or her stomach on the floor, then extends the arms so the body is supported with the hands flat on the floor and the toes on the floor. The back is straight and the head positioned so the trainee looks at the floor slightly in front of the hands. The hands are shoulder-width or slightly wider apart and are directly below the shoulders (Figure 6.68a). The wider the hands, the greater the involvement of the chest and the less the involvement of the back of the upper arms.

Movement. Keeping the back straight, the lifter lowers the body in a controlled manner by bending at the elbows until the chest touches the floor (Figure 6.68b). The lifter then raises the body back to the starting position. The back should remain straight at all times during the exercise.

Spotting and Safety. No spotting is needed. The practice of making a push-up easier by having the knees instead of the toes touch the floor has recently been questioned due to the stress that this position places on the lower back.

Muscles Strengthened. Back of upper arm (triceps), chest area (pectoralis group), and front of shoulder (anterior deltoid).

a

b

Figure 6.68 (a) Starting and finishing position for push-up. The back should remain straight throughout the exercise. (b) Bottom position for push-up; the chest should touch the floor.

Multijoint Upper Body Pulling Exercises

These exercises involve a pulling motion with the elbow and shoulder joints, a motion that is important to many sporting activities. Many resistance training equipment companies manufacture equipment for multijoint pulling exercises. This equipment often involves a pulley-and-handle arrangement.

Example Activities Muscles Are Used For.   Pulling an opponent toward oneself in wrestling or judo, tackling in football, pulling up on the pole in pole vaulting, and pulling in rowing.

Proper Technique.   These exercises are designed to train the arms, shoulders, and upper back. Therefore, the lifter should not use the lower back to get the resistance moving at the start of the pulling motion. Using the lower back to start the resistance moving can injure the lower back.

BARBELL BENT-OVER ROWING

Starting Position. Starting from a partial squat, the lifter grips a barbell with the hands slightly wider than shoulder-width and the palms facing the body, then stands up using the legs, not the back. The barbell is now touching the thighs. The lifter then bends over at the waist until the back is almost parallel to the floor. The barbell is now hanging straight down from the shoulders and is off the ground. The back is straight from the hips to the shoulders and the head is positioned so the trainee is looking slightly up. The knees are slightly bent and the feet approximately shoulder-width apart (Figure 6.69a).

Movement.   The lifter pulls the barbell upward in a controlled manner until it touches the chest. The elbows should be above the back and shoulders at the end of the pull (Figure 6.69b). Then in a controlled manner the lifter lowers the barbell back to the starting position. The back and legs should not be used to get the barbell started moving upward. The back should remain straight from the hips to the shoulders during the entire exercise.

Spotting and Safety.   Spotting is not necessary. When lifting the barbell from the floor, the lifter should use the legs and back, so as not to injure the lower back. This exercise places stress on the lower back and therefore should not be performed by individuals with a history of lower back problems. Also, due to this lower back stress, heavy resistances (less than 8 RM) should not be used. Before performing this exercise the lifter should train the lower back with some type of lower back exercise.

Muscles Strengthened.   The upper back (trapezius, rhomboids), shoulder extensors (latissimus dorsi), and back of shoulder area (posterior deltoid) are emphasized with the elbow flexors (biceps brachii, brachialis) and finger flexors also being involved in this exercise.

Figure 6.69 (a) Starting and finishing position for barbell bent-over rowing; the back is flat and almost parallel to the floor. (b) Top position for barbell bent-over rowing.

DUMBBELL BENT-OVER ROWING

Starting Position. The lifter should squat to pick up the weight. The lifter grips a dumbbell in one hand and rests the other hand on a bench. The dumbbell is held with the palm facing toward the body, and the back is straight from the hips to the shoulders. Supporting the body on the bench reduces stress on the lower back and keeps the shoulder of the nonexercising arm stationary during the exercise (Figure 6.70a).

Movement. The lifter pulls the dumbbell up until it touches the chest. The elbow should be above the shoulder and back at completion of the pulling motion (Figure 6.70b). Then in a controlled manner the lifter lowers the dumbbell back to the starting position. The legs, back, and nonexercising arm should remain stationary and the upper body should not rotate during the exercise.

Spotting and Safety. Spotting is not necessary. The lifter should use the legs and not the back when lifting the dumbbell to the starting position. Using one arm for support removes much of the stress on the lower back.

Muscles Strengthened. The upper back (trapezius, rhomboids), shoulder extensors (latissimus dorsi), and back of upper shoulder area (posterior deltoid) are developed with the elbow flexors (biceps brachii, brachialis) and finger flexors also involved in this exercise.

a

b

Figure 6.70 (a) Starting and finishing position for dumbbell bent-over rowing; one hand is placed on a bench to help support the lower back. (b) Top position for dumbbell bent-over rowing; the elbow should be higher than the shoulder.

BARBELL UPRIGHT ROWING

Starting Position. The lifter stands erect with the feet slightly wider than shoulder-width apart and holds a barbell with the palms facing toward the body. The barbell hangs straight down from the shoulders and touches the thighs. The hands are 6 inches apart or wider, the head is upright, and the shoulders are back (Figure 6.71a). The lifter normally gets the barbell into position by lifting it from the floor using the legs and not the lower back.

Movement. In a controlled manner, the lifter pulls the barbell straight up the body to the height of the collar bone and then lowers it back to the starting position. At the top of the pull the elbows should be higher than the shoulders and wrists (Figure 6.71b). The legs and back should not be used to start the barbell moving upward and should remain stationary throughout the exercise. The knees should always be slightly bent.

Spotting and Safety. Two spotters can be used, one at each end of the bar. The lifter must not use the back to start the barbell moving, because this may injure the lower back.

Muscles Strengthened. The entire shoulder area (deltoid) is emphasized in this exercise with the upper back (trapezius, rhomboids), elbow flexors (biceps brachii, brachialis), and finger flexors also being involved.

a

b

Figure 6.71 (a) Starting and finishing position for barbell upright rowing. The back should be straight and the head upright throughout the exercise. (b) Top position for barbell upright rowing; elbows should be above the bar throughout the exercise.

SEATED ROW

Starting Position.   This exercise requires special equipment, which in most cases consists of a pulley-and-handle or pulley-and-bar arrangement and a seat. Some machines have a separate handle for each hand. The lifter sits in the appropriate spot, grasps the handle or handles, and braces the feet or legs against the pads provided. The back should be straight from the hips to the shoulders and the knees should be slightly bent (Figure 6.72a). The length of the handle's cable can be adjusted on most machines so that the lifter can be positioned properly.

Movement.   In a controlled manner, the lifter pulls the handle back until it touches the chest. The elbows should be behind the back in the chest-touch position. Then the lifter slowly returns to the starting position. The entire back should not move during any portion of the exercise (Figure 6.72b).

Spotting and Safety.   Spotting is not necessary. The lower back should not be used to start the resistance moving, because this may injure the lower back.

Muscles Strengthened.   The upper back (trapezius, rhomboids), shoulder extensors (latissimus dorsi), and back of upper shoulder area (posterior deltoid) are developed by this exercise. The elbow flexors (biceps brachii, brachialis) and finger flexors are also involved in this exercise.

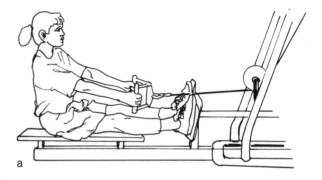

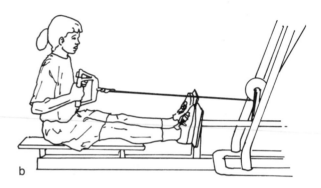

Figure 6.72   (a) Starting and finishing position for seated rowing; the knees should be slightly bent. (b) End of pulling phase of seated rowing; the elbows should be behind the back.

LAT PULL-DOWN

Starting Position.   This exercise takes its name from the major muscle involved in the motion: the latissimus dorsi, or *lat*. The exercise is performed on a lat pull-down machine, which normally consists of a high pulley with a long handle; some machines have seats and others require the trainee to sit or kneel on the floor. Some machines also have pads that can be placed on the thighs to hold the lifter down when heavy resistances are used. The lifter grasps the handle with a grip wider than shoulder-width. The lifter is positioned so that the handle can be pulled straight down from the high pulley during the exercise. The head is upright and in line with the rest of the spine, and the back is straight (Figure 6.73a).

Movement.   In a controlled manner, the lifter pulls the bar down until it touches the base of the back of the neck (Figure 6.73b), and then in a controlled manner returns to the starting position. A variation of this exercise is to pull the handle down in front of the head until it touches the top of the breastbone.

Spotting and Safety.   Spotting is not necessary. However, a spotter may pull down the handle so the lifter can grasp it after he or she is in the correct position and may take the handle from the lifter after completion of the set. Many of the handles or bars on a lat machine have a specific place to grasp. For most children this grip will be too wide, so they should grasp the handle so the upper arms are at approximately a 45-degree angle to the torso. The lifter must also take care not to bruise the base of the neck by hitting it with the bar during the pulling motion. As a child becomes stronger it may be necessary for a spotter to hold the child down by placing his or her hands on the child's shoulders near the base of the neck.

Muscles Strengthened.   The shoulder extensors (latissimus dorsi), the upper back (trapezius, rhomboids), elbow flexors (biceps brachii, brachialis), and finger flexors.

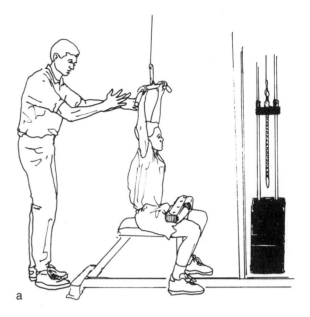

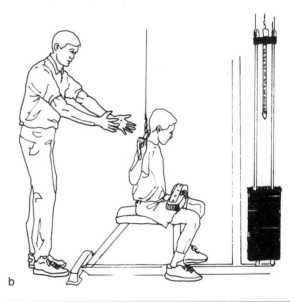

Figure 6.73   (a) Starting and finishing position for lat pull-down on a machine that has a seat and thigh pads. (b) Neck-touch position for lat pull-down with a spotter.

PULL-UP (CHIN-UP)

Starting Position.   The lifter grasps a pull-up bar with an overhand grip, with the hands shoulder-width or slightly wider apart (Figure 6.74a). Performing narrow-grip pull-ups with an underhand grip involves the elbow flexors to a greater extent than wide-grip pull-ups with an overhand grip. Another variation of this exercise is to use a very wide grip, making the exercise very similar to lat pull-downs.

Movement.   The lifter pulls the body up until the chin can be placed over the top of the bar (Figure 6.74b) and then in a controlled manner lowers the body back to the starting position. The legs should remain still during the pulling phase and should not be used to get the body moving. Many children may find it more comfortable to bend the legs at the knees or bend at the knees and cross the lower legs.

Spotting and Safety.   A spotter may help the lifter get into the starting position by grasping the lifter's waist and supporting the lifter's weight as he or she grasps the bar. The spotter may also help the lifter return to the ground safely after completion of the set. The lifter must take care coming off of the bar, especially if the height of the bar is set for an adult. If a lifter cannot perform pull-ups due to lack of strength, lat pull-downs should be performed with less than the lifter's body weight until he or she is strong enough to perform normal pull-ups.

Muscles Strengthened.   The shoulder extensors (lattissimus dorsi), upper back (trapezius, rhomboids), upper shoulder area (posterior deltoid), elbow flexors (biceps brachii, brachialis), and finger flexors.

a

b

Figure 6.74   (a) Starting and finishing position for pull-ups; the arms should be completely straight. (b) Top position for pull-ups; the lifter's chin should be above the pull-up bar.

BARBELL PULLOVER

Starting Position. The lifter lies on a bench with the feet flat on the floor or with the feet on top of the bench. The edge of the bench should be at the base of the neck. The lifter holds a barbell over the chest with a narrow grip; 6 or less inches between the hands. The barbell is held just barely off of the chest (Figure 6.75a).

Movement. In a controlled manner, the lifter slowly moves the barbell over the face and behind the top of the head and lowers it toward the floor as far as possible. Then in a controlled manner, the lifter moves the barbell back to the starting position. The angle at the elbow joint should not change during the movement (Figure 6.75b).

Spotting and Safety. A spotter is mandatory for this exercise, due to the position of the barbell over the chest and face and the possibility that the lifter will overstretch the shoulder area when the barbell is in the position closest to the floor. The spotter should stand facing the top of the lifter's head and be ready to assist if needed. The spotter can also help the lifter get the barbell into the starting position. Due to the position of the barbell over the head the resistance for this exercise must be carefully controlled and increases must be made cautiously.

Muscles Strengthened. Chest area (pectoralis), back of shoulder (posterior deltoid), and upper back (trapezius, latissimus dorsi).

Variation: Dumbbell Pullover. The lifter substitutes a dumbbell for the barbell, cupping one end of the dumbbell with both hands (Figures 6.76a and b). As with the barbell pullover, a spotter is mandatory for this exercise. If a dumbbell with collars is used, be certain the collars are tight and check their tightness frequently.

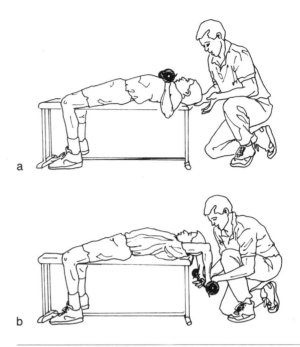

Figure 6.75 (a) Starting and finishing position for barbell pullover. (b) Bottom position for barbell pullover. Because the barbell passes over the face, a spotter is mandatory.

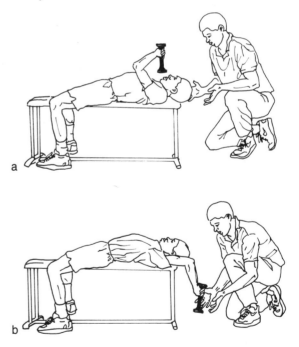

Figure 6.76 (a) Starting and finishing position for dumbbell pullover. As with the barbell pullover, a spotter is mandatory. (b) Bottom position for dumbbell pullover exercise. If a dumbbell with collars is used, make sure the collars are tight and check their tightness frequently.

Single-Joint Lower Body Exercises

Although the muscles of the lower body can be exercised by multijoint exercises (e.g., squat, power clean), single-joint lower body exercises train predominantly one muscle group of the lower body. This makes them excellent choices for rehabilitation of lower body injuries. For example, you can use knee curls to rehabilitate a hamstring pull. You can also use single-joint lower body exercises to strengthen a muscle group believed to limit performance of a skill. For example, punting a football may be improved by strengthening the knee extensors with the knee extension exercise.

Example Activities Muscles Are Used For.   Each single-joint lower body exercise emphasizes a muscle group of the lower body. Therefore, example activities the muscles are used for and the muscles strengthened are presented for each exercise.

Proper Technique.   The majority of single-joint exercises require resistance training machines. Many companies manufacture equipment for these exercises, and the technique a lifter should use will vary among machines. The following descriptions of exercises are general and apply to all resistance training equipment. Make sure you understand proper technique for the equipment available to you before you use it in a training program.

KNEE (KNEE FLEXION) CURL

Starting Position. On most equipment the lifter assumes a lying position, although on some equipment the exercise is performed in a standing position. The lying position will be described here. The lifter lies facedown with the heels underneath the pads provided, so that the pads touch the back of the ankles. The kneecaps need to be free to move during the exercise, so they should be approximately 2 inches over the edge of the bench. The trainee may grasp the edge of the bench or the handles provided on many machines (Figure 6.77a).

Movement. In a controlled manner, the lifter flexes the knees until the pads touch the buttocks (Figure 6.77b), then slowly returns to the starting position. The exercise can also be performed with only one leg at a time. This may be desirable when rehabilitating a hamstring injury, because if the exercise is performed with both legs the injured leg may merely follow the ankle pad and not really be trained.

Example Activities Muscles Are Used For. All activities for which flexing the knee and extending the hip are important: running, coming out of the blocks in sprinting, all jumping activities, and hurdling in track.

Spotting and Safety. No spotting is necessary. The lifter should avoid unnecessary jerking movements, especially of the lower back, because this may cause injury. Unless the ankle pads are adjustable, most machines will not fit small children.

Muscles Strengthened. Hamstrings and buttocks (gluteals).

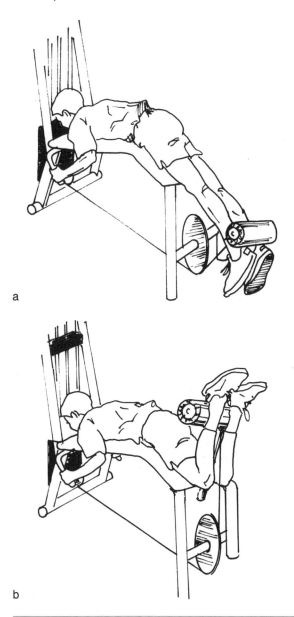

a

b

Figure 6.77 (a) Starting and finishing position for knee curl in the lying position. Unless the ankle pads are adjustable, most machines will not fit small children. (b) Heels-to-buttocks position for knee curl. The knee caps need to be free to move during this exercise, so they should be 2 inches off the bench at the start of the exercise.

KNEE EXTENSION

Starting Position.   The lifter sits on the knee-extension machine with the knees just over the edge of the seat, the back touching the back of the seat, and the fronts of the ankles touching the pads. The lifter grasps the seat or handles provided. The knees should be at slightly more than a 90-degree angle (Figure 6.78a).

Movement.   In a controlled manner, the lifter straightens the knees until they are completely straight and holds this position for 1 or 2 seconds (Figure 6.78b). Then in a controlled manner the lifter returns to the starting position. The lifter should not move the upper body in an attempt to help straighten the knees, but should use only the front of the thighs to perform the exercise.

Example Activities Muscles Are Used For.   Any activity for which straightening the knees is important: kicking a football, any jumping activity, alpine skiing, and running.

Spotting and Safety.   Spotting is not necessary. The lifter should avoid unnecessary jerking movements, especially of the lower back, because this may cause injury. Unless the ankle pads are adjustable, some machines will not fit small children. You may also need to place padding behind the child's back if it does not touch the back of the seat when he or she is positioned properly. Adjust the machine so that the knees are at not much more than a 90-degree angle, because an angle much greater than 90 degrees places undue stress on some lifters' knees. This exercise may be performed with one leg at a time.

Muscles Strengthened.   Front of thigh (quadriceps group).

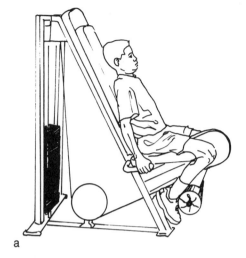
a

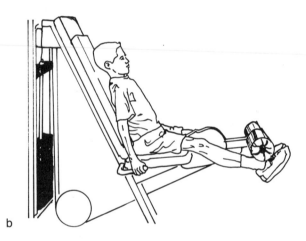
b

Figure 6.78   (a) Starting and finishing position for knee extension. A pad is used to allow the lifter's back to touch the back of the seat. (b) Top position for knee extension exercise; the knees should be completely straight.

BODY-WEIGHT CALF RAISE

Starting Position.   This is the easiest of the calf-raise exercises. The lifter stands erect with the feet flat on the floor and arms at the sides (Figure 6.79a).

Movement.   In a controlled manner, the lifter rises up onto the toes as far as possible (Figure 6.79b), then in a controlled manner returns to the starting position.

Example Activities Muscles Are Used For.   Any activity for which plantar flexion is important, including virtually all jumping and sprinting activities.

Spotting and Safety.   No spotting or safety precautions are necessary.

Muscles Strengthened.   Calf area (gastrocnemius, *soleus*).

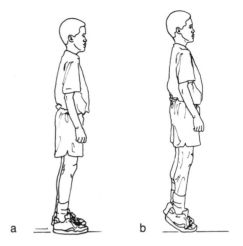

Figure 6.79   (a) Starting and finishing position for body-weight calf raise; trainee stands on the floor flat-footed. (b) Top position for body-weight calf raise; trainee stands on the toes as high as possible.

BODY-WEIGHT CALF RAISE ON A STEP

Starting Position.   This is a more difficult version of the body-weight calf raise, because standing on a step allows a greater range of motion. The lifter stands with only the toes on a step, grasping the handrail of the steps with one hand and allowing the heels to sink as low as possible (Figure 6.80a).

Movement.   In a controlled manner, the lifter rises up on the toes as far as possible (Figure 6.80b), then in a controlled manner returns to the starting position.

Example Activities Muscles Are Used For.   Any activity for which plantar flexion is important, including virtually all jumping and sprinting activities.

Spotting and Safety.   No spotting is necessary. The lifter should hold onto the handrail with one hand for balance.

Muscles Strengthened.   Calf area (gastrocnemius, soleus).

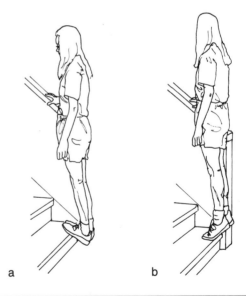

Figure 6.80   (a) Starting and finishing position for body-weight calf raise on a step; the heels are as low as possible and the toes are on the edge of a step. (b) Top position for body-weight calf raise on a step; the lifter rises up onto the toes as far as possible.

ONE-LEG BODY-WEIGHT CALF RAISE ON A STEP

Starting Position. This is more difficult than the body-weight calf raise on a step, because only one leg is used to lift the trainee's body weight. The lifter stands with the toes of only one foot on a step, grasping the handrail with one hand and allowing the heel to sink as low as possible (Figure 6.81a).

Movement. In a controlled manner, the lifter rises up onto the toes as far as possible (Figure 6.81b), then returns to the starting position. After completion of the set, the lifter performs the exercise with the other leg.

Example Activities Muscles Are Used For. Any activity for which plantar flexion is important, including virtually all jumping and sprinting activities.

Spotting and Safety. No spotting is necessary. The lifter should hold onto the handrail for balance with one hand throughout the exercise.

Muscles Strengthened. Calf area (gastrocnemius, soleus).

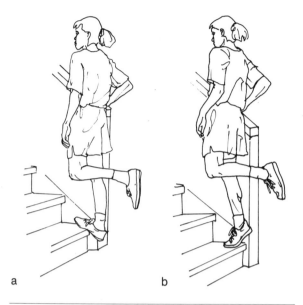

a   b

Figure 6.81 (a) Starting and finishing position for one-leg body-weight calf raise on a step; lifter stands on one leg only. (b) Top position for one-leg body-weight calf raise on a step; lifter stands on the toes as high as possible.

BARBELL CALF RAISE

Starting Position. The lifter stands erect with the barbell resting on the spines of the shoulder blades, not on the base of the neck. The lifter can either power clean and then slowly raise the barbell over the head and place it on the shoulders or take the barbell from a rack directly onto the shoulders. The lifter grasps the barbell slightly wider than shoulder width; the feet are shoulder-width apart (Figure 6.82a). To work different areas of the calf the feet can be pointed inward, outward, or straight ahead. To increase the range of motion the lifter may stand with the balls of the feet on a board or other object that is 1 or 2 inches high. A lifter can also perform calf raises on a leg press or shoulder press machine. Make sure the lifter understands how to use this equipment before attempting these exercises.

Movement. In a controlled manner, starting from the position where the heels are as low as possible, the lifter rises up onto the toes as far as possible (Figure 6.82b), then in a controlled manner returns to the starting position. The entire back is straight during all phases of the exercise.

Example Activities Muscles Are Used For. Any activity for which plantar flexion is important, including virtually all jumping and sprinting activities.

Spotting and Safety. If a barbell is used, the exercise is best spotted with two spotters, one at each end of the barbell. If the balls of the feet are elevated, be sure that whatever is used is sturdy and will not slide or tip during performance of the exercise. A very safe way for a lifter to perform this exercise is to use a power rack with the pins set slightly lower than his or her shoulder height. If a leg press is used, the lifter must be sure the feet do not slide off of the pedals during the exercise.

Muscles Strengthened. Calf area (gastrocnemius, soleus).

(continued)

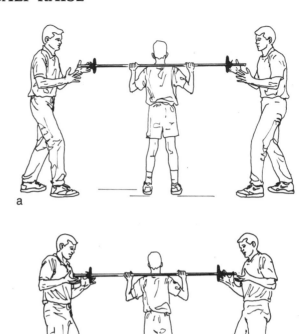

Figure 6.82 (a) Starting and finishing position for barbell calf raise; a barbell is held on the shoulders. (b) Top position for barbell calf raise; it is important to rise up onto the toes as far as possible so the calf musculature is trained throughout as much of its full range of motion as possible.

Variation: Dumbbell Calf Raise. The lifter holds a dumbbell in each hand, allowing the dumbbells to hang at the sides of the body (Figure 6.83a). The starting and finishing position and the top position (Figure 6.83b) are the same as for the barbell calf raise. When lifting the dumbbells from the floor, the lifter should use the legs and not the back. The dumbbell calf raise is easier and more comfortable for some children to perform than the barbell calf raise. However, most lifters will become strong enough to lift more weight with their calves than the weight of the dumbbells they can hold in their hands. When this happens they will have to perform some other variation of the calf raise.

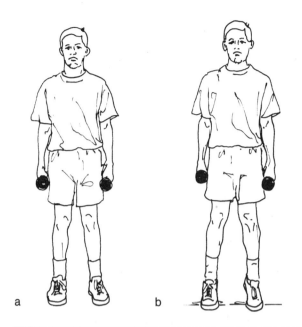

Figure 6.83 (a) Starting and finishing position for dumbbell calf raise; a dumbbell is held in each hand. (b) Top position for dumbbell calf; lifter rises up onto the toes as far as possible.

SEATED CALF RAISE

Starting Position. Calf raise machines manufactured by different companies are slightly different, so make sure the trainee understands the correct technique for the machine he or she is using. The lifter sits on the seat with the pads resting on top of the thighs just above the knees and with the heels as low as possible. The trainee may grasp the seat or the pads if desired. The back should be straight (Figure 6.84a).

Movement.   From the position where the heels are as low as possible, the lifter straightens the ankles as far as possible (Figure 6.84b), then returns to the starting position in a controlled manner.

Example Activities Muscles Are Used For.   Any activity for which plantar flexion is important, including virtually all jumping and sprinting activities.

Spotting and Safety.   Spotting is not necessary. Make sure the lifter understands how to place the resistance on the thighs and how the safety stop on the machine works to remove the resistance from the thighs. Some children's legs will be too short to fit these machines properly.

Muscles Strengthened.   Calf area (gastrocnemius, soleus).

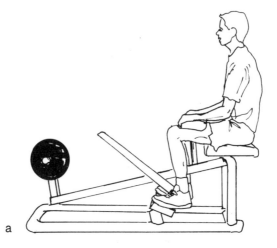

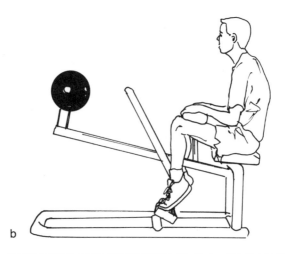

Figure 6.84   (a) Starting and finishing position for seated calf raise; the heels should be as low as possible. Resistance is normally applied with pads just above the knees. (b) Top position for seated calf raise; heels should be as far from the ground as possible.

Multijoint Lower Body Exercises

Most sports and many daily activities involve multijoint lower body movements; thus these exercises should be a part of virtually all training programs.

Example Activities Muscles Are Used For.   Virtually all lower body movements: running and jumping.

Proper Technique.   Technique for these exercises will be more difficult to master than for single-joint exercises, because multijoint exercises involve movement at several joints at the same time. Therefore, allow time for trainees to learn proper technique, and don't increase resistance until proper technique is mastered.

BODY WEIGHT SQUAT

Starting Position. The body weight squat, the easiest of the nonmachine multijoint lower body exercises, can be used as a lead-in to other squatting exercises, so proper technique is important. The feet are approximately shoulder-width apart, the toes point straight forward or slightly outward, and the feet are flat on the floor. The hands are on the hips, or the arms may hang at the sides of the body. The head is upright (Figure 6.85a).

Movement. Keeping the feet flat on the floor, the lifter bends at the knees and hips until the thighs are parallel to the floor (Figure 6.85b), then returns to the starting position. The back and head should stay as upright as possible throughout the entire movement. Some individuals will find balancing easier if the arms are brought out directly in front of the shoulders.

Spotting and Safety. No spotting or safety precautions are needed.

Muscles Strengthened. Buttocks (gluteals), front of thigh (quadriceps), back of thigh (hamstrings) and calf (gastrocnemius, soleus).

Figure 6.85 (a) Starting and finishing position for body weight squat; lifter stands with the feet shoulder-width apart. (b) Bottom position for body weight squat; thighs should be parallel to the floor.

LEG PRESS

Starting Position.   Virtually all resistance training equipment manufacturers produce a leg press machine. The majority of these are the seated, horizontally directed type. The lifter sits at the machine and adjusts the seat to the desired amount of knee bend, normally about 90 degrees. The lifter places as much as possible of the entire surface of the feet on the pedals provided and grasps the seat or the handles provided. The back rests against the backrest of the seat and the head is upright (Figure 6.86a).

Movement.   In a controlled manner, the lifter pushes the pedals out until the knees and hips are completely extended (Figure 6.86b); however, it is not necessary to lock the knees when the legs are straight. Then, in a controlled manner the lifter returns to the starting position. The back and head should remain against the backrest at all times.

Spotting and Safety.   No spotting is needed. However, the lifter must take care that the feet do not slip off of the pedals. This can occur easily when only the toes or balls of the feet are placed on the pedals. Because slight differences do exist between machines, make sure the lifter understands how to properly use the machine that's available.

Muscles Strengthened.   Buttocks (gluteals), front of thigh (quadriceps), back of thigh (hamstrings), and calf (gastrocnemius, soleus) on some machines.

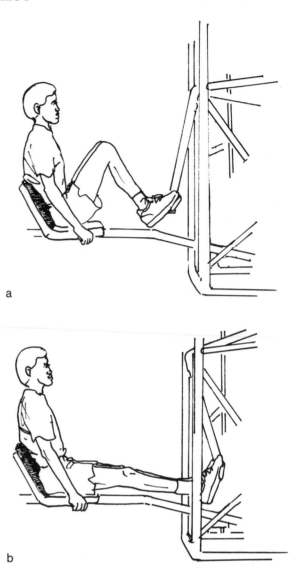

a

b

Figure 6.86   (a) Starting and finishing position for leg press; feet should be securely placed on the foot pedals of the leg press machine so they do not slip off during the exercise. (b) Knees should be straight but not locked at the end of the range of motion of the leg press.

BARBELL LUNGE

Starting Position. The lifter stands erect with a barbell resting on the spines of the shoulder blades, grasping the barbell with the hands wider than shoulder-width apart. The feet are approximately shoulder-width apart or slightly wider and are placed side by side. The head is upright (Figure 6.87a). The lifter may power clean the barbell and then place it on the shoulders or take the barbell from a rack directly onto the shoulders. Or, spotters may place the barbell on the lifter's shoulders.

Movement. The lifter slowly takes a large step forward with one leg, bends the knee of the lead leg, and lowers the body until the knee of the back leg touches the floor (Figure 6.87b). After the lifter lowers himself or herself as far as possible, the knee of the lead leg should be approximately over the ball of the foot of the lead leg. If the knee is in front of the ball of the foot, the step was not long enough; the lifter should correct this immediately, because a short step will place unnecessary torque on the knee joint. If the lead knee is over or behind the lead ankle, the step was too long or the lifter is not low enough. To return to the starting position the lifter pushes off of the floor with the lead leg, and with a series of two or three short backward steps with the lead leg returns to the side-by-side foot position. The lifter then performs the same movement using the opposite leg as the lead leg. The back should remain upright throughout the entire exercise.

Spotting and Safety. This exercise can be spotted with one or two spotters, depending upon the resistance used. If two spotters are used, they should face each other from opposite ends of the bar. When one spotter is used, he or she should stand behind the lifter and must be strong enough to take the bar from the shoulders of the lifter. Make sure the trainee's step forward is of the correct length.

Muscles Strengthened. Buttocks (gluteals), back of thigh (hamstrings) and front of thigh (quadriceps), the lower back (spinal erectors), and calf (gastrocnemius, soleus).

(continued)

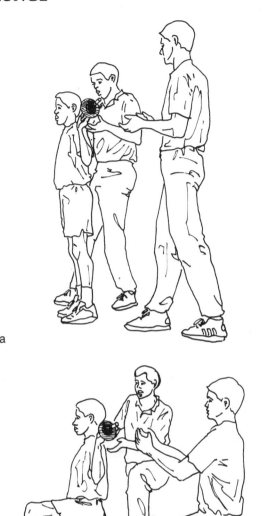

a

b

Figure 6.87 (a) Starting and finishing position for barbell lunge; barbell should be on the spines of the shoulder blades and not on the lower neck. (b) Bottom position for barbell lunge; lead knee should be over the ankle of the lead leg.

Variation: Dumbbell Lunge.   The lifter holds a dumbbell in each hand with the arms hanging at the sides of the body (Figure 6.88a). The starting and finishing position and the movement (Figure 6.88b) are the same as for the barbell lunge. Holding the dumbbells for resistance rather than carrying the barbell on the shoulders makes it easier to keep the back upright during the exercise. No spotting is necessary, because the lifter can place the dumbbells on the floor if a repetition cannot be completed. As a child becomes stronger it may be necessary to use a barbell instead of a dumbbell lunge, because the child's hands will not be strong enough to hold sufficient weight.

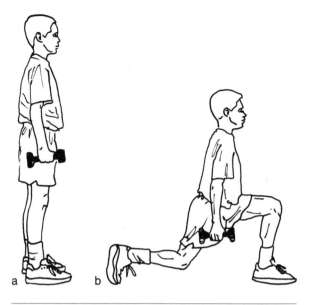

Figure 6.88 (a) Starting and finishing position for dumbbell lunge; a dumbbell is held in each hand. (b) Bottom position for dumbbell lunge; it is easier to keep the back upright in the dumbbell lunge compared to the barbell lunge.

Total Body Exercises

As the name implies, these exercises involve a large number of the major muscle groups of the body. They all involve to some extent knee, hip, and back extension. The shoulder girdle supports the resistance in some fashion during all of the exercises and in some cases is used to pull or push the resistance. The involvement of so many muscle groups and joints makes learning correct technique more difficult than for single-joint exercises. Therefore, allow lifters time to learn proper technique before incorporating these exercises into a resistance training program. Lifters should practice all of these exercises with light resistances before attempting them with heavier weights. New equipment is becoming available that allows free movement of a bar vertically, forward, and backward. Pins on this equipment can be set so the bar cannot be lowered past a particular height yet moves freely above this height. This type of equipment offers many of the advantages of free weights with some of the safety advantages of resistance machines.

Due to the large muscle mass involved in these exercises it is possible to use very heavy resistances. However, young children should not use resistances heavier than 6 RM.

Example Activities Muscles Are Used For.   Any activity for which the hips and knees are extended, including virtually all running and jumping activities.

Proper Technique.   Many times improper form is caused by the lifter attempting resistances that are too heavy and is often not evident until the last one or two repetitions of a set. Improper form is most evident in competitive individuals who want to lift maximal single repetition weights; thus you should not allow young children to attempt this regularly. A lifting belt may be worn during these exercises. The belt helps support the lower back by allowing a buildup of interabdominal pressure, which supports the back.

BACK SQUAT

Starting Position. The lifter stands with the entire back straight, eyes looking forward, feet flat on the ground, and toes pointing directly forward or slightly toward the side. The shoulders are back, and the lifter grasps the barbell with the hands wider than shoulder-width apart and the palms facing forward. The barbell rests on the spines of the shoulder blades and not on the base of the neck. The weight is supported predominantly on the shoulder blades, with the hands and arms also supporting some of the weight (Figure 6.89a). The most common way to get the barbell into the starting position is for the lifter to take it off a rack set at slightly below shoulder height. The barbell may also be placed onto the shoulders by two spotters, but this becomes more and more difficult as the resistances get heavier.

Movement. In a controlled manner the lifter slowly bends at the hips and knees until the thighs are parallel to the floor (Figure 6.89b). It is not necessary to go any lower than this, and many physicians feel going lower than this places undue stress on the knee joints. The lifter then returns to the starting position by straightening the legs; the hip and leg muscles should lift the weight, not the lower back.

Although the back will lean forward somewhat, it should remain as upright as possible throughout the exercise. The entire back should also remain rigid throughout the entire movement. Bending the lower back places undue stress on the lumbar region and makes it impossible to complete the exercise, because the weight will be out in front of the feet and the lifter will be off balance. The head should be upright, the eyes should look forward, and the neck should be in line with the rest of the spine. The head and neck should not be hyperextended, as if the lifter is looking at the ceiling. The shoulders should be kept back during the entire exercise.

At the deepest position in the squat the knees will be slightly in front of the feet. The feet should remain flat on the floor during the exercise. If they do not, you can place a weight plate or other object 1 to 2 inches high under the heels, which often allows the child to keep the feet on the floor. Elevation of the heels places more stress on the quadriceps than if the lifter keeps the feet flat on the floor. How-

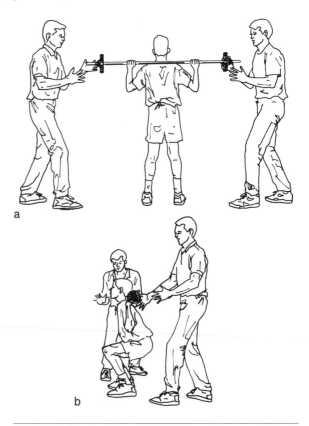

Figure 6.89 (a) Starting and finishing position for back squat; bar should be on the spines of the shoulder blades and not on the lower neck. Two spotters are shown. (b) Bottom position for back squat; the lifter does not have to go any lower than the point at which the thighs are parallel to the floor.

ever, for most people the inability to keep the feet flat on the floor is due to lack of flexibility at the ankle joint; a program of stretching the calf muscle and the Achilles' tendon will eventually allow the feet to remain flat on the floor for most individuals. When straightening the legs many people find it helpful to concentrate on bringing the hips forward and keeping the chest up, which helps to keep the back upright. Others find it helpful to concentrate on trying to push the feet through the floor rather than thinking of lifting the barbell; this also helps in keeping the back upright.

Spotting and Safety. Two spotters should be used for this exercise. A spotter stands facing each end of the barbell, watching as the child removes the barbell from the rack. The spotters then watch as each repetition is performed, ready to help the child complete the repetition by lifting up on the ends of the barbell if needed. The spotters may also completely remove the barbell from the child's shoulders if needed. The lifter can also use a power rack with the pins set at a level slightly lower than the bar's lowest position during a squat. The pins will catch the barbell if the child loses control of the barbell or cannot complete a repetition. The power rack is an added safety measure and does not replace the spotters. Any object used to elevate the child's heels must not slide or tip during the exercise and must be sturdy enough to withstand the weight of the child and barbell.

Muscles Strengthened. Buttocks (gluteals), back of thigh (hamstrings), front of thigh (quadriceps), lower back (spinal erectors), and to some extent the upper back and shoulder girdle.

FRONT SQUAT

Starting Position. The lifter stands with the entire back straight, eyes looking forward, feet flat on the ground, and toes pointing directly forward or slightly toward the side. The lifter holds the barbell in front of the neck, resting it on the upper chest, collar bones, and shoulders, grasping the barbell with the palms facing away from the body and hands slightly wider than shoulder-width. The lifter rotates the elbows upward so that the barbell rests completely on the upper chest, collar bones, and shoulders (Figure 6.90a). Carrying the weight with the arms will severely limit the amount of resistance the lifter can use.

Movement. In a controlled manner, the lifter slowly bends at the knees and hips until the upper thighs are parallel to the floor (Figure 6.90b) and then returns to the starting position. It is very important that the back stay upright and rigid, because any forward lean places the barbell in front of the feet and makes it very difficult to keep the back upright. The elbows should remain rotated upward throughout the entire exercise so that the barbell rests on the upper chest, collar bones, and shoulders and is not supported by the arms. You can place an object under the heels if the child cannot stay flat-footed during the exercise.

Spotting and Safety. Two spotters should be used for this exercise. A spotter stands facing each end of the barbell, watching as the child removes the barbell from the rack and as each repetition is performed, ready to help the child complete the repetition by lifting up on the ends of the barbell if needed. The spotters may also completely remove the barbell from the child's shoulders if needed. The lifter can perform this exercise in a power rack with the pins set at a level slightly lower than the bar's lowest position during a squat. The pins will then catch the barbell if the child loses control, or the child can place the barbell on the pins if a repetition cannot be completed. The power rack is an added safety measure and does not replace the spotters. Any object used to elevate the child's heels must not slide or tip during the exercise and must be sturdy enough to withstand the weight of the lifter and the barbell.

a

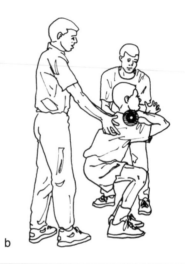

b

Figure 6.90 (a) Starting and finishing position for front squat; barbell is carried on the shoulders, upper chest, and collar bones. (b) Bottom position for the front squat; upper thighs are parallel to the floor. The elbows need to stay in front of the bar throughout the movement so that the weight is carried on the shoulders, upper chest, and collar bones and not by the arms.

Muscles Strengthened. Buttocks (gluteals), front of thigh (quadriceps), back of thigh (hamstrings), lower back (spinal erectors), and the upper back and shoulder girdle to some extent, because they are used to support the barbell.

DUMBBELL SQUAT

Starting Position.   The lifter stands erect holding a dumbbell in each hand. The back is straight, the head is upright, and the feet are approximately shoulder-width apart and pointing forward or slightly outward. The lifter can hold the dumbbells at shoulder height with the palms facing each other (Figure 6.91a). An easier position is for the lifter to hold the dumbbells so that they hang straight down at the sides from the shoulders (Figure 6.88a). Dumbbell squats should only be performed with light resistances.

Movement.   The lifter bends the knees and hips until the thighs are parallel to the floor (Figure 6.91b). The back should be kept straight and as upright as possible, and the feet should remain flat on the floor. As with all squat exercises, the entire back must remain rigid throughout the exercise.

Spotting and Safety.   Because dumbbell squats are only performed with light resistances no spotting is needed. The lifter can drop the dumbbells to the floor if really necessary. This exercise is excellent for someone who is just starting to train the legs and for a child who cannot perform a back or front squat because a light enough barbell is not available.

Muscles Strengthened.   Buttocks (gluteals), front of thigh (quadriceps), back of thigh (hamstrings), and lower back (spinal erectors), primarily; also the shoulder and upper back if the dumbbells are carried at shoulder height.

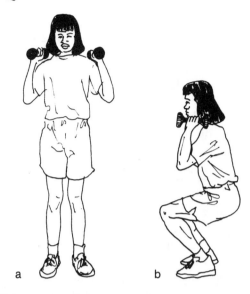

a   b

Figure 6.91 (a) Starting and finishing position for dumbbell squat with the dumbbells held at shoulder height. This exercise is a good lead-in to the front or back squat but should only be performed with light dumbbells. (b) Bottom position for dumbbell squat; same as for the front or back squat.

DEAD LIFT

Starting Position.   The lifter stands so that the bar is over the balls of the feet. The feet are shoulder-width apart and pointing forward or slightly outward. The lifter squats and grasps the bar with a mixed grip (one palm facing forward and the other backward) and with the hands slightly wider than shoulder-width apart. The upper thighs are approximately parallel to the floor. The shoulders are over the barbell, the back is rigid and arched, and the head is upright (Figure 6.92a).

Movement. The back must remain rigid throughout the entire exercise. The lifter uses the legs and hips to pull the barbell to knee height. Once the bar is past the knees, the knees and hips continue to straighten and the back starts to straighten. Once the legs and back are completely straight, the lifter ends the movement by pulling the shoulders back without arching the back (Figure 6.92b). After completely pulling the shoulders back, the lifter returns to the starting position in a controlled manner. The barbell should be kept as close as possible to the body during the entire motion. A common mistake is for a lifter to start to straighten the legs without locking the back. This results in no movement of the barbell as the knees and hips straighten. This means the trainee straightens the hips and knees using the strongest muscles of the body, but without moving the weight, so the lower back must then move the resistance. Rounding the back during the pulling motion is also a common technique problem that should be avoided, because it can result in lower back injury.

Spotting and Safety.   Because it is virtually impossible for the lifter to drop the barbell on himself or herself, no spotting is needed. If the barbell cannot be lifted, it can easily be returned to the floor. However, don't allow lifters to intentionally drop the barbell to the

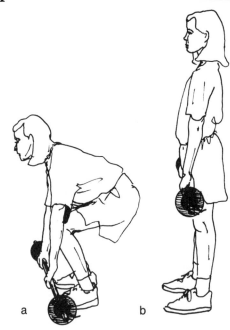

Figure 6.92   (a) Starting and finishing position for dead lift; the back should be straight and rigid so that as soon as the knees and hips start to straighten the weight moves upward and the back does not become round or bent. (b) Top position for dead lift; the shoulders should be back and the back not excessively arched.

floor, because this can damage the floor and the barbell. In addition, dropping the barbell eliminates the lowering or eccentric portion of the lift, which is part of the training stimulus. A large amount of weight can be lifted in a dead lift; however, don't allow lifters to sacrifice technique to lift more weight, because this can result in injury.

Muscles Strengthened.   Buttocks (gluteals), lower back (spinal erectors), back of thigh (hamstrings), front of thigh (quadriceps), upper back (trapezius, rhomboids), shoulder area (deltoids), and finger flexors.

Ballistic Overhead Lifts

These advanced lifts should not be taught until the lifter has at least several months of resistance training. These lifts involve use of the leg and hip muscles to propel a barbell into an overhead position. These exercises were not included with the multijoint upper body pushing exercises because the legs supply the majority of the force to raise the barbell overhead. The back, shoulders, and arms provide some propulsion to the bar but mostly act to stabilize the bar overhead. The lifter should practice all of these exercises with a broomstick before attempting them with an unloaded light barbell. The weight on the bar should be increased very gradually as the child's technique improves. The use of bumper plates is recommended when the child can use heavier resistances. Bumper plates are weight plates that have rubber rings around them or are made completely of a rubberlike material, so if they are dropped and hit the floor they are not damaged and cause little or no damage to the floor. The smallest bumper plates available are 5 kilograms (11 pounds) each. A clear area at least 10 feet square needs to be available to allow ample space for the child to drop the barbell to the floor if necessary.

Example Activities Muscles Are Used For. Shot putting and jumping.

Proper Technique. The legs supply most of the force to get the weight overhead. In order to perform these exercises correctly, the lifter must keep the back straight, locked, and upright throughout the entire movement, including the portion of the exercise in which the weight is stabilized overhead. Inability to keep the back straight is normally due to weak abdominals and lower back muscles. Thus you should include exercises to strengthen these areas when teaching a lifter to perform ballistic overhead lifts.

PUSH PRESS

Starting Position. The lifter stands with the feet shoulder-width apart and pointing directly forward or slightly outward, the back erect, the head upright, the grip slightly wider than shoulder-width, and the elbows rotated forward and upward so the barbell rests on the front of the shoulders, upper chest, and collar bones (Figure 6.93a). To get into the starting position the lifter can take the barbell from a rack or perform a power clean.

Movement. Keeping the barbell on the shoulders and using control, the lifter bends the knees and hips slightly (Figure 6.93b) and then quickly and forcibly extends them and rises up onto the toes, thrusting the bar straight up from the shoulder and past the face. The lifter should control the extension of the knees and hips and the rising onto the toes so that enough force is developed to thrust the bar to only slightly higher than the top of the head (Figure 6.93c). Then by pushing with the arms and shoulders, the lifter presses the bar overhead (Figure 6.93d). After the knees and hips are extended, they should not be rebent to lower the body in relation to the barbell, because this will remove a portion of the pressing motion to get the barbell overhead. After briefly holding the barbell overhead, in a controlled manner the lifter slowly lowers the barbell back to the shoulders for the next repetition. The knees may bend slightly just as the bar contacts the upper chest, collar bones, and shoulders to cushion the landing of the bar. The upper and lower back should remain rigid and upright during the entire exercise.

Spotting and Safety. Due to the ballistic nature of this exercise, spotters should not be used. The exercise should be performed on a platform, and individuals other than the lifter should not be allowed on the platform during performance of the exercise. If a repetition cannot be completed, the lifter should lower the barbell back to the shoulders, chest, and collar bones. If the barbell moves too far out in front of the child, it should be allowed to drop to the platform. The lifter can also perform this exercise in a power rack with the pins set slightly lower than the lifter's lowest position during the knee and hip bend. The pins of the power rack will catch the barbell if the lifter loses control of it. The lifter may have to tilt the head slightly back to avoid hitting the chin with the barbell as it leaves the shoulders.

Muscles Strengthened. Front of thigh (quadriceps), buttocks (gluteals), back of thigh (hamstrings), back of upper arm (triceps), entire upper and lower back and shoulder area.

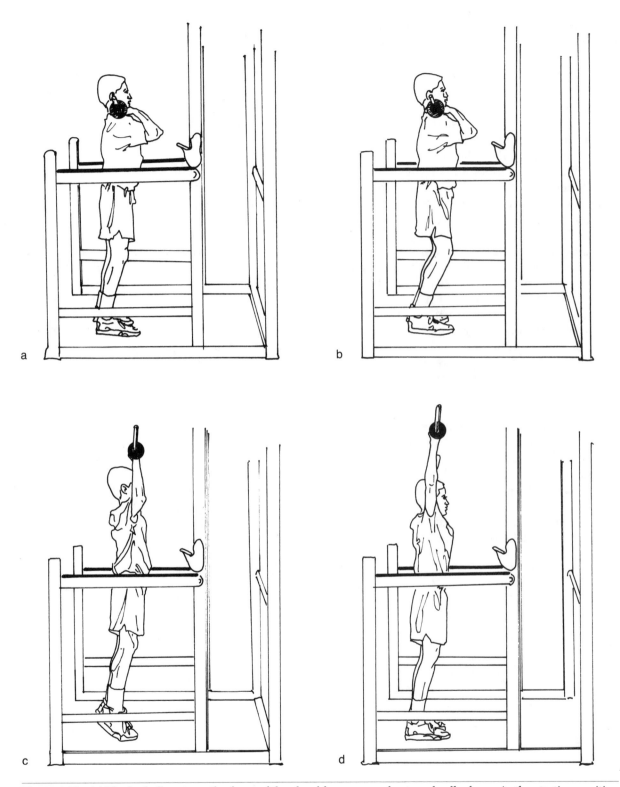

Figure 6.93 (a) The barbell rests on the front of the shoulders, upper chest, and collar bones in the starting position of the push press. (b) The lifter bends slightly at the knees and hips. (c) Using the legs, the lifter propels the barbell to slightly higher than the top of the head. (d) The lifter then presses the barbell to the overhead position by fully extending the arms.

PUSH JERK

Starting Position. The lifter stands with the feet shoulder-width apart and pointing forward or slightly outward, the back erect, the head upright, the grip slightly wider than shoulder-width, and the elbows rotated forward and upward so the barbell rests on the front of the shoulders, upper chest, and collar bones (Figure 6.94a). To get into the starting position the lifter can take the barbell from a rack or perform a power clean.

Movement. Keeping the barbell on the shoulders and using control, the lifter bends slightly at the knees and hips (Figure 6.94b). The lifter then extends the knees and hips maximally, rising onto the toes and thrusting the barbell overhead. The object is to use the legs to propel the barbell completely overhead. After the trainee has completely extended the lower body quickly, he or she bends the knees and hips slightly so that the barbell can be caught with the arms completely extended (Figure 6.94c). Then the lifter straightens the knees and hips and stands with the bar overhead (Figure 6.94d). If the force from the lower body is not sufficient to get the barbell completely overhead, the lifter may have to partially press the barbell overhead. The lifter should use a pressing movement anyway at the end of the leg drive to help stabilize the barbell overhead. The lifter briefly holds the bar overhead and then slowly lowers it back to the shoulders, collar bones, and chest area to perform the next repetition. The entire back must remain upright and rigid throughout the exercise.

Spotting and Safety. Due to the ballistic nature of this exercise, spotters should not be used. The exercise should be performed on a platform. Individuals other than the lifter should not be allowed on the platform during performance of the exercise. If a repetition cannot be completed, the lifter should lower the barbell back to the starting position on the shoulders, chest, and collar bones. If the barbell moves too far out in front of the lifter, it should be allowed to drop to the platform. The exercise can also be performed in a power rack with the pins set slightly lower than the lifter's lowest position during the knee and hip bend. The pins of the power rack will catch the barbell if the lifter loses control of it. The lifter may have to tilt the head back slightly to avoid hitting the chin with the barbell as it leaves the shoulders.

Muscles Strengthened. Front of thigh (quadriceps), buttocks (gluteals), hamstrings, back of upper arm (triceps), and entire upper and lower back and shoulder area.

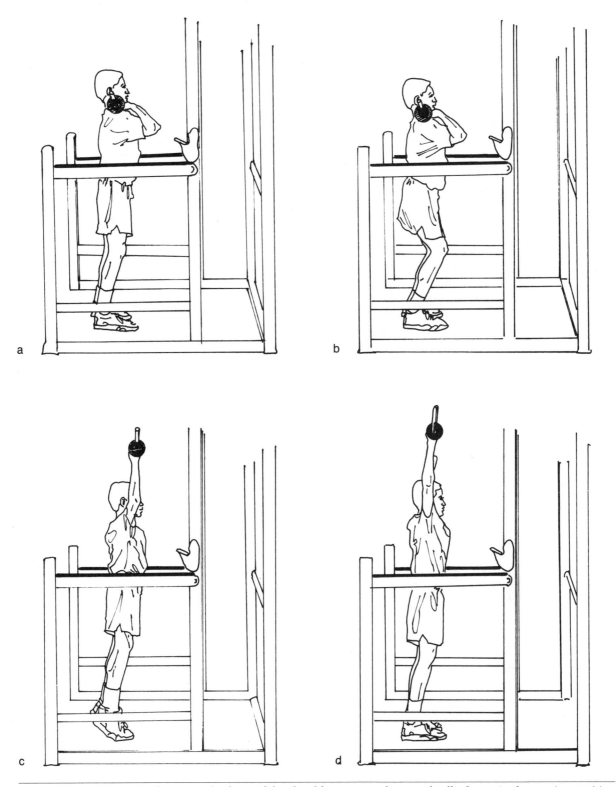

Figure 6.94 (a) The barbell rests on the front of the shoulders, upper chest, and collar bones in the starting position of the push jerk. (b) The lifter bends at the knees and hips. (c) The lifter straightens the knees and hips to propel the barbell to a full overhead position. (d) After catching the barbell overhead the lifter straightens the knees.

Ballistic Total Body Exercises

There are two main categories of ballistic total body exercises: cleans and snatches. These advanced exercises require the lifter to rapidly accelerate the barbell in order to successfully complete the exercise. Many people believe these exercises are very useful, because in most sports success is determined by an athlete's ability to accelerate against a resistance. The first technique described is the power clean. The three subsequent exercises, the clean pull from floor, floor-to-knees clean partial pull, and second pull clean partial pull, are variations of the power clean. You can use clean pull variations when teaching clean pull technique and to strengthen the muscles involved in the power clean motion. The advantage of clean pull variations is that some aspects of the power clean are removed, which reduces the difficulty. Yet the variations strengthen the leg, hip, shoulder, and back muscles in a power-oriented exercise.

Then the power snatch is described, followed by its three variations: the snatch pull from floor, floor-to-knees snatch partial pull, and second pull snatch partial pull. As with clean pull variations, you can use snatch pull variations when teaching exercise technique and to strengthen the muscles involved in the power snatch motion. Snatch pull variations omit some aspects of the power snatch and are therefore less difficult. However, the variations strengthen the leg, hip, shoulder, and back muscles in a power-oriented exercise.

Example Activities Muscles Are Used For.   Virtually all running and jumping activities.

Proper Technique.   As with all total body exercises, you must allow lifters time to learn proper lifting technique for these exercises before including them in the training program. Due to the ballistic nature of these exercises, lifters must use less resistance than is used for exercises like squats in which the exercise movement can be completed slowly. Proper technique for ballistic total body exercises requires that the back remain straight and rigid. You should teach these exercises only to children who have had several months of resistance training and who have demonstrated the maturity to follow directions. Continue to supervise and teach as exercise technique is refined.

POWER CLEAN

Starting Position. The lifter stands with the feet hip-width apart or slightly wider and pointing straight forward or slightly to the side. The barbell is over the balls of the feet. The lifter bends over and grasps the barbell, with the hands slightly wider than shoulder-width apart and both palms facing backward. The back is arched and tight and the thighs are approximately parallel to the floor. The head is upright and the eyes look at a point 2 to 3 yards in front of the lifter. The shoulders are above or slightly in front of the bar, and the elbows are completely straight. The feet are flat on the ground but the majority of weight is on the heels (Figure 6.95a, page 160).

Movement. Although the lift is separated into various phases and positions for this description, the lifter does not stop or hesitate at each of these positions but performs the entire movement fluidly and explosively.

The lifter pulls the barbell to knee height by straightening the knees, keeping the bar close to the shins (Figure 6.95b). Until the barbell is slightly above the knees, the angle of the entire back to the floor is the same as in the starting position. This means the entire initial pull is with the legs. During the initial pull to knee height, the lifter's weight will move from the heels to over the arches of the feet. The pull to the knees is done at a moderate speed but in a controlled manner.

When the bar is past the knees, the second pull starts. This portion of the pull must be done very quickly and explosively. Once the bar is past the knees the trainee's weight should again be over the arches of the feet, but the lifter should be able to wiggle the toes. The hips should be driven toward the bar, which should allow the knees to rebend slightly. Until the bar is slightly above the knees, the angle of the back to the floor should not change. Once the bar is past the knees, as the hips are driven forward and upward, the back starts to assume an upright position, but the shoulders should still be directly above or slightly in front of the bar (Figure 6.95c). From this position, where the barbell is at approximately the lower third of the thighs and the knees have rebent slightly, the lifter performs a very rapid and explosive movement similar to a vertical jump. The hips and knees are rapidly straightened

as the back becomes upright, the shoulders are over the bar, and the bar is near the top of the thighs (Figure 6.95d). The lifter straightens the ankles as if jumping and shrugs the shoulders as if trying to touch them to the ears (Figure 6.95e). The pull from thigh level to the shoulder shrug resembles the knee and hip movement of a vertical jump.

Until now the elbows have remained straight as if the arms were cables attached to the barbell. Only after the trainee has risen onto the toes and shrugged the shoulders do the elbows start to bend. Now the trainee starts to pull on the barbell, in a motion similar to upright rowing. The elbows bend but are kept out to the sides and above the barbell. During this pulling motion the lifter flexes the wrists as if doing a wrist curl, keeping the barbell very close to the body (Figure 6.95f). The lifter should not pull on the barbell as if trying to do an arm curl with the elbows below the barbell.

The lifter must now catch the barbell at the shoulders. After pulling the barbell as high as possible, the lifter rapidly drops the elbows underneath the barbell and catches it (Figure 6.95g). The feet should leave the ground as the lifter pulls the bar as high as possible and starts to drop underneath the bar to catch it. The feet may land on the ground slightly wider apart than they were during the pull, although they should not be placed excessively wide upon landing. The feet should not land in a position in front of or behind their position during the pull. To catch the bar, the lifter rapidly rotates the elbows down and underneath the barbell and then up and in front of the barbell. The elbows rotate around the barbell; the barbell should not move forward or backward during this movement. While the elbows are being rotated, the lifter bends the knees slightly, drops underneath the barbell, and catches it on the upper chest, collar bones, and fronts of the shoulders. The lifter should drop just far enough to get underneath the barbell (Figure 6.95h). If the trainee drops too far, the barbell will crash onto the shoulders and upper chest.

For the lifter to get under the bar and catch it at the shoulders, he or she must accelerate the bar by performing the lift quickly and explosively. Once the barbell is resting on the shoulders and upper chest, the lifter continues to bend the knees a little more to cushion the barbell's landing. The lifter then straightens the knees and stands completely erect (Figure 6.95i). To return the barbell to the floor, the lifter rotates the elbows backward and carefully lowers the barbell to the floor, performing the pulling motion in reverse order. Due to the height of the barbell, it may hit floor with some velocity. However, it should not be dropped to the floor.

The pull to the knees is done at a moderate speed but in a controlled manner. However, once the knees are rebent after the bar is pulled over the kneecaps, all movements until the barbell is caught are fast and explosive.

Spotting and Safety.   Due to the ballistic nature of this lift, spotting is impossible. If the child misses an attempt to power clean the barbell, the barbell will fall so quickly that by the time a spotter reacts the barbell will be on the floor. It is recommended that the lifter use a platform free of other equipment and people when performing this exercise. In addition, bumper plates should be used when the child can perform the lift with the lightest bumper plates available (5 kilograms or 11 pounds each).

Muscles Strengthened.   Buttocks (gluteals), front of thigh (quadriceps), back of thigh (hamstrings), lower back (spinal erectors), upper back (trapezius, rhomboids), and shoulder area (deltoids).

CLEAN PULL FROM FLOOR (CLEAN HIGH PULL)

Starting Position.   The lifter stands with the feet hip-width apart or slightly wider and pointing straight forward or slightly to the side. The barbell is over the balls of the feet. The lifter bends over and grasps the barbell, with the hands slightly wider than shoulder-width apart and both palms facing backward. The back is arched and tight and the thighs are approximately parallel to the floor. The head is upright and the eyes look at a point 2 to 3 yards in front of the lifter. The shoulders are above or slightly in front of the bar, and the elbows are completely straight. The feet are flat on the ground but the majority of weight is on the heels (Figure 6.95a, page 160).

Movement.   The lifter pulls the barbell to knee height by straightening the knees, keeping the bar close to the shins (Figure 6.95b). Until the barbell is slightly above the knees, the angle of the entire back to the floor is the same as in the starting position. This means the entire initial pull is with the legs. During the initial pull to knee height, the lifter's weight will move from the heels to over the arches of the feet. The pull to the knees is done at a moderate speed but in a controlled manner.

When the bar is past the knees, the second pull starts. This portion of the pull must be done very quickly and explosively. Once the bar is past the knees the trainee's weight is over the arches of the feet, but the lifter should be able to wiggle the toes. The hips should be driven toward the bar, which should allow the knees to rebend slightly. Until the bar is slightly above the knees, the angle of the back to the floor should not change. Once the bar is past the knees, the back starts to assume an upright position, but the shoulders should still be directly above the bar (Figure 6.95c). From this position, where the barbell is at approximately the lower third of the thighs and the knees have rebent slightly, the lifter performs a very rapid and explosive movement similar to a vertical jump. The hips and knees are rapidly straightened as the back becomes upright. The shoulders are over the bar, and the bar is near the top of the thighs (Figure 6.95d). The lifter straightens the ankles as if jumping and shrugs the shoulders as if trying to touch them to the ears (Figure 6.95e). The pull from thigh level to the shoulder shrug resembles the knee and hip movement of a vertical jump.

Until now the elbows have remained straight as if the arms were cables attached to the barbell. Only after the trainee has risen onto the toes and shrugged the shoulders do the elbows start to bend. Now the trainee starts to pull on the barbell, in a motion similar to upright rowing. The elbows bend but are kept out to the sides and above the barbell. During this pulling motion the lifter flexes the wrists as if doing a wrist curl, keeping the barbell very close to the body (Figure 6.95f). The lifter should not pull on the barbell as if trying to do an arm curl with the elbows below the barbell.

After the bar is pulled as high as possible, the lifter returns it to the floor.

Spotting and Safety. No spotting is needed. The lifter should use a platform that is free of other equipment and people. Bumper plates should be used when the child can perform the lift with the lightest bumper plates available (5 kilograms or 11 pounds each).

Muscles Strengthened. Buttocks (gluteals), front of thigh (quadriceps), back of thigh (hamstrings), lower back (spinal erectors), upper back (trapezius, rhomboids), and shoulder area (deltoids).

FLOOR-TO-KNEES CLEAN PARTIAL PULL

Starting Position. The lifter stands with the feet hip-width apart or slightly wider and pointing straight forward or slightly to the side. The barbell is over the balls of the feet. The lifter bends over and grasps the barbell, with the hands slightly wider than shoulder-width apart and both palms facing backward. The back is arched and tight and the thighs are approximately parallel to the floor. The head is upright and the eyes look at a point 2 to 3 yards in front of the lifter. The shoulders are above or slightly in front of the bar, and the elbows are completely straight. The feet are flat on the ground but the majority of weight is on the heels of the feet (Figure 6.95a, page 160).

Movement. The lifter pulls the barbell to knee height by straightening the knees, keeping the bar close to the shins (Figure 6.95b). The lifter then returns the bar to the floor. The lifter should perform the movement in a controlled manner and concentrate on technique.

Spotting and Safety. No spotting is needed. Give the lifter constant feedback on technique.

Muscles Strengthened. Buttocks (gluteals), front of thigh (quadriceps), lower back (spinal erectors), upper back (trapezius, rhomboids), and shoulder area (deltoid).

SECOND PULL CLEAN PARTIAL PULL (THIGH LEVEL TO FINISH)

Starting Position. The lifter stands with the feet hip-width apart or slightly wider and pointing straight forward or slightly to the side. The lifter grasps a barbell from a rack with the hands slightly wider than shoulder-width apart and both palms facing backward. The barbell is at the lower third of the thighs (Figure 6.95c, page 160); it is either held in this position or supported on blocks or in a rack. The shoulders are above or slightly in front of the bar, and the elbows are completely straight. The feet are flat on the floor but the majority of weight is over the arches of the feet. The knees are slightly bent.

Movement. The lifter performs a very rapid and explosive movement similar to a vertical jump. The knees and hips are rapidly straightened as the back becomes upright. The shoulders are over the bar, and the bar is near the top of the thighs (Figure 6.95d). The lifter straightens the ankles as if jumping and shrugs the shoulders as if trying to touch them to the ears (Figure 6.95e). The pull from thigh level to the shoulder shrug resembles the knee and hip movement of a vertical jump.

Until now the elbows have remained straight as if the arms were cables attached to the barbell. Only after the trainee has risen onto the toes and shrugged the shoulders do the elbows start to bend. Now the trainee starts to pull on the barbell, in a motion similar to upright rowing. The elbows bend but are kept out to the sides and above the barbell. During this pulling motion the lifter flexes the wrists as if doing a wrist curl, keeping the barbell very close to the body (Figure 6.95f). The lifter should not pull on the barbell as if trying to do an arm curl with the elbows below the barbell.

At this point the lifter may finish in one of two ways: The simplest way is to pull the barbell as high as possible, then return it to the floor.

The second way of finishing involves catching the barbell. To catch the barbell, the lifter rapidly drops the elbows underneath the barbell and catches it (Figure 6.95g). The feet should leave the ground as the lifter pulls the bar as high as possible and starts to drop underneath the bar to catch it. The feet may land on the ground slightly wider apart than they were during the pull, although they should not be placed excessively wide and should not land in a position in front of or behind their previous position. To catch the bar, the lifter rapidly rotates the elbows down and underneath the barbell and then up and in front of the barbell; the barbell should not move forward or backward during this movement. While the elbows are being rotated, the lifter bends the knees slightly, drops underneath the barbell, and

catches it on the upper chest, collar bones, and fronts of the shoulders. The lifter should drop just far enough to get underneath the barbell (Figure 6.95h). If the lifter drops too far, the barbell will crash onto the shoulders and chest. For the lifter to get under the bar and catch it at the shoulders, he or she must accelerate the bar by performing the lift quickly and explosively. Once the barbell is resting on the shoulders and upper chest, the lifter continues to bend the knees a little more to cushion the barbell's landing. The lifter then straightens the knees and stands completely erect (Figure 6.95i). To return the barbell to the floor, the lifter rotates the elbows backward and carefully lowers the barbell to the floor, performing the pulling motion in reverse order. Due to the height of the barbell, it may hit the floor with some velocity. However, it should not be dropped to the floor.

Spotting and Safety.   No spotting is needed. The lifter should use a platform that is free of other equipment and people. Bumper plates should be used when the lifter can perform the lift with the lightest bumper plates available (5 kilograms or 11 pounds each).

Muscles Strengthened.   Buttocks (gluteals), front of thigh (quadriceps), back of thigh (hamstrings), lower back (spinal erectors), upper back (trapezius, rhomboids), and shoulder area (deltoids).

POWER SNATCH

Starting Position.   To determine the correct grip for the power snatch, have the lifter stand erect with the right arm straight out to the side of the body parallel to the floor, with the hand clenched in a fist. Measure the distance from the *acromion process* (the most lateral bony protuberance of the spine of the shoulder blade) of the left shoulder to the knuckles of the right hand; this is the approximate grip width (Figure 6.96a, page 162). This grip is wider than that used in the power clean, which means that the shoulders and hips are closer to the ground in the starting position. The back is arched and locked, the head is upright, and the shoulders are above the bar (Figure 6.96b). The feet are

flat on the ground, approximately hip-width or slightly wider, and pointing straight ahead or slightly to the sides. The body weight is predominantly over the heels of the feet. The bar is close to the shins and is above the balls of the feet.

Movement.   This lift is described in stages and by various positions. However, when the lift is performed the lifter does not stop or hesitate at these positions but performs the entire lift fluidly and explosively.

Because the bar is caught overhead for this exercise, the lifter must use a lighter weight than used in a power clean. Due to the lighter weight used, the lifter can move the weight faster in a power snatch.

To begin, the lifter pulls the barbell to knee height by beginning to straighten the knees. The angle of the back to the floor should stay the same and the shoulders should remain over the barbell (Figure 6.96c). Once the barbell is past the knees, the lifter drives the hips forward and upward and rebends the knees slightly (Figure 6.96d). The barbell is at thigh level and the shoulders are above the barbell. Now the second pull begins, the portion of the exercise in which the barbell must really be accelerated.

The lifter rapidly extends the knees and hips and the back starts to assume an upright position (Figure 6.96e). The barbell is close to the thighs and the shoulders are still over the bar. The body weight is moving more toward the front of the foot but the toes can still be wiggled. The lifter rises up onto the toes and shrugs the shoulders (Figure 6.96f). The pull from the floor to rising up onto the toes should resemble a vertical jump.

Up to this point the elbows have remained completely straight. Now the elbows bend and the lifter pulls the barbell higher with the arms and shoulders (Figure 6.96g). The elbows should remain above the barbell during this motion and the wrists should flex. The lifter rapidly bends at the knees, not at the waist, and rapidly rotates the elbows down and to the front (Figure 6.96h). The lifter's feet may leave the floor as he or she moves underneath the bar. The feet may land on the ground slightly wider than they were during the pull. However, they should not be excessively wide and they should not land in front of or behind their position during the pull. As the barbell passes the head, the lifter pushes with the arms and shoulders so that the barbell is supported overhead and held approximately over the ears (Figure 6.96i). The knees should bend only enough to allow the lifter to get underneath the barbell, normally no more than 90 degrees. Once the barbell is overhead the lifter should pull with the hands and arms as if trying to stretch the bar; this will help stabilize the bar overhead. The lifter straightens the knees and assumes an upright stance (Figure 6.96j), then in a controlled fashion lowers the barbell back to the floor.

Spotting and Safety. No spotting is needed. If the lifter cannot complete a repetition, the barbell should be returned to the floor. The lifter should use a platform clear of other equipment and individuals and should use bumper plates whenever possible. Give the lifter constant feedback on proper technique, especially when he or she is learning the lift. There is a possibility that the lifter will lose control of the barbell behind the head and have to "dump" it behind him or her. Therefore, shoulder flexibility is important. From the overhead position, using a broomstick or similar rod, a lifter should be able to rotate at the shoulders and, keeping the elbows straight, touch the lower back with the rod. If the lifter can do this movement, dumping the barbell behind the back will be easier.

Muscles Strengthened. Buttocks (gluteals), front of thigh (quadriceps), back of thigh (hamstrings), lower back (spinal erectors), upper back (trapezius, rhomboids), and shoulder area (deltoids).

SNATCH PULL FROM FLOOR (SNATCH HIGH PULL)

Starting Position. The lifter stands with the back arched and locked, the head upright, and the shoulders above the bar. The feet are flat on the ground, approximately hip-width apart or slightly wider and pointing straight ahead or slightly to the sides. The body weight is predominantly over the heels. The lifter holds the bar close to the shins and above the balls of the feet (Figure 6.96b, page 162), using a grip width as determined by measuring from the acromion process to the knuckles (Figure 6.96a).

Movement. The lifter pulls the barbell to knee height by beginning to straighten the knees. The angle of the back to the floor stays the same and the shoulders remain over the barbell (Figure 6.96c). The lifter drives the hips forward and upward and rebends the knees slightly (Figure 6.96d), so the barbell is at thigh level and the shoulders are above the barbell.

The lifter rapidly extends the knees and hips and starts to straighten the back (Figure 6.96e). The barbell is close to the thighs and the shoulders are still over the bar. The body weight shifts forward but the lifter can still wiggle the toes. The lifter rises up onto the toes and shrugs the shoulders (Figure 6.96f). The pull resembles a vertical jump.

Now the elbows bend and the lifter pulls the barbell higher with the arms and shoulders (Figure 6.96g). After reaching the highest point, the lifter returns the barbell to the floor.

Spotting and Safety. No spotting is needed. If the lifter cannot complete a repetition, the barbell should be returned to the floor. The lifter should use a platform that is free of other equipment and lifters and should use bumper plates if possible. Give the lifter constant feedback about proper technique, especially when he or she is learning the lift. Be sure the lifter has adequate shoulder flexibility to dump the barbell behind him or her if necessary.

Muscles Strengthened. Buttocks (gluteals), front of thigh (quadriceps), back of thigh (hamstrings), lower back (spinal erectors), upper back (trapezius, rhomboids), and shoulder area (deltoids).

FLOOR-TO-KNEES SNATCH PARTIAL PULL

Starting Position. The lifter stands with the back arched and locked, the head upright, and the shoulders above the bar. The feet are flat on the ground, approximately hip-width apart or slightly wider and pointing straight ahead or slightly to the sides. The body weight is predominantly over the heels of the feet. The lifter holds the bar close to the shins and the bar is above the balls of the feet (Figure 6.96b, page 162), using a grip width as determined by measuring from the acromion process to the knuckles (Figure 6.96a).

Movement. The lifter pulls the barbell to knee height by beginning to straighten the knees. The angle of the back to the floor stays the same and the shoulders remain over the barbell (Figure 6.96c). Once the bar is at knee height it is returned to the floor in a controlled manner.

Spotting and Safety. No spotting is needed. If the lifter cannot complete a repetition, the barbell should be returned to the floor. The lifter should use a platform that is free of other equipment and lifters and should use bumper plates if possible. Give the lifter constant feedback about proper technique, especially when he or she is learning the lift.

Muscles Strengthened. Buttocks (gluteals), front of thigh (quadriceps), back of thigh (hamstrings), lower back (spinal erectors), upper back (trapezius, rhomboids), and shoulder area (deltoids).

SECOND PULL SNATCH PARTIAL PULL (THIGH LEVEL TO FINISH)

Starting Position. The lifter stands with the back arched and locked, the head upright, and the shoulders above the bar. The bar is at thigh level (Figure 6.96d, page 162). Either the lifter holds the bar at this position or it rests on blocks. The lifter grips the bar as if performing a power snatch. The feet are flat on the ground, approximately hip-width apart or slightly wider and pointing straight ahead or slightly to the sides. The body weight is predominantly over the arches of the feet.

Movement. The lifter uses a lighter weight for this exercise than is used in a second pull clean partial pull; thus, the lifter can perform the movements more quickly. The lifter rapidly extends the knees and hips and starts to straighten the back (Figure 6.96e). The barbell is close to the thighs and the shoulders are still over the bar. The body weight shifts forward but the lifter can still wiggle the toes. The lifter rises up onto the toes and shrugs the shoulders (Figure 6.96f). This pull resembles a vertical jump.

Now the elbows bend and the lifter pulls the barbell higher with the arms and shoulders (Figure 6.96g). At this point the lifter may finish in one of two ways. The simplest way is to pull the barbell as high as possible, then return it to the floor.

To finish the second way, the lifter rapidly bends at the knees and rotates the elbows down and to the front (Figure 6.96h). The feet may leave the floor but should land in about the same position, perhaps slightly wider. The lifter pushes the barbell with the arms and shoulders so it is supported overhead (Figure 6.96i). Now the lifter straightens the knees and stands upright (Figure 6.96j), then lowers the barbell to the floor. The entire motion of the exercise should be performed fluidly and explosively.

Spotting and Safety. No spotting is needed. If the lifter cannot complete a repetition, the barbell should be returned to the floor. The lifter should use a platform that is free of other equipment and lifters and should use bumper plates if possible. Give the lifter constant feedback about proper technique, especially when he or she is learning the lift. Be sure the lifter has adequate shoulder flexibility to dump the barbell behind him or her if necessary.

Muscles Strengthened. Buttocks (gluteals), front of thigh (quadriceps), back of thigh (hamstrings), lower back (spinal erectors), upper back (trapezius, rhomboids), and shoulder area (deltoids).

Figure 6.95, Power Clean   (a) Starting position for power clean; the back and shoulders are above or slightly in front of the bar, the hands are shoulder-width apart or slightly wider, and the feet are hip-width apart or slightly wider. (b) The pull to the knees; the angle of the back to the floor is the same as in the starting position. (c) The pull to the lower one-third of the thighs; the shoulders are above or slightly in front of the bar. (d) The pull to the tops of the thighs; the legs are straight and the back is more upright, but the shoulders are still above or slightly in front of the bar. (e) The rise to the toes; the elbows are still straight and the shoulders are shrugged.

(f) Top portion of the pull; the elbows remain above the bar as it is pulled with the arms. (g) Preparation for the catch; after pulling the bar as high as possible the athlete bends at the knees and hips and rotates the elbows around the bar. (h) Preparation for completion of the catch; the lifter finishes rotating the elbows and starts to straighten the legs to assume a full standing position. (i) Completion; the lifter completely straightens the legs and is in a full standing position. For the **Clean Pull From Floor (Clean High Pull)**, follow figures a-f. For the **Floor-to-Knees Clean Partial Pull**, follow figures a-b. For the **Second Pull Clean Partial Pull (Thigh Level to Finish)**, follow figures c-i.

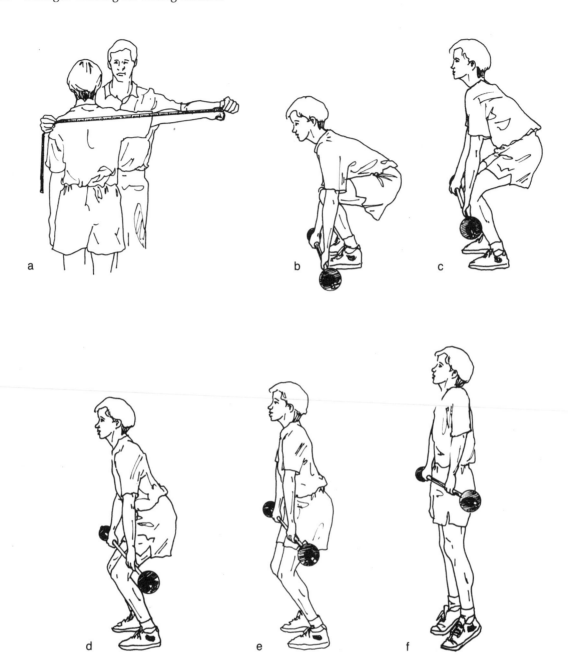

Figure 6.96, Power Snatch   (a) Measuring the distance from the left acromion process to the knuckles of the right hand to determine the approximate grip width for the power snatch. (b) Starting position for power snatch; the back is straight, the shoulders are above or slightly in front of the bar, and the feet are approximately hip-width apart or slightly wider. (c) The pull to the knees; the angle of the back to the floor is the same as it was in the starting position and the shoulders are still above or slightly in front of the bar. (d) The pull to midthigh level; the shoulders are still above or slightly in front of the bar. (e) The pull to upper thigh level; when the bar is at this level the elbows are still straight and the shoulders still above or slightly in front of the bar. (f) The rise to the toes; the elbows are still straight and the shoulders are shrugged.

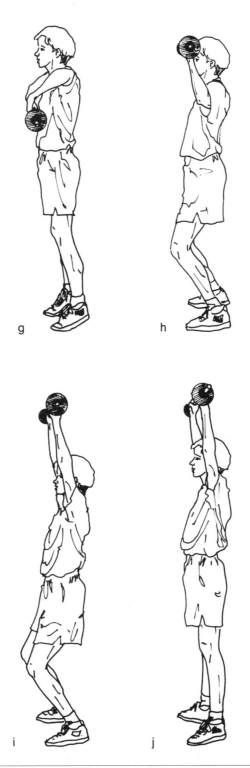

g   h

i   j

(g) The pull above waist level; the elbows are still above the bar. (h) Preparation to catch the barbell; after the bar is pulled as high as possible the knees are bent and the elbows are rotated under the bar. (i) The initial overhead position; the knees are bent as the lifter moves underneath the bar. (j) The standing position. For the **Snatch Pull From Floor (Snatch High Pull)** follow figures a-g. For the **Floor-to-Knees Snatch Partial Pull** follow figures a-c. For the **Second Pull Snatch Partial Pull (Thigh Level to Finish)** follow figures d-j.

Chapter 7

Strength Training Programs for Fitness and Sports

It's important that you guard against too much specialization too early in a young athlete's career. In other words, all resistance training programs for young athletes should include exercises for the major muscle groups of the body. After a young athlete has established an adequate strength/power base, he or she can slowly and carefully begin a more sport-specific program.

The chapter contains sample programs for the child interested in improving physical fitness and performance in various sports. The chapter begins with a basic program for children, followed by descriptions of sport-specific programs. These examples along with the information in chapter 4 provide a starting point from which you can develop a resistance training program for a particular sport. Following the basic

program for each sport are additional exercises that you can add to the program as the child's needs change and the child matures. Also included are exercises for the older, more experienced young athlete (approximately 15 years of age or older) who is ready for more advanced resistance training programs for sports. These advanced exercises require a greater emphasis on exercise technique; therefore, be sure the lifter understands basic concepts of resistance exercise before you introduce these advanced exercises.

The young athlete must understand the program and be enthusiastic about it. Often parents, teachers, and coaches try to implement programs that are too aggressive or too advanced for children; a child may be physically but not mentally able to tolerate certain exercise demands. You must communicate with the child and involve him or her in the development of the program's goals. This involvement allows the child to demonstrate motivation and desires and develop a positive attitude about the program.

You can enhance self-esteem, achievement, and physical development by allowing the child to only compete against himself or herself in training. Also realize that a child's perspective of the program may be different from yours. This includes everything from the reward systems used to the satisfactions gained.

Although we can provide basic guidelines, one program will not fit all children; individualization is ultimately the only way to address the diversity among children. Programs are starting points from which you can make appropriate reductions or advancements. A successful individualized resistance training program allows for individual progression in the day-to-day changes in exercise, resistance, rest periods, sets, and repetitions. Indeed, individualization of resistance training programs is vital for their ultimate success. Individualization will enhance program adherence and effectiveness. By individualizing a program, the various variables (see Chapter 4), such as resistance used, rest between sets and exercises, volume of the workout or training period (sets × reps × resistance), exercise choices, etc. are manipulated in response to the child's ability to adapt and succeed with the training. For example, a resistance too heavy for a child would need to be lightened the next day, or a child may be too tired the day after a workout which increased the total number of sets (i.e., volume increases) and the volume has to be lowered the next day. Changing the characteristics of the workout in response to the child's ability to tolerate the exercise or improve is an important part of the art of individualizing the program. One cannot just grind out the same old sets, reps, etc. day after day. Successful monitoring of the training program can lead to more optimal productive program manipulations. Keeping track of what is being done and how the child feels are vital components in making the right choices day to day and week to week as to what is going to be the workout plan.

Some of the sport-specific programs in the chapter include certain injury-prevention exercises. This is because some sports have very specific sites of injury that are not addressed by the exercises in the standard program. Performing specialized exercises will help prevent injury in the part of the body where the sport stress is greatest.

When a child performs various advanced exercises (e.g., power clean), the resistance should always allow 6 or more repetitions, even though the lifter may not perform this many. For example, a program in this chapter may specify 5 repetitions with a 6- to 8-RM load. Although the resistance is light enough to allow 6 to 8 repetitions, the lifter performs 5 repetitions. Since the technique must be perfect, the repetitions cannot be performed properly if fatigue becomes a factor. Thus, the loading reference is given in terms of an RM range that should allow more repetitions than actually performed. In other words, the load is heavier with a 6- to 8-RM reference than with an 8- to 10-RM reference.

Basics of Seasonal Training

The diversity of children's schedules can make it difficult to organize exercise training into various training periods. However, the following programs differentiate between preseason, off-season, and in-season to associate periods of time with specific phases of a competitive sport season. In general, each of these training periods has characteristics and goals as follows:

- Off-Season: This program is used to develop general overall body strength and local muscular endurance. Special attention is given to total conditioning and a balanced program. Adequate rest is allowed for recovery and exercise tolerance is increased. This training period is normally the longest in duration.
- Preseason: Program changes are made to develop strength, power, and local muscular endurance in muscle groups predominantly used in a particular sport. This training period usually runs 6 to 12 weeks.
- In-Season: The primary goal is to maintain the training gains made in the off-season and preseason programs. Special attention is given to joints susceptible to injury in the target sport. This constitutes the training done during the sport's season.

Active-Child and Sport-Specific Programs

Prepubescents or pubescents should not perform programs designed for collegiate or professional athletes. The ability of these athletes to improve in strength using advanced programs is in part due to their many years of well-planned resistance training. Advanced programs often involve daily lifting of very heavy resistances (1 to 3 RM), which is not recommended for prepubescents. Forcing prepubescents or pubescents to perform programs designed for mature athletes can result in excessive fatigue and possible injury.

Following are example programs for any active child who wants to increase muscular strength/power or local muscular endurance, as well as sport-specific programs for different youth sports. These are basic guidelines for program construction and must be modified to meet the individual's situation (i.e., equipment availability, time, tolerance for exercise, and resistance training experience). Although the program can be performed on any 3 days of the week, you should allow at least 1 day between training sessions to promote adequate recovery. Initially, plan the exercise order so that the lifter alternates between arm and leg exercises. This will provide for better recovery within the exercise session.

You can use the active-child program that uses resistance training equipment as a lead-in to a sport-specific program. In developing a sport-specific program, incorporate all information concerning periodization (preseason, in-season, off-season) and weekly variation (light, moderate, heavy days). In addition, draw upon information previously discussed concerning learning proper exercise technique, increases in resistance, and the physiological and psychological age of a child, in short, all information concerning designing and implementing a resistance program.

Incorporate the additional injury-prevention exercises into the program, especially if the child has a history of injury to the specific joint or muscles trained by a listed exercise. In some programs, exercises can be periodized for resistance in this phase, which means that the resistance used can vary from the suggested RM to a 6-RM resistance. Normally, the heavier resistances are incorporated in the last weeks of the phase. Add the additional or replacement exercises to the training program, or use them to replace an exercise that trains the same muscle groups to add variation to the training.

Active Child
(Body Weight- and Partner-Resisted Exercise)

As with all exercise programs, you must take care not to overwork the trainees during the initial training sessions. Instruct the trainees to perform only one set of each exercise during the first two to three training sessions. During the next two to three sessions two sets of each exercise should be performed. Thereafter, the trainees perform the program as outlined with three sets of each exercise.

You can use the following guidelines with either a circuit or a set-repetition format. To use a *circuit format*, the lifter performs one set of an exercise, then moves to the next exercise after a predetermined rest period. If two or three sets of the exercises are to be performed, the lifter repeats the entire circuit two or three times. With a *set-repetition format*, the lifter performs all sets of a particular exercise before moving to the next exercise. The sets and exercises in a set-repetition format are separated by predetermined rest periods.

Year-Round Program—Body Weight or Partner Resisted

The lifter performs exercises in the order listed.
Warm-Up—General exercise consisting of jogging or cycling for about 5 minutes followed by a general stretching routine

- Push-Up
- Body-weight squat
- Self-resisted elbow curl
- Calf raise
- Partner-resisted lateral arm raise
- Lying back extension
- Bent-leg sit-up

Approximate Time

- Two to three training sessions per week with at least 1 day separating sessions
- 25 to 45 minutes per session

Additional or Replacement Exercises

- Progression to resistance equipment exercises

Advanced Exercises

- Progression to resistance equipment exercises. Note that not all body weight–resisted exercises are simple or beginning exercises. Push-ups and pull-ups may be very difficult if the trainee is unable to perform at least six repetitions. In this case, using exercise equipment will allow the lifter to progress to body weight–resisted exercises.

Program Notes—Body Weight–Resisted/Partner-Resisted Program

- Format: set-repetition or circuit
- Number of sets or circuits: one initially; lifter progresses to three
- Resistance: 10 to 12 RM
- Rest periods between sets and exercises: 2 minutes initially; lifter progresses to 1 minute
- Repetitions per set for abdominal exercises: 20-30
- Other: The lifter should move through the full range of motion for each exercise.

Partner resistance must be applied smoothly. If applying resistance becomes difficult, or if body weight exercises are too difficult or too easy to perform, have the lifter use resistance training equipment.

Active Child
(Resistance Exercise Equipment)

When children use resistance training equipment, several factors concerning safety cannot be overemphasized. The equipment must physically fit the children, and you must continually stress spotting and proper technique. You must maintain proper conduct in the resistance training facility and have adult supervision at all times. The lifter must control the resistance throughout the entire range of motion of an exercise, and increases in the resistance must be controlled and gradual. Finally, you must individualize program progression for each exercise. These factors ensure the safety of the trainees and prevent damage to equipment.

The child's age and resistance training experience will impact the program. A 16- to 17-year-old may be able to perform the entire program, whereas a 10- to 11-year-old may have to limit the exercise program to three or four multijoint exercises and a few selected single-joint exercises in order to tolerate the workout. Because an example program can only act as a guideline, examples will either overshoot or undershoot most individuals' abilities to perform the program as well as tolerate and recover from the physical stress imposed by a workout. You must assign children programs that are appropriate for their ages and experience. Use sound judgment, and monitor the training sessions as each child progresses to more advanced training programs. Initially, alternate the order of exercise between muscle groups. Use additional or replacement exercises to make the program more advanced and to provide variety.

Year-Round Program—Resistance Equipment

The lifter performs exercises in the order listed.

Warm-Up—General exercise consisting of jogging or cycling for about 5 minutes followed by a general stretching routine.

- Bench press
- Leg press or back squat
- Elbow curl
- Knee curl (using one leg at a time or both legs at once)
- Overhead press
- Knee extension (using one leg at a time or both legs at once)
- Lat pull-down
- Calf raise
- Bent-leg sit up

Approximate Time

- Two to three training sessions per week with at least 1 day separating sessions
- 25 to 55 minutes per session

Additional or Replacement Exercises

- Lunge
- Dumbbell exercises

- Seated row
- Reverse elbow curl
- Internal and external shoulder rotation exercise

Advanced Exercises

- Dead lift
- Clean pull from the thigh or knee level (no more than five repetitions per set)

Program Notes—Resistance Equipment Program

- Format: set-repetition or circuit
- Number of sets or circuits: one set of each exercise for the first six to nine training sessions; two sets for the next three to six training sessions; three sets thereafter
- Resistance: 12 to 15 RM initially
- Rest periods between sets and exercises: 2 minutes initially; lifter progresses to 1-1/2 minutes
- Repetitions per set for abdominal exercises: 20-30
- Other: The lifter can initially choose half of the listed exercises and add one exercise per training session until all of the listed exercises are performed. The lifter should increase resistances slowly and in small increments.

Stress proper technique at all times. When adding or replacing exercises, be sure the lifter has learned proper exercise technique before you allow increases in resistance. If an exercise is replaced, make sure that the muscles it trains are used in other exercises so that proper muscular balance is maintained.

When varying a program over the year and during the week, use the information presented in chapter 4 concerning periodization and heavy, medium, and light sessions.

Baseball

Baseball involves short periods in which a player uses maximal power, such as swinging a bat, throwing the ball, and sprinting to a base. Maximal throwing velocity in adult baseball players has a significant relationship to shoulder adduction and elbow extension strength. Professional pitchers have been shown to have stronger shoulder muscles than players at other positions. Most athletic trainers agree that resistance training can help prevent the shoulder pain commonly called pitcher's shoulder. In addition, most coaches agree that power and short sprint ability are important characteristics for a baseball player.

The exercises listed here are for players of all positions. You may wish to have pitchers perform more shoulder exercises, as outlined in the shoulder rotator cuff exercises in chapter 6, to help prevent shoulder injury. The program stresses overall body strength with emphasis upon the shoulder area. The program includes abdominal and lower back exercises so that power developed by the legs can be transferred to the upper body during throwing and hitting. As the program progresses, the lifter performs the abdominal and lower back exercises with a twisting motion to strengthen the muscles involved in rotating the hips, which occurs in throwing or hitting.

Off-Season Program—Baseball

The lifter performs exercises in the order listed. Italics indicate exercises that can be periodized for resistance within this phase.

Warm-Up—General exercise consisting of jogging or cycling for about 5 minutes followed by a general stretching routine.

- *Shoulder press*
- *Leg press or back squat*
- *Bench press*
- Calf raise
- Triceps extension
- Knee curl
- Lat pull-down
- Knee extension
- Abdominal exercise

Approximate Time

- Three training sessions per week with at least 1 day separating sessions
- 30 to 50 minutes per session

Additional Injury-Prevention Exercises

- Shoulder adduction and shoulder extension
- Shoulder rotator cuff exercise
- Shoulder internal rotation and shoulder external rotation

Additional or Replacement Exercises

- Seated row
- Lower back exercise
- Wrist curl
- Gripping exercise

Advanced Exercises

- Dead lift

Off-Season Program Notes— Baseball

- Format: set-repetition
- Number of sets: one initially; lifter works up to three
- Resistance: 8 to 15 RM; for variation, change the resistance for large muscle group exercises to as high as 6 RM for older children
- Rest periods between sets and exercises: 2 minutes for large muscle group exercises; 90 seconds for small muscle group exercises (e.g., wrist curls)
- Repetitions per set for abdominal exercises: 20 to 25
- Other: The lifter performs shoulder adduction using a high pulley or as a partner exercise. To perform it with a high pulley the lifter grasps the handle of the high pulley with one hand and stands with that side of the body toward the high pulley. Then the lifter adjusts his or her position so that the arm is slightly below parallel to the floor. Keeping the elbow slightly bent, the lifter pulls the arm toward the body until the hand touches the upper thigh, then in a controlled manner returns to the starting position. After the desired number of repetitions have been completed, the lifter performs the exercise with the opposite arm.

  To perform partner-resisted shoulder adduction, the lifter stands with one arm held out to the side, slightly below parallel to the floor. A partner stands behind the lifter and places his or her hand below the lifter's elbow. As the lifter moves the arm toward the body, the partner resists. The lifter repeats with the other arm.

Preseason Program—Baseball

The lifter performs exercises in the order listed.

Warm-Up—General exercise consisting of jogging or cycling for about 5 minutes followed by a general stretching routine.

- Dumbbell incline bench press
- Lunge
- Upright rowing
- Knee extension
- Pullover
- Knee curl
- Abdominal exercise with a twist

Approximate Time

- Three training sessions per week with at least 1 day separating sessions
- 30 to 50 minutes per session

Additional Injury-Prevention Exercises

- Shoulder extension
- Shoulder adduction
- Shoulder rotator cuff exercise

Additional or Replacement Exercises

- Wrist curl
- Tricep extension

Advanced Exercises

- None

Preseason Program Notes— Baseball

- Format: set-repetition
- Number of sets: two to three
- Resistance: 10 RM initially; 6 to 8 RM near end of phase
- Rest periods between exercises: 1-1/2 to 2 minutes initially; 2 to 3 minutes near end of phase
- Repetitions per set for abdominal exercises: 20 to 30

In-Season Program—Baseball

The lifter performs exercises in the order listed.

Warm-Up—General exercise consisting of jogging or cycling for about 5 minutes followed by a general stretching routine.

- Pullover
- Lunge
- Triceps extension
- Calf raise
- Upright rowing
- Abdominal exercise with a twist

Approximate Time

- Two training sessions per week with at least 1 day separating sessions
- 25 to 30 minutes per session

Additional Injury-Prevention Exercises	• Internal and external shoulder rotator cuff exercise • Wrist curl or wrist roller
Additional or Replacement Exercises	• None
Advanced Exercises	• None
In-Season Program Notes— Baseball	• Format: set-repetition • Number of sets: three • Resistance: 8 to 10 RM • Rest periods between sets and exercises: 1-1/2 to 2 minutes • Repetitions per set for abdominal exercises: 20 to 30

Basketball

In basketball the abilities to jump, rebound, and shoot are important. Resistance training can improve vertical jumping ability, ability to grasp the ball, and passing ability, and it may improve a player's shooting range by strengthening upper body muscles. As players grow older, adequate size and muscle mass for the physical style of play used today can also be enhanced with a resistance training program.

For many years, basketball players and coaches were afraid of lifting weights (they did not want to become too muscle-bound to shoot the ball well), but resistance training is now considered an important part of player development. Lack of sufficient leg strength has been shown to contribute to susceptibility of knee injury; thus, exercises to strengthen the muscles of the knee joint are important for basketball players. Exercises for the ankle should also be part of a sport-specific program for basketball.

Off-Season Program—Basketball

The lifter performs exercises in the order listed. Italics indicate exercises that can be periodized for resistance in this phase.

Warm-Up—General exercise consisting of jogging or cycling for about 5 minutes followed by a general stretching routine.

• *Bench press*
• *Back squat or leg press*
• Lat pull-down
• Knee curl
• Overhead press
• Calf raise
• Abdominal exercise

Approximate Time	• Three training sessions per week with at least 1 day separating sessions • 35 to 45 minutes per session
Additional Injury-Prevention Exercises	• Knee extension

Additional or Replacement Exercises
- Lunge
- Pullover
- Wrist curls or wrist roller

Advanced Exercises
- The lifter should perform no more than five repetitions per set using 8- to 10-RM resistance for advanced exercises. If an advanced exercise is used, it should be performed at the beginning of the training session. These exercises can be periodized for resistance in this phase.
- Power clean or clean pull from the knee or thigh level

Off-Season Program Notes— Basketball
- Format: set-repetition
- Number of sets: three
- Resistance: 10 to 12 RM
- Rest periods between sets and exercises: 2 to 3 minutes
- Repetitions per set for abdominal exercises: 20 to 25

Preseason Program—Basketball

The lifter performs exercises in the order listed.
Warm-Up—General exercise consisting of jogging or cycling for about 5 minutes followed by a general stretching routine.

- Close-grip bench press
- Lunge
- Knee curl
- Overhead dumbbell press
- Knee extension
- Lat pull-down
- Calf raise
- Reverse elbow curl
- Abdominal exercise (including twisting sit-up)

Approximate Time
- Three training sessions per week with at least 1 day separating sessions
- 30 to 45 minutes per session

Additional Injury-Prevention Exercises
- None

Additional or Replacement Exercises
- Seated row
- Wrist roller or wrist curl

Advanced Exercises
- The lifter performs no more than five repetitions per set using 8- to 10-RM resistance for advanced exercises. If an advanced exercise is used, it should be performed at the beginning of the training session.
- Power clean or clean pull from thigh or knee level
- Power snatch or snatch pull from thigh or knee level

Preseason Program Notes— Basketball
- Format: Circuit
- Number of circuits: one initially; lifter works up to three
- Resistance: 8 to 10 RM
- Rest periods between sets and exercises: 1 to 1-1/2 minutes; reduce rest periods after lifter can perform three circuits
- Repetitions per set for abdominal exercises: 20 to 30

In-Season Program—Basketball

The lifter performs exercises in the order listed.

Warm-Up—General exercise consisting of jogging or cycling for about 5 minutes followed by a general stretching routine.

- Back squat or leg press
- Dumbbell overhead press
- Lat pull-down
- Knee curl
- Bench press
- Knee extension
- Reverse elbow curl
- Calf raise
- Abdominal exercise

Approximate Time

- One to two training sessions per week with at least 1 day separating sessions
- 25 to 30 minutes per session

Additional Injury-Prevention Exercises

- None

Additional or Replacement Exercises

- Incline dumbbell bench press
- Lunge
- Behind-the-neck press
- Wrist exercise

Advanced Exercises

- The lifter should perform no more than five repetitions per set using 8- to 10-RM resistance for advanced exercises. If an advanced exercise is used, it should be performed at the beginning of the training session.
- Power clean or clean pull from the knee or thigh level
- Snatch pull from knee or thigh level
- Push press

In-Season Program Notes— Basketball

- Format: circuit
- Number of circuits: two to three
- Resistance: 8 to 10 RM
- Rest periods between sets and exercises: 1 minute
- Repetitions per set for abdominal exercises: 20 to 30

Distance Running

The major goals of a resistance training program for distance runners are to prevent injury and to increase local muscular endurance. To meet these goals, the athlete can use resistances of 10 RM or lighter and for the most part can incorporate short rest periods between sets and exercises. Resistances of 10 RM or lighter will increase strength to some extent but not to the same degree as heavier resistances of 6 to 8 RM. Recent information suggests that resistance training does increase performance of endurance athletes. Increasing strength and local muscular endurance of postural support muscles in the trunk helps the runner maintain proper form. Improved leg strength helps in hill running and in "kick" performance at the end of the race. Furthermore, resistance training can enhance bone density and the strength of tendons and ligaments, thus preventing injury (e.g., stress fractures).

Off-Season Program—Distance Running

The lifter performs exercises in the order listed.

Warm-Up—General exercise consisting of jogging or cycling for about 5 minutes followed by a general stretching routine.

- Dumbbell incline press
- Back squat or leg press
- Overhead press
- Knee curl
- Calf raise
- Bent-over rowing
- Abdominal exercise
- Shoulder shrug

Approximate Time

- Two to three training sessions per week with at least 1 day separating sessions
- 30 to 45 minutes per session

Additional Injury-Prevention Exercises

- Knee extension

Additional or Replacement Exercises

- Lat pull-down

Advanced Exercises

- None

Off-Season Program Notes— Distance Running

- Format: circuit
- Number of circuits: work up to three
- Resistance: 15 to 20 RM
- Rest periods between exercises: 2 minutes initially; reduce after lifter can perform three circuits
- Repetitions per set for abdominal exercises: 20 to 25

Preseason Program—Distance Running

The lifter performs exercises in the order listed.

Warm-Up—General exercise consisting of jogging or cycling for about 5 minutes followed by a general stretching routine.

- Overhead press
- Lunge
- Bent-over rowing
- Calf raise
- Shoulder shrug
- Lower back exercise
- Abdominal exercise
- Shoulder lateral raise

Approximate Time

- Two training sessions per week with at least 1 day separating sessions
- 20 to 30 minutes per session

Additional Injury-Prevention Exercises	• Knee extension • Knee curl
Additional or Replacement Exercises	• Lat pull-down • Seated row • Elbow curl
Advanced Exercises	• None
Preseason Program Notes— Distance Running	• Format: circuit • Number of circuits: two to three • Resistance: 10 to 12 RM • Rest periods between sets and exercises: 1 minute or less • Repetitions per set for abdominal exercises: 20 to 25 • Other: Include twisting abdominal exercises in the program.

In-Season Program—Distance Running

The lifter performs exercises in the order listed.

Warm-Up—General exercise consisting of jogging or cycling for about 5 minutes followed by a general stretching routine.

- Shoulder shrug
- Lunge
- Overhead press
- Calf raise
- Bent-over rowing
- Knee curl
- Arm curl
- Abdominal exercise

Approximate Time	• One to two training sessions per week with at least 1 day separating sessions • 15 to 25 minutes per session
Additional Injury-Prevention Exercises	• Knee extension
Additional or Replacement Exercises	• Lat pull-down • Narrow-grip bench press
Advanced Exercises	• None
In-Season Program Notes— Distance Running	• Format: circuit • Number of circuits: one to three • Resistance: 12 to 15 RM • Rest periods between sets and exercises: 30 to 60 seconds • Repetitions per set for abdominal exercises: 20 to 30

Football

Playing football requires speed, strength, and power. The requirements for each position are somewhat different, yet improving these three factors with resistance training can contribute to enhanced sport performance and prevent injury. In this sport, being physically prepared to play is vital for injury prevention.

Quarterbacks need to stress exercises for the shoulders. All players need to perform exercises for the neck, shoulders, knees, and ankles, areas in which injury frequently occurs.

Off-Season Program—Football

The lifter performs exercises in the order listed. Italics indicate exercises that can be periodized for resistance within this phase.

Warm-Up—General exercise consisting of jogging or cycling for about 5 minutes followed by a general stretching routine.

- *Bench press*
- *Squat or leg press*
- Overhead press
- Knee curl
- Seated row
- Knee extension
- Elbow curl
- Abdominal exercise

Approximate Time

- Three training sessions per week with at least 1 day separating sessions
- 60 to 70 minutes per session

Additional Injury-Prevention Exercises

- Neck exercise
- Shoulder rotator cuff exercises
- Calf raise

Additional or Replacement Exercises

- *Dead lift*
- Lat pull-down
- Lunge
- *Front squat*
- *Narrow-grip bench press*

Advanced Exercises

- The lifter should perform no more than five repetitions per set using 8- to 10-RM resistance for advanced exercises. If an advanced exercise is used, it should be performed at the beginning of the training session.
- Power clean or clean pull from knee or thigh level
- Power snatch or snatch pull from knee or thigh level

Off-Season Program Notes— Football

- Format: set-repetition
- Number of sets: two to three
- Resistance: 10 to 12 RM
- Rest periods between sets and exercises: 2 to 3 minutes
- Repetitions per set for abdominal exercises: 20 to 30
- Other: Quarterbacks and offensive linemen perform supplemental shoulder girdle exercises.

Preseason Program—Football

The lifter performs exercises in the order listed. Italics indicate exercises that can be periodized for resistance within this training phase.

Warm-Up—General exercise consisting of jogging or cycling for about 5 minutes followed by a general stretching routine.

- *Incline bench press*
- *Back squat*
- Lat pull-down
- Knee curl
- Reverse elbow curl or elbow curl
- Abdominal exercise
- Shoulder internal rotation and shoulder external rotation (especially for quarterbacks)

Approximate Time

- Three training sessions per week with at least 1 day separating sessions
- 30 to 45 minutes per session

Additional Injury-Prevention Exercises

- Calf raise
- Additional shoulder rotator cuff exercises
- Neck exercise
- Knee extension

Additional or Replacement Exercises

- *Narrow-grip bench press*
- Seated row or bent-over rowing
- *Bench press*
- Wrist curl
- Dead lift

Advanced Exercises

- The lifter should perform no more than five repetitions per set using 8- to 10-RM resistance for advanced exercises. If an advanced exercise is used, it should be performed at the start of the training session.
- Power clean or clean pull from knee or thigh level
- Power snatch or snatch pull from knee or thigh level

Preseason Program Notes— Football

- Format: set-repetition
- Number of sets: three
- Resistance: 8 to 10 RM
- Rest periods between sets and exercises: 1-1/2 to 2 minutes
- Repetitions per set for abdominal exercises: 20 to 30

In-Season Program—Football

The lifter performs exercises in the order listed.

Warm-Up—General exercise consisting of jogging or cycling for about 5 minutes followed by a general stretching routine.

- Overhead press
- Back squat
- Bench press
- Knee curl
- Neck exercise
- Knee extension
- Shoulder internal rotation and shoulder external rotation
- Abdominal exercise

Approximate Time

- One to two training sessions per week with at least 1 day separating sessions
- 25 to 45 minutes per session

Additional Injury-Prevention Exercises	• None
Additional or Replacement Exercises	• Incline bench press • Seated row • Lat pull-down • Lunge • Front squat • Calf raise • Narrow-grip bench press
Advanced Exercises	• The lifter should perform no more than five repetitions per set using an 8- to 10-RM resistance for advanced exercises. If an advanced exercise is used, it should be performed at the beginning of the training session. • Power clean or clean pull from knee or thigh level • Power snatch or snatch pull from knee or thigh level
In-Season Program Notes— Football	• Format: set-repetition or circuit • Number of sets or circuits: two to three • Resistance: 8 to 10 RM • Rest periods between sets and exercises: 1 to 2 minutes • Repetitions per set for abdominal exercises: 20 to 30

Gymnastics

Gymnastics requires the athlete to control his or her body through various strength and balance moves. A gymnast needs high levels of strength/power and local muscular endurance to complete movements, retain body positions, and perform winning routines. Resistance training complements the practice of gymnastics by improving strength and endurance and thus helping to prevent injury.

Off-Season Program—Gymnastics

The lifter performs exercises in the order listed. Italics indicate exercises that can be periodized for resistance within this phase of training.

Warm-Up—General exercise consisting of jogging or cycling for about 5 minutes followed by a general stretching routine.

• *Bench press*
• *Squat or leg press*
• Shoulder front raise
• Knee curl
• Abdominal exercise
• Shoulder lateral raise
• Knee extension
• Lat pull-down

Approximate Time

• Three training sessions per week with at least 1 day separating sessions
• 20 to 60 minutes per session

Additional Injury-Prevention Exercises	• Shoulder internal rotation and shoulder external rotation • Wrist curl or wrist roller
Additional or Replacement Exercises	• Triceps extension • *Incline press* • Lunge • *Close-grip bench press* • Bent-over rowing • Overhead press
Advanced Exercises	• The lifter should perform no more than five repetitions per set at 8- to 10-RM resistance for advanced exercises. If an advanced exercise is used, it should be performed at the beginning of the training session. • Power clean, clean pull, power snatch, or snatch pull from knee or thigh level
Off-Season Program Notes— Gymnastics	• Format: set-repetition • Number of sets: 3 to 5 • Resistance: 10 to 12 RM • Rest periods between sets and exercises: 1 to 2 minutes • Repetitions per set for abdominal exercises: 20 to 30

Preseason Program—Gymnastics

The lifter performs exercises in the order listed. Italics indicate exercises that can be periodized for resistance within this phase of training.

Warm-Up—General exercise consisting of jogging or cycling for about 5 minutes followed by a general stretching routine.

• *Lunge*
• *Overhead dumbbell press*
• Knee curl
• *Lat pull-down*
• Calf raise
• *Incline or bench press using dumbbells*
• Front shoulder raise
• Abdominal exercise with twist
• Shoulder lateral dumbbell raise

Approximate Time	• Two to three training sessions per week with at least 1 day separating sessions • 15 to 45 minutes per session
Additional Injury-Prevention Exercises	• Shoulder rotator cuff exercises
Additional or Replacement Exercises	• Knee extension • *Seated row* • Lower back exercise
Advanced Exercises	• The lifter should perform no more than five repetitions per set at 8- to 10-RM resistance for advanced exercises. If an advanced exercise is used, it should be performed at the beginning of the training session. • Power clean, clean pull, power snatch, or snatch pull from knee or thigh level

Preseason Program Notes—Gymnastics

- Format: set-repetition
- Number of sets: one to three
- Resistance: 8 to 10 RM
- Rest periods between sets and exercises: 1-1/2 minutes
- Repetitions per set for abdominal exercises: 20 to 30

In-Season Program—Gymnastics

The lifter performs exercises in the order listed.

Warm-Up—General exercise consisting of jogging or cycling for about 5 minutes followed by a general stretching routine.

- Overhead press
- Lunge
- Bench press
- Calf raise
- Seated row
- Abdominal exercise

Approximate Time

- One to two training sessions per week with at least 1 day separating sessions
- 15 to 25 minutes per session

Additional Injury-Prevention Exercises

- Shoulder rotator cuff exercises
- Wrist curl or wrist roller

Additional or Replacement Exercises

- Front squat
- Shoulder anterior, posterior, and lateral dumbbell raises
- Lat pull-down
- Knee curl
- Knee extension
- Narrow-grip bench press

Advanced Exercises

- The lifter should perform no more than five repetitions of power clean or power snatch exercises per set using 8- to 10-RM resistance for advanced exercises. If an advanced exercise is used, it should be performed at the beginning of the training session.
- Push press
- Power clean, clean pull, power snatch, or snatch pull from knee or thigh level

In-Season Program Notes—Gymnastics

- Format: circuit
- Number of circuits: one to three
- Resistance: 8 to 10 RM
- Rest periods between sets and exercises: 1 to 1-1/2 minutes
- Repetitions per set for abdominal exercises: 20 to 30

Ice Hockey

Ice hockey is a high-speed anaerobic sport that requires skating and stick-handling ability for successful performance. As a contact sport, its physical demands are great. Resistance training can provide the strength/power and high-intensity local muscular endurance of the legs, back, and arms needed for successful hockey performance and can help prevent injuries of the ankles, knees, back, and shoulders. Resistance exercise can also help improve speed and control of movement during the high-speed activity of skating. Adequate local muscular endurance of the legs and back is especially important for young hockey players who are trying to improve their toleration of long periods of play on the ice.

Off-Season Program—Ice Hockey

The lifter performs exercises in the order listed. Italics indicate exercises that can be periodized for resistance within this phase of training.

Warm-Up—General exercise consisting of jogging or cycling for about 5 minutes followed by a general stretching routine.

- *Bench press*
- *Squat or leg press*
- *Overhead press*
- Knee curl
- Seated row
- Calf raise
- Elbow curl
- Abdominal exercise

Approximate Time

- Three training sessions per week with at least 1 day separating sessions
- 55 to 60 minutes per session

Additional Injury-Prevention Exercises

- Knee extension

Additional or Replacement Exercises

- *Dead lift*
- Reverse elbow curl
- Lunge
- Lat pull-down
- Wrist roller or wrist curl
- Reverse wrist curl

Advanced Exercises

- The lifter should perform no more than five repetitions per set using 8- to 10-RM resistance for advanced exercises. If an advanced exercise is used, it should be performed at the beginning of the training session.
- Power clean, clean pull, power snatch, or snatch pull from knee or thigh level

Off-Season Program Notes— Ice Hockey

- Format: set-repetition
- Number of Sets: three
- Resistance: 10 to 12 RM
- Rest periods between sets and exercises: 1-1/2 to 2 minutes
- Repetitions per set for abdominal exercises: 20 to 30

Preseason Program—Ice Hockey

The lifter performs exercises in the order listed.

Warm-Up—General exercise consisting of jogging or cycling for about 5 minutes followed by a general stretching routine.

- Lunge
- Reverse elbow curl
- Dead lift
- Knee curl
- Abdominal exercise with twists
- Calf raise

Approximate Time
- Three training sessions per week with at least 1 day separating sessions
- 25 to 36 minutes per session

Additional Injury-Prevention Exercises
- Wrist curl or roller
- Shoulder rotator cuff exercises

Additional or Replacement Exercises
- Elbow curl
- Bent-over row
- Overhead press
- Dumbbell bench press
- Lower back exercise
- Reverse wrist curl

Advanced Exercises
- The lifter should perform no more than five repetitions per set using 8- to 10-RM resistance for advanced exercises. If an advanced exercise is used, it should be performed at the beginning of the training session.
- Power clean, clean pull, power snatch, or snatch pull from knee or thigh level

Preseason Program Notes— Ice Hockey
- Format: set-repetition; near the end of the phase a circuit format can be used
- Number of sets: three
- Resistance: 8 to 10 RM
- Rest periods between sets and exercises: 1 to 1-1/2 minutes
- Repetitions per set for abdominal exercises: 20 to 30

In-Season Program—Ice Hockey

The lifter performs exercises in the order listed.

Warm-Up—General exercise consisting of jogging or cycling for about 5 minutes followed by a general stretching routine.

- Overhead press
- Single-leg knee extension
- Dumbbell fly
- Single-leg knee curl
- Bench press
- Calf raise
- Abdominal exercise
- Seated row

Approximate Time
- One to two training sessions per week with at least 1 day separating sessions
- 15 to 30 minutes per session

Additional Injury-Prevention Exercises
- Wrist curl or roller
- Shoulder rotator cuff exercises

Additional or Replacement Exercises

- Lower back exercise
- Lunge
- Incline bench press
- Reverse wrist curl

Advanced Exercises

- The lifter should perform no more than five repetitions per set using 8- to 10-RM resistance for advanced exercises. If an advanced exercise is used, it should be performed at the beginning of the training session.
- Power clean, clean pull, power snatch, or snatch pull from the knee or thigh level

In-Season Program Notes—Ice Hockey

- Format: circuit
- Number of circuits: 2
- Resistance: 8 to 10 RM
- Rest periods between sets and exercises: 1 minute; for variation 30 seconds to 1-1/2 minutes
- Repetitions per set for abdominal exercises: 20 to 30

Racket Sports (Tennis, Squash, and Racquetball)

Racket sports have a high anaerobic component. Resistance training can improve the player's ability to recover from short, high-intensity spurts of exercise involved with each rally and to hit shots with greater power and control. Strength can also help prevent injury to the shoulder, back, knees, and ankles. Thus, resistance training that includes sport-specific components to improve skills and prevent injuries can benefit the young player.

Off-Season Program—Racket Sports

The lifter performs exercises in the order listed. Italics indicate exercises that can be periodized for resistance within this phase of training.

Warm-Up—General exercise consisting of jogging or cycling for about 5 minutes followed by a general stretching routine.

- *Back squat or leg press*
- *Bench press*
- Knee curl
- *Overhead press*
- Lat pull-down
- Shoulder side raise
- Abdominal exercise

Approximate Time

- Three training sessions per week with at least 1 day separating sessions
- 35 to 50 minutes per session

Additional Injury-Prevention Exercises

- Shoulder internal rotation and shoulder external rotation
- Wrist roller or wrist curl
- Shoulder rotator cuff exercises

Additional or Replacement Exercises	• *Seated row* • Lower back exercise • Dumbbell incline press • Calf raise • Knee extension • Front squat • Reverse wrist curl
Advanced Exercises	• Advanced exercises can be introduced toward the end of this phase. The lifter should perform no more than five repetitions per set using 8- to 10-RM resistance for advanced exercises. If an advanced exercise is used, it should be performed at the beginning of the training session. • Power clean, power snatch, clean pull, and snatch pull
Off-Season Program Notes— Racket Sports	• Format: set-repetition • Number of sets: two to three • Resistance: 10 to 12 RM • Rest periods between sets and exercises: 1-1/2 to 2 minutes • Repetitions per set for abdominal exercises: 20 to 30

Preseason Program—Racket Sports

The lifter performs exercises in the order listed.

Warm-Up—General exercise consisting of jogging or cycling for about 5 minutes followed by a general stretching routine.

• Lunge
• Bent-over dumbbell rowing
• Knee curl
• Dumbbell fly
• Calf raise
• Reverse wrist curl or wrist curl
• Abdominal exercise with twist

Approximate Time	• Three training sessions per week with at least 1 day separating sessions • 25 to 40 minutes per session
Additional Injury-Prevention Exercises	• Shoulder internal rotation and shoulder external rotation • Shoulder rotator cuff exercises
Additional or Replacement Exercises	• Pullover • Knee extension • Seated row
Advanced Exercises	• The lifter should perform no more than five repetitions per set using 8- to 10-RM resistance for advanced exercises. If an advanced exercise is used, it should be performed at the beginning of the training session. • Clean pull or snatch pull from the knee or thigh level
Preseason Program Notes— Racket Sports	• Format: circuit; for variation, set-repetition • Number of sets or circuits: two to three • Resistance: 8 to 10 RM

- Rest periods between sets and exercises: 1 minute; for variation, 30 seconds to 1-1/2 minutes
- Repetitions per set for abdominal exercises: 20 to 30

In-Season Program—Racket Sports

The lifter performs exercises in the order listed.

Warm-Up—General exercise consisting of jogging or cycling for about 5 minutes followed by a general stretching routine.

- Back squat or leg press
- Dumbbell overhead press
- Knee curl
- Seated row
- Knee extension
- Bent over rowing
- Calf raise
- Twisting abdominal exercise

Approximate Time

- One to two days per week with at least 1 day separating sessions
- 30 to 45 minutes per session

Additional Injury-Prevention Exercises

- Shoulder internal rotation and shoulder external rotation
- Reverse wrist curl and wrist curl
- Wrist roller
- Shoulder rotator cuff exercises
- Front squat

Additional or Replacement Exercises

- Lower back exercise
- Lunge

Advanced Exercises

- None

In-Season Program Notes— Racket Sports

- Format: circuit
- Number of circuits: two
- Resistance: 8 to 10 RM
- Rest periods between sets and exercises: 1 minute
- Repetitions per set for abdominal exercises: 20 to 30

Soccer

Soccer presents a unique set of physical demands to the young athlete: cardio-vascular endurance, sprint speed, ball-handling ability, and physical power to kick the ball for passing or shots on goal. Younger players must develop leg strength to perform soccer skills and improve performance; neck strength is also vital for absorbing and tolerating the forces involved with heading the ball. Resistance training can contribute to improved leg, neck, and total body strength/power of the young soccer player. Furthermore, resistance training can improve muscle and connective tissue strength, which will help prevent injury. A total conditioning program, including resistance exercise, will help the young soccer player perform better and decrease injuries.

Off-Season Program—Soccer

The lifter performs exercises in the order listed. Italics indicate exercises that can be periodized for resistance during this phase.

Warm-Up—General exercise consisting of jogging or cycling for about 5 minutes followed by a general stretching routine.

- *Back squat or leg press*
- *Bench press*
- Knee curl
- Lat pull-down
- Abdominal exercise with twist
- Calf raise

Approximate Time

- Three training sessions per week with at least 1 day separating sessions
- 25 to 45 minutes per session

Additional Injury-Prevention Exercises

- Knee extension
- Neck exercise

Additional or Replacement Exercises

- Front squat
- Lunge
- Overhead press

Advanced Exercises

- The lifter should perform no more than five repetitions per set using 8- to 10-RM resistance for advanced exercises. If an advanced exercise is used, it should be performed at the beginning of the training session.
- Clean pull and snatch pull from knee level

Off-Season Program Notes—Soccer

- Format: circuit
- Number of circuits: two to three
- Resistance: 12 to 15 RM
- Rest periods between sets and exercises: 1 to 2 minutes
- Repetitions per set for abdominal exercises: 20 to 30

Preseason Program—Soccer

The lifter performs exercises in the order listed.

Warm-Up—General exercise consisting of jogging or cycling for about 5 minutes followed by a general stretching routine.

- Lunge
- Pullover
- Knee curl
- Dumbbell shoulder press
- Neck exercise
- Abdominal exercise (twisting)

| **Approximate Time** | • Three days per week with at least 1 day separating sessions |
| | • 25 to 40 minutes per session |

Additional Injury-Prevention Exercises
- Calf raise
- Knee extension

Additional or Replacement Exercises
- Dumbbell incline bench press
- Dumbbell bench press
- Front or back squat

Advanced Exercises
- The lifter should perform no more than five repetitions per set using 8- to 10-RM resistance for advanced exercises. If an advanced exercise is used, it should be performed at the beginning of the training session.
- Clean pull or snatch pull from knee or thigh level

Preseason Program Notes—Soccer
- Format: set-repetition or circuit
- Number of sets or circuits: two to three
- Resistance: 8 to 10 RM
- Rest periods between sets and exercises: 1 to 1-1/2 minutes
- Repetitions per set for abdominal exercises: 20 to 30

In-Season Program—Soccer

The lifter performs exercises in the order listed.

Warm-Up—General exercise consisting of jogging or cycling for about 5 minutes followed by a general stretching routine.

- Lunge
- Dumbbell shoulder press
- Knee curl
- Bent-over row
- Calf raise
- Neck exercises
- Abdominal exercise

Approximate Time
- One to two training sessions per week with at least 1 day separating sessions
- 20 to 35 minutes per session

Additional Injury-Prevention Exercises
- Knee extension

Additional or Replacement Exercises
- Bench press
- Narrow-grip bench press
- Incline bench press
- Dumbbell fly
- Elbow curl

Advanced Exercises
- The lifter should perform no more than five repetitions per set using 8- to 10-RM resistance for advanced exercises. If an advanced exercise is used, it should be performed at the beginning of the training session.
- Clean pull or snatch pull from knee or thigh level

In-Season Program Notes—Soccer
- Format: circuit
- Number of circuits: two to three

- Resistance: 8 to 10 RM
- Rest periods between sets and exercises: 1 minute
- Repetitions per set for abdominal exercises: 20 to 30

Swimming

Power of the upper body—the chest, back of arm, front of arm, shoulder, and upper back—has a significant effect on swimming performance. In addition, during the crawl, backstroke, and fly, the legs supply some propulsive force through knee and hip flexion and extension. During the breaststroke, hip adduction and abduction are also important. Resistance training can help prevent shoulder pain commonly referred to as swimmer's shoulder. Injury prevention for the shoulder, even for divers, is very important for swimmers. A properly designed resistance program can improve swimming performance and aid in injury prevention.

The exercises presented are for swimming in general. You should modify them to meet the specific needs of a particular athlete. For example, for a child who swims the breaststroke add hip adduction and abduction exercises to the program. For a distance swimmer, keep the number of repetitions per set in the 12- to 15-RM range during the preseason and maintenance programs. You can also reduce rest periods for distance swimmers in the preseason and in-season training sessions to 1 minute or less, so that the body can develop and increase toleration to high-intensity exercise. For an in-season program, exercises can be performed in a circuit fashion to save time.

Off-Season Program—Swimming

The lifter performs exercises in the order listed. Italics indicate exercises that can be periodized for resistance within this training phase.

Warm-Up—General exercise consisting of jogging or cycling for about 5 minutes followed by a general stretching routine.

- *Bench press*
- *Back squat or leg press*
- Lat pull-down
- Knee curl
- Shoulder lateral raise
- Seated row
- Abdominal exercise

Approximate Time

- Three training sessions per week with at least 1 day separating sessions
- 30 to 50 minutes per session

Additional Injury-Prevention Exercises

- Shoulder rotator cuff exercises

Additional or Replacement Exercises

- Dip
- Knee extension
- Elbow curl
- Pullover

Advanced Exercises

- The lifter should perform no more than five repetitions per set using 8- to 10-RM resistance for advanced exercises. If an advanced exercise is used, it should be performed at the beginning of the training session.
- Power clean or clean pull from knee or thigh level (especially for sprinters)

Off-Season Program Notes—Swimming

- Format: set-repetition
- Number of sets: three
- Resistance: 12 to 15 RM
- Rest periods between sets and exercises: 2 minutes
- Repetitions per set for abdominal exercises: 20 to 30

Preseason Program—Swimming

The lifter performs exercises in the order listed.

Warm-Up—General exercise consisting of jogging or cycling for about 5 minutes followed by a general stretching routine.

- Lat pull-down
- Back squat or leg press
- Pullover
- Knee curl
- Dumbbell fly
- Knee extension
- Arm curl
- Abdominal exercise

Approximate Time

- Two to three training sessions per week with at least 1 day separating sessions
- 30 to 45 minutes per session

Additional Injury-Prevention Exercises

- Shoulder side raise
- Shoulder anterior raise
- Shoulder posterior raise
- Shoulder rotator cuff exercises

Additional or Replacement Exercises

- Dip
- Incline dumbbell press

Advanced Exercises

- The lifter should perform no more than five repetitions per set using 8- to 10-RM resistance for advanced exercises. If an advanced exercise is used, it should be performed at the beginning of the training session.
- Power clean, clean pull, or snatch pull from knee or thigh level

Preseason Program Notes—Swimming

- Format: circuit
- Number of circuits: three
- Resistance: 8 to 10 RM
- Rest periods between sets and exercises: 1 minute
- Repetitions per set for abdominal exercises: 20 to 30

In-Season Program—Swimming

The lifter performs exercises in the order listed.

Warm-Up—General exercise consisting of jogging or cycling for about 5 minutes followed by a general stretching routine.

- Lat pull-down
- Knee extension
- Shoulder internal rotation and shoulder external rotation
- Knee curl
- Shoulder side raise
- Abdominal exercise
- Shoulder anterior raise
- Pullover
- Shoulder posterior raise

Approximate Time

- One to two training sessions per week with at least 1 day separating sessions
- 25 to 40 minutes per session

Additional Injury-Prevention Exercises

- Shoulder rotator cuff exercises

Additional or Replacement Exercises

- Bench press
- Narrow-grip bench press
- Lunge
- Back squat or leg press

Advanced Exercises

- The lifter should perform no more than five repetitions per set using 8- to 10-RM resistance for advanced exercises. If an advanced exercise is used, it should be performed at the beginning of the training session.
- Power clean, clean pull, or snatch pull from knee or thigh level

In-Season Program Notes— Swimming

- Format: circuit
- Number of circuits: two to three
- Resistance: 8 to 10 RM
- Rest periods between sets and exercises: 30 seconds to 1 minute
- Repetitions per set for abdominal exercises: 20 to 30

Track and Field—Jumps

The long jump, high jump, and pole vault can be divided into two phases: the approach run and the actual jump or vault. Speed during the approach run is more important for the long jump and pole vault than for the high jump, but all events depend upon leg strength for the jump or vault. Pole vaulters also need upper body strength. The program presented stresses leg strength and power for performance of these events. In addition, upper body exercises are included for the pole vaulter.

Off-Season Program—Jumps

The lifter performs exercises in the order listed. Italics indicate exercises that can be periodized for resistance during this training phase.

Warm-Up—General exercise consisting of jogging or cycling for about 5 minutes followed by a general stretching routine.

- *Bench press*
- *Back squat or leg press*
- Upright rowing
- Knee curl
- Shoulder press
- Calf raise
- Elbow curl
- Abdominal exercise
- Lat pull-down (can be periodized for pole vaulters)

Approximate Time	• Three training sessions per week with at least 1 day separating sessions • 40 to 60 minutes per session
Additional Injury-Prevention Exercises	• Knee extension
Additional or Replacement Exercises	• Triceps extension (for pole vaulters) • Lunge • Seated row • Incline press
Advanced Exercises	• The lifter should perform no more than five repetitions per set using 8- to 10-RM resistance for advanced exercises. If an advanced exercise is used, it should be performed at the beginning of the training session. • Clean or snatch pulls from knee or thigh level
Off-Season Program Notes—Jumps	• Format: set-repetition • Number of sets: three • Resistance: 10 to 12 RM • Rest periods between sets and exercises: 2 minutes • Repetitions per set of abdominal exercises: 20 to 30

Preseason Program—Jumps

The lifter performs exercises in the order listed.
Warm-Up—General exercise consisting of jogging or cycling for about 5 minutes followed by a general stretching routine.

- Dumbbell bench press
- Lunge
- Upright rowing
- Knee curl
- Overhead press
- Calf raise
- Pull-up or lat pull-down
- Abdominal exercise

Approximate Time	• Three training sessions per week with at least 1 day separating sessions • 20 to 50 minutes per session
Additional Injury-Prevention Exercises	• Knee extension

| Additional or Replacement Exercises | • Dumbbell incline press
• Seated row
• Elbow curl
• Back squat |

Advanced Exercises

- The lifter should perform no more than five repetitions per set using 8- to 10-RM resistance for advanced exercises. If an advanced exercise is used, it should be performed at the beginning of the training session.
- Power snatch or snatch pull from knee or thigh level

Preseason Program Notes—Jumps

- Format: set-repetition
- Number of sets: one to three
- Resistance: 8 to 10 RM
- Rest periods between sets and exercises: 2 minutes
- Repetitions per set for abdominal exercises: 20 to 30

In-Season Program—Jumps

The lifter performs exercises in the order listed.

Warm-Up—General exercise consisting of jogging or cycling for about 5 minutes followed by a general stretching routine.

- Overhead press
- Front or back squat or leg press
- Pull-up or lat pull-down (especially for pole vaulters)
- Knee curl
- Seated row
- Calf raise
- Abdominal exercise with twist

Approximate Time

- One to two training sessions per week with at least 1 day separating sessions
- 30 to 50 minutes per session

Additional Injury-Prevention Exercises

- Knee extension

Additional or Replacement Exercises

- Narrow-grip bench press
- Dead lift
- Upright rowing

Advanced Exercises

- The lifter should perform no more than five repetitions per set using 8- to 10-RM resistance for advanced exercises. If an advanced exercise is used, it should be performed at the beginning of the training session.
- Power snatch or snatch pull from knee or thigh level

In-Season Program Notes—Jumps

- Format: set-repetition
- Number of sets: two to three
- Resistance: 7 to 9 RM
- Rest periods between sets and exercises: 1-1/2 to 2 minutes
- Repetitions per set for abdominal exercises: 20 to 30

Track and Field—Throws
(Shot Put and Discus)

Because throws are short-term, high-powered events, increases in strength and power will improve an athlete's performance in these events. However, maximal bench press ability does not have a strong relationship to performance in these events. Stronger relationships to performance are shown by power-oriented lifts, such as the power clean and snatch. Therefore, you should include these exercises in the resistance program as the child gets older and advances in these events, and you should de-emphasize the bench press. Overhead lifts should also be part of the program for these events. Emphasize technique and carefully monitor resistance for these exercises.

Off-Season Program—Throws

The lifter performs exercises in the order listed. Italics indicate exercises that can be periodized for resistance in this phase.

Warm-Up—General exercise consisting of jogging or cycling for about 5 minutes followed by a general stretching routine.

- *Bench press*
- *Back squat or leg press*
- *Overhead press*
- Knee curl
- Lat pull-down
- Calf raise
- Dumbbell fly
- Abdominal exercise

Approximate Time
- Three training sessions per week with at least 1 day separating sessions
- 40 to 60 minutes per session

Additional Injury-Prevention Exercises
- Wrist curl
- Wrist roller
- Shoulder rotator cuff exercise

Additional or Replacement Exercises
- Knee extension
- Lower back exercise
- Triceps extension
- Pullover
- Lunge
- Leg press

Advanced Exercises
- The lifter should perform no more than five repetitions per set using 8- to 10-RM resistance for advanced exercises. If an advanced exercise is used, it should be performed at the beginning of the training session.
- Power clean or clean pull from knee or thigh level

Off-Season Program Notes— Throws
- Format: set-repetition
- Number of sets: three
- Resistance: 10 to 12 RM
- Rest periods between sets and exercises: 2 to 3 minutes
- Repetitions per set for abdominal exercises: 20 to 30

Preseason Program—Throws

The lifter performs exercises in the order listed. Italics indicate exercises that can be periodized for resistance in this phase.

Warm-Up—General exercise consisting of jogging or cycling for about 5 minutes followed by a general stretching routine.

- *Front squat*
- Dumbbell shoulder press
- *Dead lift*
- Dumbbell incline press
- Knee curl
- Calf raise
- Abdominal exercise with twist

Approximate Time
- Three training sessions per week with at least 1 day separating sessions
- 45 to 60 minutes per session

Additional Injury-Prevention Exercises
- Wrist curl
- Wrist roller
- Shoulder internal rotation and shoulder external rotation

Additional or Replacement Exercises
- Lunge
- Knee extension
- Elbow curl
- Bench press
- Narrow-grip bench press
- Back squat
- Leg press

Advanced Exercises
- The lifter should perform no more than five repetitions per set using 8- to 10-RM resistance for advanced exercises. If an advanced exercise is used, it should be performed at the beginning of the training session.
- Power clean and power snatch
- Clean and snatch pulls from floor, knee, or thigh level

Preseason Program Notes— Throws
- Format: set-repetition
- Number of sets: three
- Resistance: 8 RM
- Rest periods between sets and exercises: 1-1/2 to 3 minutes
- Repetitions per set for abdominal exercises: 20 to 30

In-Season Program—Throws

The lifter performs exercises in the order listed.

Warm-Up—General exercise consisting of jogging or cycling for about 5 minutes followed by a general stretching routine.

- Back or front squat
- Incline press
- Dead lift
- Dumbbell fly
- Knee curl
- Abdominal exercise

Approximate Time

- One to two training sessions per week with at least 1 day separating sessions
- 35 to 60 minutes per session

Additional Injury-Prevention Exercises

- Wrist curl
- Wrist roller
- Shoulder internal rotation and shoulder external rotation

Additional or Replacement Exercises

- Leg press
- Bench press
- Dumbbell incline press
- Knee extension
- Calf raise
- Lunge

Advanced Exercises

- The lifter should perform no more than five repetitions per set using 8- to 10-RM resistance for advanced exercises. If an advanced exercise is used, it should be performed at the beginning of the training session.
- Power snatch and power clean from the floor, knee, and thigh levels
- Snatch pull and clean pull from the floor, knee, or thigh levels

In-Season Program Notes— Throws

- Format: set-repetition
- Number of sets: two to three
- Resistance: 6 to 8 RM
- Rest periods between sets and exercises: 1-1/2 to 3 minutes
- Repetitions per set for abdominal exercises: 20 to 30
- Other: Technique practice in the throwing skills is necessary in order to successfully transfer strength and power gains to the events. In-season programs should stress maintenance of total body power development and technique enhancement.

Track—Sprints

Sprinting is a high-power output, short-duration event (100 meters) as well as a high-power, local muscular endurance event (200 and 400 meters). A program for sprinting should be designed to meet the needs of a particular individual and to meet the needs of a particular sprint event. For example, 200- and 400-meter sprinters may use shorter rest periods (30 seconds to 1 minute) between sets and exercises than 100-meter sprinters, especially during the preseason and in-season programs. Hundred-meter sprinters may switch to 8-RM resistances in the late preseason, because the 100-meter event requires higher power output than the 200- to 400-meter events.

Off-Season Program—Sprints

The lifter performs exercises in the order listed. Italics indicate exercises that can be periodized for resistance during this phase.

Warm-Up—General exercise consisting of jogging or cycling for about 5 minutes followed by a general stretching routine.

- *Back squat or leg press*
- *Bench press*
- Knee curl
- Upright rowing
- Knee extension
- Lat pull-down
- Calf raise
- Abdominal exercise

Approximate Time
- Three training sessions per week with at least 1 day separating sessions
- 45 to 60 minutes per session

Additional Injury-Prevention Exercises
- None

Additional or Replacement Exercises
- *Incline press*
- Low-back exercise
- Lunge

Advanced Exercises
- The lifter should perform no more than five repetitions per set using 8- to 10-RM resistance for advanced exercises. If an advanced exercise is used, it should be performed at the beginning of the training session.
- Power clean or clean pull from knee or thigh level

Off-Season Program Notes— Sprints
- Format: set-repetition
- Number of sets: one to three
- Resistance: 8 to 10 RM
- Rest periods between sets and exercises: 1-1/2 to 3 minutes
- Repetitions per set for abdominal exercises: 20 to 30

Preseason Program—Sprints

The lifter performs exercises in the order listed.

Warm-Up—General exercise consisting of jogging or cycling for about 5 minutes followed by a general stretching routine.

- Lunge
- Dumbbell bench press or dumbbell incline press
- Single-leg knee curl
- Single-leg knee extension
- Calf raise
- Abdominal exercise with twist

Approximate Time
- Three training sessions per week with at least 1 day separating sessions
- 35 to 55 minutes per session

Additional Injury-Prevention Exercises

• None

Additional or Replacement Exercises

• Pullover
• Back squat or leg press
• Lat pull-down
• Dead lift

Advanced Exercises

• The lifter should perform no more than five repetitions per set using 8- to 10-RM resistance for advanced exercises. If an advanced exercise is used, it should be performed at the beginning of the training session.
• Power clean or power snatch from floor, knee, or thigh level
• Clean pull or snatch pull from floor, knee, or thigh level

Preseason Program Notes— Sprints

• Format: circuit for 200- and 400-meter sprinters; set-repetition for 100-meter sprinters
• Number of sets or circuits: one to three
• Resistance: 10 to 12 RM for 200- and 400-meter sprinters; up to 6 RM for 100-meter sprinters
• Rest periods between sets and exercises: 30 seconds to 1 minute for 200- and 400-meter sprinters; 2 to 3 minutes for 100-meter sprinters
• Repetitions per set for abdominal exercises: 20 to 30

In-Season Program—Sprints

The lifter performs exercises in the order listed.
Warm-Up—General exercise consisting of jogging or cycling for about 5 minutes followed by a general stretching routine.

• Dumbbell bench press or dumbbell incline press
• Lunge
• Seated row or dumbbell bent-over row
• Calf raise
• Abdominal exercise with a twist
• Knee curl

Approximate Time

• One to two training sessions per week with at least 1 day separating sessions
• 20 to 45 minutes per session

Additional Injury-Prevention Exercises

• Knee extension

Additional or Replacement Exercises

• Lat pull-down
• Shoulder shrug
• Dumbbell elbow curl
• Dumbbell fly
• Front or back squat

Advanced Exercises

• The lifter should perform no more than five repetitions per set using 8- to 10-RM resistance for advanced exercises. If an advanced exercise is used, it should be performed at the beginning of the training session.
• Clean pull and snatch pull from knee or thigh level

In-Season Program Notes—Sprints

- Format: set-repetition or circuit
- Number of sets or circuits: two to three
- Resistance: 10 to 12 RM for 200- and 400-meter sprinters; 8 RM for 100-meter sprinters
- Rest periods between sets and exercises: 30 seconds to 1 minute for 200- and 400-meter sprinters; 1 to 2 minutes for 100-meter sprinters and for sprints of less than 100 meters
- Repetitions per set for abdominal exercises: 20 to 30

Volleyball

In volleyball, blocking, vertical jumping, passing (bumping), and spiking are skills crucial to success. By increasing leg and total body strength and power, an athlete can enhance vertical jumping ability. Shoulder rotator cuff strength and upper body and abdominal development are vital for spiking and serving. In addition, increased shoulder, leg, and hip strength will help prevent injury. Unilateral leg strength is vital for skills involving one leg. Resistance exercise can provide positive changes in these physical capabilities.

Off-Season Program—Volleyball

The lifter performs exercises in the order listed. Italics indicate exercises that can be periodized for resistance in this training phase.

Warm-Up—General exercise consisting of jogging or cycling for about 5 minutes followed by a general stretching routine.

- *Back squat or leg press*
- *Overhead press*
- Dumbbell bench press or dumbbell incline press
- Knee curl
- Lat pull-down
- Calf raise
- Abdominal exercise with twist

Approximate Time

- Three training sessions per week with at least 1 day separating sessions
- 45 to 60 minutes per session

Additional Injury-Prevention Exercises

- Shoulder internal rotation and shoulder external rotation
- Shoulder rotator cuff exercises

Additional or Replacement Exercises

- Knee extension
- Pullover
- Seated row
- Elbow curl
- Front squat

Advanced Exercises

- The lifter should perform no more than five repetitions per set using 8- to 10-RM resistance for advanced exercises. If an advanced exercise is used, it should be performed at the beginning of the training session.
- Power clean and clean pull from knee or thigh level

Off-Season Program Notes—Volleyball

- Format: set-repetition
- Number of sets: two to three
- Resistance: 10 to 12 RM
- Rest periods between sets and exercises: 1-1/2 minutes
- Repetitions per set for abdominal exercises: 20 to 30

Preseason Program—Volleyball

The lifter performs exercises in the order listed. Italics indicate exercises that can be periodized for resistance in this phase.

Warm-Up—General exercise consisting of jogging or cycling for about 5 minutes followed by a general stretching routine.

- *Lunge*
- *Overhead press*
- Shoulder anterior raise
- Knee curl
- Shoulder side raise
- Calf raise
- Abdominal exercise with twist

Approximate Time

- Three training sessions per week with at least 1 day separating sessions
- 25 to 45 minutes per session

Additional Injury-Prevention Exercises (to perform training day)

- Shoulder internal rotation and shoulder external rotation
- Shoulder rotator cuff exercises

Additional or Replacement Exercises

- Reverse elbow curl
- Dumbbell fly
- Pullover
- Leg press
- Knee extension

Advanced Exercises

- The lifter should perform no more than five repetitions per set using 8- to 10-RM resistance for advanced exercises. If an advanced exercise is used, it should be performed at the beginning of the training session.
- Power clean and clean pull from the knee or thigh level
- Snatch pull from midthigh level

Preseason Program Notes—Volleyball

- Format: circuit
- Number of circuits: two to three
- Resistance: 8 to 10 RM
- Rest periods between sets and exercises: 1 to 1-1/2 minutes; for variation, can be periodized between 1 and 2 minutes
- Repetitions per set for abdominal exercises: 20 to 30

In-Season Program—Volleyball

The lifter performs exercises in the order listed.

Warm-Up—General exercise consisting of jogging or cycling for about 5 minutes followed by a general stretching routine.

- Overhead press or push press
- Single-leg knee extension

- Seated row
- Single-leg knee curl
- Abdominal exercise with twist
- Calf raise

Approximate Time

- One to two training sessions per week with at least 1 day separating sessions
- 20 to 35 minutes per session

Additional Injury-Prevention Exercises (to perform training day)

- Shoulder internal rotation and shoulder external rotation
- Shoulder rotator cuff exercises

Additional or Replacement Exercises

- Bench press
- Shoulder lateral raise
- Lat pull-down
- Arm curl
- Front squat
- Lunge

Advanced Exercises

- The lifter should perform no more than five repetitions per set using 8- to 10-RM resistance for advanced exercises. If an advanced exercise is used, it should be performed at the beginning of the training session.
- Power clean, clean pull, or snatch pull from the knee or thigh level

In-Season Program Notes— Volleyball

- Format: circuit
- Number of circuits: two to three
- Resistance: 8 to 10 RM
- Rest periods between sets and exercises: 1 minute
- Repetitions per set for abdominal exercises: 20 to 30

Wrestling

Junior high school and high school wrestling requires the ability to perform high-intensity exercise for 5 to 6 minutes per match. Back, hip, leg, and whole body movement strength is vital for throws, takedowns, and escapes. Thus, a wrestler's training should include structural, multijoint, total body movements. Furthermore, toleration of high-intensity exercise is also of great concern. Because of the high intensity of wrestling, the body relies upon anaerobic energy from the lactic acid energy source. In order to offset nausea, dizziness, and fatigue often associated with this type of exertion, the rest periods need to be gradually decreased in the resistance training cycle, from 1-1/2 minutes to 30 seconds. This will help the wrestler adapt to the type of stress encountered in a match.

Off-Season Program—Wrestling

The lifter performs exercises in the order listed. Italics indicate exercises that can be periodized for resistance during this phase.
Warm-Up—General exercise consisting of jogging or cycling for about 5 minutes followed by a general stretching routine.

- *Bench press*
- *Back squat or leg press*
- *Dead lift*
- Overhead press
- Seated row
- Knee curl
- Lat pull-down
- Elbow curl
- Abdominal exercise

Approximate Time
- Three training sessions per week with at least 1 day separating sessions
- 40 to 60 minutes per session

Additional Injury-Prevention Exercises
- Shoulder rotator cuff exercises
- Knee extension

Additional or Replacement Exercises
- Front squat
- Calf raise
- Neck exercises

Advanced Exercises
- The lifter should perform no more than five repetitions per set using 8- to 10-RM resistance for advanced exercises. If an advanced exercise is used, it should be performed at the beginning of the training session.
- Power clean or power snatch from floor, knee, or thigh level
- Clean pull or snatch pull from floor, knee, or thigh level

Off-Season Program Notes— Wrestling
- Format: set-repetition
- Number of sets: two to three
- Resistance: 10 to 12 RM
- Rest periods between sets and exercises: 1-1/2 to 2 minutes
- Repetitions per set for abdominal exercises: 20 to 30

Preseason Program—Wrestling

The lifter performs exercises in the order listed.

Warm-Up—General exercise consisting of jogging or cycling for about 5 minutes followed by a general stretching routine.

- Lunge
- Dumbbell bench press or dumbbell incline press
- Dead lift
- Neck exercise
- Dumbbell overhead press
- Bent-over row
- Knee curl
- Lat pull-down
- Abdominal exercise with twist

Approximate Time
- Two to three training sessions per week with at least 1 day separating sessions
- 25 to 50 minutes per session

Additional Injury-Prevention Exercises
- Shoulder rotator cuff exercises
- Lower back exercise
- Knee extension

Additional or Replacement Exercises	• Bench press • Shoulder press • Seated row • Leg press • Back squat
Advanced Exercises	• The lifter should perform no more than five repetitions per set using 8- to 10-RM resistance for advanced exercises. If an advanced exercise is used, it should be performed at the beginning of the training session. • Power clean or power snatch from floor, knee, or thigh level • Clean pull or snatch pull from floor, knee, or thigh level
Preseason Program Notes— Wrestling	• Format: circuit • Number of circuits: three • Resistance: 8 to 10 RM • Rest periods between sets and exercises: gradually decreased from 1-1/2 minutes to 30 seconds • Repetitions per set for abdominal exercises: 20 to 30 • Other: Carefully monitor the athlete's toleration to the short rest periods.

In-Season Program—Wrestling

The lifter performs exercises in the order listed.

Warm-Up—General exercise consisting of jogging or cycling for about 5 minutes followed by a general stretching routine.

• Bench press
• Dead lift
• Single-leg knee curl
• Elbow curl
• Single-leg knee extension
• Seated row
• Abdominal exercise

Approximate Time	• One to two training sessions per week with at least 1 day separating sessions • 25 to 45 minutes per session
Additional Injury-Prevention Exercises	• Shoulder rotator cuff exercises
Additional or Replacement Exercises	• Lunge • Leg press • Narrow-grip bench press
Advanced Exercises	• The lifter should perform no more than five repetitions per set using 8- to 10-RM resistance for advanced exercises. If an advanced exercise is used, it should be performed at the beginning of the training session. • Power clean or power snatch from floor, knee, or thigh level • Clean pull or snatch pull from floor, knee, or thigh level
In-Season Program Notes— Wrestling	• Format: set-repetition or circuit • Number of sets or circuits: one to three • Resistance: 8 RM • Rest periods between sets and exercises: 1 to 2 minutes • Repetitions per set for abdominal exercises: 20 to 30

Additional Readings

Amos, J., & Calvin, N. (1987). Burlingame High School girl's basketball in-season strength program. *National Strength and Conditioning Association Journal*, **9**(2), 48-49.

Ball, R. (1989). The basketball jump shot: A kinesiological analysis with recommendations for strength and conditioning programs. *National Strength and Conditioning Association Journal*, **11**(5), 4-12.

Bartlett, L.R., Storey, M.D., & Simons, B.D. (1989). Measurement of upper extremity torque production and its relationship to throwing speed in the competitive athlete. *American Journal of Sports Medicine*, **17**, 89-91.

Baumhofer, L. (1986). The backstroke. *National Strength and Conditioning Association Journal*, **8**(3), 5-12.

Behm, D. (1988). A kinesiological analysis of the tennis service. *National Strength and Conditioning Association Journal*, **10**(5), 4-13.

Behm, D. (1987). Strength and power conditioning for racquet sports. *National Strength and Conditioning Association Journal*, **9**(1), 37-40.

Bennett, J.G., & Stauber, W.T. (1986). Evaluation and treatment of anterior knee pain using eccentric exercise. *Medicine and Science in Sports and Exercise*, **18**, 526-530.

Brown, L.P., Niehues, S.L., Harrah, A., Yavorsky, P., & Hirshman, H.P. (1988). Upper extremity range of motion and isokinetic strength of the internal and external rotators in major league baseball players. *American Journal of Sports Medicine*, **16**, 577-585.

Burgener, M. (1987). Year round periodization for high school football. *National Strength and Conditioning Association Journal*, **9**(4), 60-61.

Butler, R., & Rogness, K. (1984). Strength training for the advanced volleyball player. *National Strength and Conditioning Association Journal*, **5**(6), 34-37.

Butler, R., & Rogness, K. (1983). Strength training for the young volleyball player. *National Strength and Conditioning Association Journal*, **5**(3), 66-68.

Ciccantelli, P. (1987). Year round strength and conditioning program for soccer. *National Strength and Conditioning Association Journal*, **9**(4), 31-34.

Cicullo, J.V., & Stevens, G.G. (1989). The prevention and treatment of injuries to the shoulder in swimming. *Sports Medicine*, **7**, 182-204.

Cipriano, N. (1987). Physical conditioning principles and protocols for amateur freestyle wrestling. *National Strength and Conditioning Association Journal*, **9**(4), 44-49.

Cipriano, N. (1988). Supplemental conditioning exercises and training protocols for the amateur wrestler. *National Strength and Conditioning Association Journal*, **10**(5), 32-34.

Coburn, S. (1987). Tests and measurements for wrestling at Worland High School. *National Strength and Conditioning Association Journal*, **9**(3), 29-30.

Coaches Roundtable. (1983). Strength and conditioning for baseball. *National Strength and Conditioning Association Journal*, **5**(3), 11-19.

Emmert, W. (1984). The slap shot strength and conditioning program for hockey at Boston College. *National Strength and Conditioning Association Journal*, **6**(2), 46, 68, 71, 73.

Goebel, R. (1984). Eleven-week jump training for women's basketball. *National Strength and Conditioning Association Journal*, **6**(4), 59-71.

Goranson, G. (1981). Kip strength: Explosive power for Olympic gymnastics. *National Strength and Conditioning Association Journal*, **3**(3) 4-6.

Gowan, I.D., Jobe, F.W., Tibone, J.E., Perry, J., & Moyers, D.R. (1987). A comparative electromyographic analysis of the shoulder during pitching—professional versus amateur pitchers. *American Journal of Sports Medicine*, **15**, 586-590.

Hickson, R.C., Pvorak, B.A., Gorostiaga, E.M., Kurowski, T.T., & Foster, C. (1988). Potential for strength and endurance training to amplify endurance performance. *Journal of Applied Physiology*, **65**, 2285-2290.

Hilyer, J., & Hunter, G. (1990). A year round strength development and conditioning program for men's basketball. *National Strength and Conditioning Association Journal*, **11**(6), 16-17.

Hichcock, W. (1988). Individualized strength and conditioning program for women's basketball. *National Strength and Conditioning Association Journal*, **10**(5), 28-30.

Jacobs, P. (1987). The overhand baseball pitch: A kinesiological analysis and related strength-conditioning programming. *National Strength and Conditioning Association Journal*, **9**, 5-13, 78-79.

James, S. (1987). Periodization of weight training for women's gymnastics. *National Strength and Conditioning Association Journal*, **9**(1), 28-31.

Kenyon, S. (1987). Year round computerized high school program. *National Strength and Conditioning Association Journal*, **9**(4), 57-59.

Kraemer, W.J. (1983). Strength training for collision sports. In A. Weltman and C.G. Spain (Eds.), *Proceedings of White House Symposium on Physical Fitness and Sports Medicine* (pp. 60-62). Washington, DC: President's Council on Physical Fitness and Sports.

Kraemer, W.J. (1984). The challenge of training the three-sport athlete. *National Strength and Conditioning Association Journal*, **6**(5), 50-52.

Kraemer, W.J. (1982). The physiological basis for conditioning in wrestling. *National Strength and Conditioning Association Journal*, **4**(3), 24-25.

Kraemer, W.J., & Richardson, T. (1984). Wrestling bridging the gap. *National Strength and Conditioning Association Journal*, **6**(1), 40-41, 66-67, & 70.

Kroll, W. (1982). Conditioning for basketball. *National Strength and Conditioning Association Journal*, **5**(2), 24-26.

Mannine, K., & DiAngelo, C. (1983). Perspectives and programs in high school basketball and baseball conditioning. *National Strength and Conditioning Association Journal*, **4**(6), 52-54.

McKenzie Gillam, G., & Semenick, D. (1985). Basketball bioenergetics bridging the gap. *National Strength and Conditioning Association Journal*, **6**(6), 44, 45, 71, 72-73.

Miller, J. (1987). Medicine ball training for throwers. *National Strength and Conditioning Association Journal*, **9**(1), 32-33.

Olgjo, B. (1987). UCLA soccer weight training. *National Strength and Conditioning Association Journal*, **9**(1), 43-46.

Pearson, D., & Wallace, D. (1984). Winter strength conditioning program at Ball State University. *National Strength and Conditioning Association Journal*, **6**(1), 28-30.

Pedegana, L.R., Elsner, R.C., & Roberts, D. (1982). The relationship of upper extremity strength to throwing speed. *American Journal of Sports Medicine*, **10**, 352-354.

Poprawski, B. (1987). Aspects of strength, power and speed in shot put training. *National Strength and Conditioning Association Journal*, **9**(6), 39-41.

Railsback, D. (1987). The pole vault. *National Strength and Conditioning Association Journal*, **9**(2), 5-9, 79-80.

Richardson, T., Schmotzer, P., Brandenburg, J., & Kraemer, W. (1983). Improved rebounding performance through strength training. *National Strength and Conditioning Association Journal*, **4**(6), 6-7, 70-71.

Rodeo, S. (1984). Swimming the breaststroke: A kinesiological analysis and considerations for strength training. *National Strength and Conditioning Association Journal*, **6**(4), 4-6, 79-81.

Rowland, T.W. (1989). Oxygen uptake and endurance fitness in children: A developmental perspective. *Pediatric Exercise Science*, **1**, 313-328.

Simmons, J., & Hill, T. (1984). Year round strength and conditioning program for volleyball at the University of Southern California. *National Strength and Conditioning Association Journal*, **6**(4), 57-58.

Shankman, G. (1983). Comprehensive yearly conditioning for Lassiter High School Football, Marietta, Ga. *National Strength and Conditioning Association Journal*, **5**(2), 67-68.

Sharp, R. (1986). Muscle strength and power as related to competitive swimming. *Journal of Swimming Research*, **2**, 5-10.

Stewart, K. (1977). Conditioning for tennis. *Towards an understanding of human performance* (pp. 262-266). Ithaca, NY: Movement Press.

Steward, T. (1988). Strength training for wrestling. *National Strength and Conditioning Association Journal*, **10**(4), 32-34.

Symons, R. (1989). Weight training conditioning for cross-country runners. *National Strength and Conditioning Association Journal*, **11**(5), 57-59.

Trachtenberg, A. (1988). Conditioning drills for soccer. *National Strength and Conditioning Association Journal*, **10**(4), 50-52.

Vermeil, A. (1989). Training components for basketball. *National Strength and Conditioning Association Journal*, **10**(6), 64-66.

Appendix

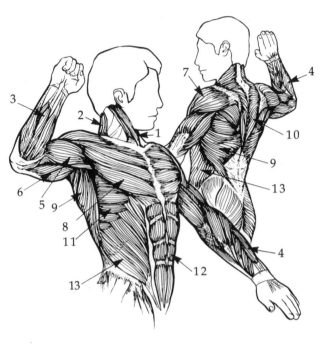

Upper Body Musculature

1. Neck flexors
2. Neck extensors
3. Forearm and finger flexors
4. Forearm and finger extensors
5. Biceps
6. Triceps
7. Deltoid
8. Pectoralis group
9. Latissimus dorsi
10. Trapezius
11. Serratus anterior
12. Rectus abdominis
13. Transverse abdominis

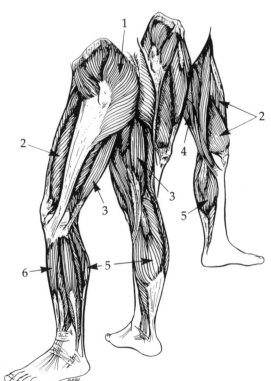

Leg Musculature

1. Gluteal group
2. Quadriceps group
3. Hamstring group
4. Leg adductor group
5. Plantar flexor group
6. Dorsiflexor group

Glossary

acromion process—Most lateral bony protuberance of the spine of the shoulder blade

aerobic—Using oxygen to break down carbohydrates, fats, and proteins for energy

amenorrhea—Temporary absence of menstruation

anaerobic—Using energy stored in muscles or energy obtained from breakdown of carbohydrates without oxygen

apophyseal insertion—Site of tendon insertion into bone

articular cartilage—Cartilage on the surface of a joint

back extensor—Muscle involved in straightening the back

ballistic—Dynamic muscular movements

barbell—A bar to which varying weights are attached; usually held with both arms

biceps brachii—Elbow flexor of upper arm

bilateral exercise—Using both arms or legs at the same time to perform an exercise

bodybuilding—A sport in which muscle size, definition, and symmetry determine the winner

brachialis—Elbow flexor of upper arm

bumper plate—Weight plate surrounded by a rubber ring or completely made of rubberlike material

circuit format—Training format in which a lifter performs one set of each exercise in a group in succession, normally with little rest between exercises

clavicle—Collar bone

delayed-onset muscle soreness—Pain or soreness in the muscle which peaks 24 to 48 hours after exercise

deltoid—Muscle on outside shoulder area

dumbbell—Small weight of fixed resistance; usually held with one arm

dynamic concentric—A muscle contraction during which muscle shortens and movement occurs

dynamic eccentric—A muscle contraction during which muscle lengthens and movement occurs

endurance—The ability of the muscle to execute repeated contractions

epiphyseal plate—Growth plate at ends of long bones

equipment fit—How the individual's body (limb lengths, height) fits the resistance training machine

EZ curl bar—A bar designed with bends for ease with curling exercises

fixed-form exercise—Exercise using a machine

free-form exercise—Exercise using free weights

free weights—Weights not part of an exercise machine (i.e., barbells and dumbbells)

frequency—Number of times per week resistance training is performed

gastrocnemius—Calf muscle

gluteals—Muscle of the buttock

glycogen—A storage form of carbohydrate in the body

hamstring—Muscle on the back of the thigh that flexes the knee and extends the hip

hip flexor—Muscle that attaches the lower back or hip to the upper thigh

humerus—Upper arm bone

hypertrophy—Increase in muscle size

infraspinatus—Muscle of the rotator cuff

intensity—Resistance used in an exercise

isokinetic—Relating to muscle contractions using a specialized piece of equipment which allows maximal force at a set speed of movement

isometric—Relating to a muscle contraction during which no movement takes place

lactic acid—Metabolic by-product of anaerobic metabolism

latissimus dorsi (lat)—Large muscle on the upper back that extends the upper arm

levator scapulae—Muscle of upper back and neck area that raises the shoulder blade or tilts the neck to one side

lumbar lordosis—Anterior bending of lower spine often accompanied by forward tilting of pelvis

lumbar region—Lower back

machine—Resistance training equipment that dictates the direction of the exercise movement and the body position

maturation—Progress toward adulthood

maximal strength testing—Lifting as much weight as possible for one repetition

menarche—Beginning of menstrual function

mineralization—Deposit of minerals in bone

oblique—Muscle on side of abdominal area

Osgood-Schlatter's disease—Degeneration of the bone at the site where the patellar tendon attaches to the tibia

osteochondritis dissecans—Separation of a portion of the articular cartilage from the joint surface

osteoporosis—Decrease in bone mass that increases fragility of bones

pec deck—Resistance training machine that trains the pectoralis muscle group

pectoralis—Major muscle group of the chest

periodization—Training method which allows for systematic changes in the intensity and volume of exercise

plateau—Period during training when no observable progress is made

progressive overload—Gradual increase in exercise stress (e.g., accomplished by increasing intensity or volume of training)

quadriceps—Muscle group on front of thigh

range of motion—Movement allowed by the body's joints and body position in a particular exercise

repetition (rep)—One resistance exercise movement

repetition maximum (RM)—Maximum number of repetitions possible with a given resistance

resistance—Weight lifted

resistance training—The use of various methods or equipment to provide an external force to exercise against

rhomboid—Muscle of the upper back that pulls the shoulder blade towards the backbone

rotator cuff—Group of muscles that rotate upper arm in shoulder joint and stabilize the upper arm in the shoulder joint

scapulae—Shoulder blades

serratus anterior—Muscle that pulls the shoulder blade away from the backbone located at the side of the rib cage

set—Group of repetitions

set-repetition format—Training in which the lifter performs the desired number of sets of an exercise before moving to the next exercise

soleus—Calf muscle under gastrocnemius

specificity—Principle which states adaptations occur only in the muscles used in the exercise

spinal erector—Muscles in the back which straighten the back

spotter—Individual responsible for the safety of a trainee who is performing a lift

strength—A muscle's ability to produce maximal force

subscapularis—Muscle of the rotator cuff

supraspinatus—Back of the upper shoulder

teres minor—Muscle of the rotator cuff

timed training session—Training in which a specified length of time is given to perform an exercise and to rest between exercises

trapezius—Muscle of the back that connects shoulder and shoulder blade to neck and back

triceps—Major muscle on back of upper arm

unilateral exercise—Single-arm or single-leg exercise

variation—Process of changing exercise variables to provide a different training stimulus

volume—A measure of the total work (sets × repetitions × resistance) for a given exercise, training session, or training period

weight lifting—An Olympic competitive sport in which the highest total poundage in two lifts—snatch, and clean and jerk— determine the winner

Index

A complete weight training package

Weight Training

Steps to Success

**Thomas R. Baechle, EdD, CSCS, and
Barney R. Groves, PhD, CSCS**

1992 • Paper • 208 pp • Item PBAE0451
ISBN 0-88011-451-7 • $14.95 ($21.95 Canadian)

Weight Training Video

Steps to Success

(57-minute videotape)

1993 • 1/2" VHS • Item MBAE0243
ISBN 0-87322-485-X • $29.95 ($44.95 Canadian)

Weight Training: Steps to Success is the first book to provide students a balanced, self-paced program *and* the knowledge they need to design a customized weight training program. It includes a basic program and alternative exercises for lever-arm and cam-type machines as well as free weights.

Weight Training: Steps to Success features a 16-step progression of proven techniques that help students prevent injuries and maximize progress. Students will learn why each concept or exercise is important, the keys to correct technique, how to correct common errors, how to practice each exercise in realistic ways, specific performance goals for each drill, and how to evaluate proper technique.

By following the practice procedures and drills noted, students will also learn how to

- perform exercises in a safe and time-efficient manner,
- make needed changes in program intensity,
- warm up and cool down properly,
- select appropriate exercises for each large muscle group,
- follow easy-to-difficult drills,
- chart their workouts, and
- design programs that meet their personal training goals.

Sequential illustrations and helpful tips, or the "keys to success," provide students with anatomical and biomechanical information for correct lifting and spotting techniques.

Weight Training: Steps to Success not only provides the knowledge students need to safely participate in weight training, but also challenges them to develop their own programs.

Companion Video

The companion videotape to *Weight Training: Steps to Success* shows viewers everything they need to know to start a well-balanced weight training program. It's excellent for strength and fitness instructors, coaches, and others who are interested in teaching beginners how to safely and effectively lift weights.

Step by step, the video demonstrates how to perform the same 19 exercises that are covered in the book. The video makes learning easy by using slow motion, freeze-frames, and graphics to show viewers the proper positioning and lifting technique for each exercise. It also gives tips on choosing the right equipment and presents exercise programs for three different types of equipment—free weights, single- or multistation pivot machines, and cam machines.

While the *Weight Training Video* is designed for students who are just starting out, it's also great for those who have lifted weights before but have never had formal instruction in weight training. It's full of informative demonstrations that give students a sound base of weight training knowledge and allow them to visualize the methods described in the book.

Together, these three weight training resources—the instructor guide, participant book, and companion video—are a powerful, high quality instructional package for successful teaching and learning.

Human Kinetics
The Premier Publisher for Sports & Fitness
http://www.humankinetics.com/

2335

To request more information or to place your order,
U.S. customers call **TOLL-FREE 1-800-747-4457**.
Customers outside the U.S. use appropriate telephone number/
address shown in the front of this book.